Siege Warfare
During the
Hundred Years
War

Siege Warfare During the Hundred Years War

'Once More unto the Breach ...'

Peter Hoskins

Pen & Sword
MILITARY

AN IMPRINT OF PEN & SWORD BOOKS LTD
YORKSHIRE – PHILADELPHIA

First published in Great Britain in 2018 by
PEN & SWORD MILITARY
An imprint of Pen & Sword Books Ltd
Yorkshire – Philadelphia

Copyright © Peter Hoskins, 2018

ISBN 978-1-47383-432-3

Typeset by Concept, Huddersfield, West Yorkshire.
Printed and bound in England by TJ International Ltd. PadstowPL28 8RW

Pen & Sword Books Ltd incorporates the Imprints of Aviation, Atlas, Family
History, Fiction, Maritime, Military, Discovery, Politics, History, Archaeology,
Select, Wharncliffe Local History, Wharncliffe True Crime, Military Classics,
Wharncliffe Transport, Leo Cooper, The Praetorian Press, Remember When,
White Owl, Seaforth Publishing and Frontline Publishing.

For a complete list of Pen & Sword titles please contact
PEN & SWORD BOOKS LTD
47 Church Street, Barnsley, South Yorkshire, S70 2AS, England
E-mail: enquiries@pen-and-sword.co.uk
Website: www.pen-and-sword.co.uk
or
PEN & SWORD BOOKS
1950 Lawrence Rd, Havertown, PA 19083, USA
E-mail: uspen-and-sword@casematepublishers.com
Website: www.penandswordbooks.com

For Josephine
13 December 1942 to 11 January 2016

Contents

List of Maps and Plans xi

List of Plates xii

Acknowledgements xiii

Preface xiv

Glossary xvii

1. The Hundred Years War   1
   Causes of the Hundred Years War   1
   The Outbreak of War and the English Ascendancy, 1337–1360   3
   The French Recovery, 1369–1389   8
   An Uneasy Truce, 1389–1415   8
   A Return to War, 1415–1444   10
   The Truce of Tours, 1444–1449, and the Defeat of the English   14

2. Siege Warfare   16
   The Characteristics of a Siege   16
   The Strategic Context   19
   The Conventions of Siege Warfare   22
   Costs   25

3. Fortifications – Attack and Defence   27
   Fortifications   27
   Siege Techniques   29
   Countermeasures   34
   The Politics and Economics of Defence   36
   The Organization of Defence   38

4. The English Ascendancy, 1337–1360   39
   Cambrai, 1339   39
   Tournai, 1340   40
   Aquitaine, 1345–1346   46
   La Réole, 1345–1346   48
   Aiguillon, 1346   49
   Calais, 1346–1347   53

Breteuil, 1356 63

Romorantin, 1356 64

Reims, 1359–1360 66

5. The French Recovery, 1369–1389 70

Réalville, 1369 72

Duravel, 1369 72

La Roche-sur-Yon, 1370 73

Limoges, 1370 74

Montpon-Ménestérol, 1370–1371 77

Soubise, 1372 78

Chizé, 1373 79

Brest and Derval, 1373 80

La Réole, 1374 82

St-Sauveur-le-Vicomte, 1374–1375 84

Bergerac, 1377 86

St-Macaire, 1377 88

Cherbourg, 1378 88

Nantes, 1380–1381 90

Ypres, 1383 92

The Truce of Leulinghem, 1389 97

6. From Harfleur to the Death of Henry V, 1415–1422 99

Harfleur, 1415 99

Caen, 1417 107

Falaise, 1417–1418 110

Louviers, 1418 111

Pont-de-l'Arche, 1418 112

Rouen, 1418–1419 114

Between Rouen and Montereau 120

Montereau, 1420 122

Melun, 1420 123

Between Melun and Meaux 126

Meaux, 1421–1422 129

Cosne, 1422 132

7. From the Death of Henry V to the Siege of Orléans, 1422–1429 134

Meulan, 1423 134

Le Crotoy, 1423–1424 136

Cravant, 1423 137

Compiègne, Gaillon and Ivry-la-Bataille, 1424 138

Guise, 1424–1425 140

Mont-St-Michel, 1424–1425 141
Pontorson, 1427 142
Montargis, 1427 143
La Gravelle, 1427 144
Orléans, 1428–1429 144

8. From Orléans to the Truce of Tours, 1429–1444 160
Jargeau, 1429 160
Beaugency-sur-Loire, 1429 160
Charles VII's Coronation Campaign 162
La Charité-sur-Loire, 1429 164
Compiègne, 1430 164
Louviers, 1431 166
St-Céneri-le-Gérei, 1432 167
Lagny-sur-Marne, 1432 169
St-Valery-sur-Somme, 1433 170
St-Céneri-le-Gérei, 1433 171
Sillé-le-Guillaume, 1433 172
Creil, 1434 172
St-Denis, 1435 173
Paris, 1436 175
Calais, 1436 176
Le Crotoy, 1437 178
Meaux, 1439 179
Avranches, 1439 181
Harfleur, 1440 182
Creil, 1441 184
Pontoise, 1441 184
Tartas, 1441–1442 186
Dieppe, 1442–1443 187
The Truce of Tours 188

9. The Expulsion of the English from France, 1449–1453 190
Verneuil-sur-Avre, 1449 190
Vernon, 1449 192
Harcourt, 1449 192
Rouen, 1449 193
Harfleur, 1449 196
Honfleur, 1450 197
The Beginning of the End 198
Bayeux, 1450 198

Caen, 1450 199

Falaise, 1450 201

Cherbourg, 1450 201

The Recovery of Aquitaine: the First Campaign, 1450–1451 203

Mauléon, 1449 204

Montguyon, 1451 205

Blaye, 1451 205

Bordeaux, 1451 206

Bayonne, 1451 207

The Recovery of Aquitaine: the Second Campaign, 1452–1453 208

Cadillac, 1453 209

Bordeaux, 1453 209

Conclusion 211

Appendix I: Summary of Outcomes of Sieges 213

Appendix II: Duration of Sieges 214

Notes 218

Bibliography 223

Index 226

List of Maps and Plans

Maps

Northern France, 1337–1360 41

Flanders 42

South-west France, 1337–1360 47

Southern France, 1369–1389 71

Northern France, 1369–1389 81

Normandy, 1415–1422 100

Northern France, 1415–1422 121

Northern France, 1422–1429 135

France, 1429–1444 161

Normandy, 1429–1444 163

Normandy, 1449–1450 191

Aquitaine, 1450–1453 204

Plans

Harfleur in the fifteenth century 101

Caen, 1418 109

Rouen, 1418–1419 115

Orléans, 1428–1429 145

List of Plates

Carcassonne.

The castle at Arques-la-Bataille.

The keep at Vernon.

The barbican of Picquigny castle.

Angers castle.

Mangonel.

Springald.

Bricole.

Trebuchet.

Couillard.

Battering ram.

Belfry.

Bombard.

La Réole castle.

The thirteenth-century watch tower in Calais.

Rodin's sculpture of the Burghers of Calais.

The Rouen gate at Harfleur.

Graville Priory.

Caen castle.

The Tour St-Vigor at Pont-de-l'Arche.

The keep of Rouen castle.

Fécamp castle.

Dieppe castle.

The ramparts of St-Lô.

Bonport abbey.

The Porte du Prêtre gate at Mantes-la-Jolie.

The perimeter tower of St Martin at Mantes-la-Jolie.

Ramparts in Beauvais.

The Château des Tourelles at Vernon.

Vestiges of Chizé castle.

Acknowledgements

First of all I should like to thank Rupert Harding at Pen & Sword for having the confidence to carry this project forward despite books on the medieval period being somewhat of a niche market. Thanks also to Scott Hall for his cover illustration for this the third of my books to which he has contributed. On matters of substance my thanks to a fine French historian, Guilhem Pépin, steeped in the history of Gascony and the Black Prince for his sharing with me his newly discovered information concerning the sack of Limoges in 1370. My thanks to Rebecca Sewell and Nicolas Savy for permission to use their photographs. Finally, and by no means least, thank you to Professor Anne Curry for her support in my endeavours over several years, and for passing me a copy of the transcription of the College of Arms MS M9, folios 31–66v. Professor Anne Curry, Dr Andy King, Dr Craig Lambert and Dr Dan Spencer also generously made papers and articles available which had escaped me. I am also grateful to Anne and Andrew Vallance for their helpful reviews of my manuscript – errors remain mine!

Preface

Siege warfare had a more important role during the Hundred Years War than one would believe in view of the attention given to dramatic set-piece battles such as Crécy and Agincourt. Shakespeare's famous speech for King Henry in *Henry V* (act III, scene I) which begins 'Once more unto the breach, dear friends, once more; or close the wall up with our English dead!' is often associated with the battle of Agincourt. Indeed, the BBC used the speech to introduce an item on the 600th anniversary of the battle in October 2015. This is perhaps not surprising since *Henry V* in its entirety is widely associated solely with the battle. However, the span of action in the play is much broader, covering events in England before the English invasion of 1415 through the Battle of Agincourt to the Treaty of Troyes in 1420 and the marriage of Henry to Catherine de Valois. Henry's famous speech relates to the siege of Harfleur and not to the battle. This misunderstanding of the context of the speech is, however, no more than a reflection of the place of the great battles of the Hundred Years War such as Crécy, Poitiers and Agincourt in the popular imagination of the English.

Sieges, other than the stories of the burghers of Calais when the town surrendered in 1347 and of Joan of Arc at the siege of Orléans in 1429, garner little attention. However, sieges and the capture of castles and towns were far more numerous than pitched battles during the Hundred Years War, and the holding or loss of towns and castles proved in the end to be of greater strategic importance than battles. The conquest of Normandy and much of northern France by Henry V was due to his successful campaign of taking towns and castles in 1417 and the years that followed. He could not have launched that campaign without Agincourt under his belt, but it was the taking of the great towns of Normandy such as Caen and Rouen which brought the Normans and others in northern France into his allegiance, and not Agincourt.

Victories in pitched battles were, of course, important, and those of Crécy and Poitiers in particular with the capture of King John II were crucial in establishing the English ascendancy which resulted in the Treaty of Brétigny in 1360. On the French side it was the battle of Formigny in

1450 which finished all hope for the English of holding on to Normandy and that of Castillon in 1453 which led to the expulsion of the English from Aquitaine, leaving the English with nothing other than the Calais Pale. However, the disintegration of English power in the years before Castillon stemmed more from the French driving the English out of towns and fortresses than from victory on the battlefield. Earlier in the war the reversal from 1369 onwards of the English ascendancy was due to the French strategy of King Charles V of concentrating on the capture of towns and fortresses and avoiding pitched battle at almost all costs. Edward III, the architect of the English success in the first phase of the Hundred Years War, is much more famous for his victory at Crécy in 1346 than for his capture of Calais after almost a year of siege. Yet the taking of Calais had a more lasting importance for the English prosecution of the war than the somewhat ephemeral victory at Crécy the year before.

The focus on battles is, of course, understandable: the clashes of armoured men-at-arms or the success of English and Welsh archers against the nobility of France are much more dramatic than often long drawn-out sieges which frequently ended in surrender rather than in assault. Indeed, many ended in failure with the besiegers breaking camp and abandoning the siege, often leaving materiel and weapons behind them. Even within the context of the siege of Harfleur Shakespeare's famous speech for Henry before the walls of the town owes its dramatic effect to the prospect of the town being taken by storm. The following scene when the captain of the town surrenders to Henry is much more prosaic and considerably less well known. Henry V spent much more time and effort in sieges than in battle. Indeed, his premature death was due to dysentery, the only too familiar scourge of besiegers, contracted at the siege of Meaux in 1422; he did not die a glorious death in combat on the field of battle. However, sieges were not without their drama: the siege of a well-defended town, and indeed its defence, was not for the faint-hearted with hand-to-hand combat, fighting underground during mining and counter-mining, and the effects of stone-throwing and gunpowder artillery.

This book cannot hope to restore the balance entirely, and it certainly does not cover anything like the totality of the innumerable sieges conducted over this period. However, it traces the course of the war through the story of some of the sieges of the Anglo-French wars between the years 1337 and 1453 that have now become known collectively as the Hundred Years War and, I hope, shows how important they were to the ebb and flow of fortunes. Some of the sieges must obviously be included: Calais,

Harfleur, Rouen, Meaux (where Henry V contracted the dysentery which was to kill him) and Orléans (famous for the part played by Joan of Arc). For the rest, those that I have chosen serve as milestones to take the reader through the progress of the war, as well as showing the importance and nature of contemporary siege warfare. The choice has also been dictated to some extent by the information available. Many sieges of places which by their location would be expected to be significant receive scant attention from the chroniclers and subsequent historians. Inevitably I shall have missed some that will seem more important to some readers. I can only apologize in advance.

A word of caution is also required. Numbers quoted by chroniclers need to be taken with a good deal of caution. They were often in conveniently round figures and frequently exaggerated. Much work has been done in recent years on how many and who served in garrisons and armies, particularly for English armies. However, accurate figures for many of the sieges and battles which feature in this book have not been subject to this rigour. Nevertheless, I have mentioned the figures to give some idea of scale.

Glossary

Arrière-ban – a general proclamation by the King of France to raise men by extending the summons to join the army to tenants and vassals of his immediate vassals.

Bailli – an officer in France with administrative and military responsibilities for a particular town or area.

Ballista – a large crossbow, often mounted on a stand, using either tension with the string drawn back mechanically or torsion with twisted ropes to propel a bolt.

Barbican – a fortification built in front of a gate to improve its defence.

Bastide – in the south-west of France a fortified town, more generally a field fortification.

Bastille – a field fortification or masonry tower or fortress.

Belfry – a wooden, mobile siege tower allowing men to shoot over walls into towns or fortresses or cross the walls without scaling ladders.

Bombard – a large, heavy cannon.

Bouches inutiles – literally 'useless mouths', inhabitants of a besieged place considered to be of no value to the defence and a burden on supplies and thus a threat to the ability to continue to hold out.

Boulevard – an earthwork fortification, sometimes to support cannon.

Bourg – many French towns, particularly in the south-west, were divided into two parts: the *bourg* and the *cité*. Usually the *cité* was the oldest of the two, often based on earlier Roman towns. It was also often administered by the Church or a local lord. The *bourg* was usually the newer part and subject to civil administration.

Bricole – a stone-throwing machine operated by human traction launching small projectiles for anti-personnel purposes rather than bombardment of fortifications.

Caltrop – a small spiked object, in the shape of a tetrahedron about 5cm in height, used to disrupt the movement of men and horses.

Chevauchée a mounted expedition moving at speed, exemplified by the Crécy campaign of 1346 and the Black Prince's raids of 1355 and 1356.

Cité – *see* **Bourg**.

Composition – a treaty defining terms of surrender of a town or fortress.

Constable – the chief military officer of the crown.

Couillard – a form of trebuchet with two articulated counterweights.

Ecorcheurs – literally 'skinners': bands of mercenaries or discharged soldiers who pillaged the French countryside for their own gain.

Greek Fire – an incendiary material which stuck to surfaces and was difficult to extinguish.

Hoardings – wooden constructions added to battlements which extended beyond the wall to allow defenders to drop projectiles vertically.

Interval tower – a tower built on the walls of a town or fortress between gates and projecting forward to allow flanking fire along the walls.

Keep – commonly a rectangular tower surrounded by a perimeter wall enclosing one or several baileys or courtyards.

Machicolations – masonry constructions added to battlements, similar to wooden hoardings, which extended beyond the wall to allow defenders to drop projectiles vertically.

Mangonel – a stone-throwing machine operated by a fixed counterweight.

Marshal – a senior military officer, sometimes in command of the cavalry or more broadly as commander of a force or army.

Oriflamme – a banner which when carried in battle in the presence of the King of France indicated that no quarter would be given.

Provost – an officer appointed to maintain law and order or to fulfil a military function.

Ribald – small multi-barrelled guns firing lead shot.

Routiers – bands of discharged soldiers or soldiers of fortune living by pillaging the French countryside.

Seneschal – a senior administrative officer appointed by the Crown.

Springald – *see* **Ballista**.

Tonnelon – a machine using winches or counterweights to raise men on a platform to the height of walls either to aid assault or allow shooting into a town or fortress.

Trebuchet – a stone-throwing machine operated by an articulated counterweight giving greater stability and accuracy than a mangonel.

Trepan – a battering ram with a steel spike designed to dislodge stones from fortifications.

Chapter 1

The Hundred Years War

Sieges, like the great battles of the Hundred Years War, mean little out of the context of the broader history of the war, particularly as the strategies adopted by both sides evolved throughout the war. It was only in the nineteenth century that historians coined the term 'the Hundred Years War' to cover the conflict between the English and French kings between 1337 and 1453. The name is somewhat misleading since it gives the impression of a period of continual warfare, whereas there were several distinct phases of war interspersed by periods of truce and peace, and the strategies employed varied between these phases. The English strategy in the reign of Edward III from the outbreak of war in 1337 until his death in 1377 was largely one of mobile warfare through mounted raids called *chevauchées*. There were numerous sieges, most notably those of Tournai in 1340 and Calais in 1346–1347, but overall the objectives of the strategy were to take the war deep into enemy territory and to bring the French to battle if the circumstances were right. This strategy has been described by the historian Clifford J. Rogers as being focused on people rather than places, with a key objective to bring the French to battle in favourable circumstances for the English. Under Henry V, and until the end of the war, the emphasis of English strategy changed. Bringing the French to battle was still an objective, but taking and holding towns to establish English rule took primacy. On the French side, the major successes of Charles V in driving the English out of the territories ceded by the Treaty of Brétigny and by his grandson Charles VII in finally expelling the invaders were largely attributable to the retaking of towns and fortresses and the re-establishment of French rule in lands which had gone over to the English.

Causes of the Hundred Years War

There were two underlying causes of the war which started in 1337: the homage claimed by the French kings from the kings of England for their lands in France, and the English claim to the throne of France.

The anomaly whereby English kings owed homage to the kings of France can be traced back to William the Conqueror, who was both King

William I of England and Duke of Normandy. The situation was exacerbated when Henry II came to the throne in 1154. He had acquired extensive lands in south-western France through his marriage to Eleanor of Aquitaine. Thus he, and subsequent English kings, ruled the Duchy of Aquitaine centred on the city of Bordeaux. The status of Aquitaine was a persistent cause of dispute between the kings of England and France, with kings of France demanding homage from the English kings who proclaimed their right to full sovereignty as Dukes of Aquitaine. In the years immediately preceding the Hundred Years War there were protracted diplomatic wrangles between Edward III and Philip VI. Matters came to a head in 1337 with a dispute over the extradition from England of a French exile, Robert of Artois, a one-time adviser to Philip. Edward refused to return Robert to France, and Philip declared Edward's Duchy of Aquitaine forfeit. With war coming Edward revoked his homage for Aquitaine.

The issue of homage for Aquitaine should have been resolved by the Treaty of Brétigny of 1360 between Edward III and John II of France after the English victory at Poitiers in 1356. Under a protocol associated with the treaty Edward III agreed to renounce his claim to the throne of France in return for French agreement that he should hold Aquitaine in full sovereignty. Unfortunately, King John II died in 1364 before these terms were put into effect, and the issue remained in the forefront of the quarrel between England and France. In 1369 Charles V reclaimed sovereignty over Aquitaine and Edward III took up the title of King of France once more. In 1399, on his father's accession as Henry IV, the thirteen-year-old future Henry V was named Duke of Aquitaine, but the dispute over sovereignty came into sharp focus again in early 1401 when the French king, as a deliberate slight to Henry IV, named the Dauphin Louis, his eldest son and hence heir to the throne, Duke of Guienne (the French name for Aquitaine). The importance of resolving the dispute over sovereignty for Aquitaine was not lost on the young Henry, and it was a central tenet of his policy towards France after his accession as King Henry V in 1413.

The second cause of the war was the claim of English kings to the crown of France. On the death of the French King Charles IV in 1328 the closest male successor was Edward III of England through his mother Isabella, sister to Charles IV and daughter of Philip IV.

The crux of the matter was whether the crown could be passed through the female line. The French view was that a woman could not inherit the crown and that she could not, therefore, pass this right to her son. Thus, Philip, the next closest male successor, who could trace his lineage back to Philip III through an unbroken male line, assumed the title King Philip VI – the first of the Valois dynasty. There was a somewhat desultory attempt by the English to lay claim to the throne on behalf of the fifteen-year-old Edward III. This received short shrift in France, and there the matter lay until the third year of the war in 1340 when Edward formally laid claim to the crown of France.

It is not clear whether or not Edward held this claim as a serious war aim. Since, in the Treaty of Brétigny, he was prepared to trade the claim to the throne for sovereignty over Aquitaine it may have been simply a way of encouraging allies and exerting negotiating pressure on Philip VI and his successor John II. With the failure to implement the treaty the issue remained unresolved throughout the rest of Edward III's life and the remainder of the war.

The Outbreak of War and the English Ascendancy, 1337–1360

First Moves

In May 1337 Philip VI's decision that the Duchy of Aquitaine should be forfeit due to Edward III's refusal to deliver Robert of Artois into the hands of the French led to Edward's revocation of homage. Philip had already proclaimed the *arrière-ban* to summons a royal army. The war which was to span the reigns of five French and five English kings and known to us now as the Hundred Years War had been unleashed.

At the start of the war both kings expected that Aquitaine and the south-west of France would be the principal theatre of operations. Indeed, in the first years of the war there were some French incursions into Aquitaine, where a small number of English reinforcements had been despatched. Also there was some cross-channel raiding by both sides, but as events unfolded it became apparent to the English and the French that the main focus would be to the north and neither king went to the south-west.

In the north attention turned to the Low Countries where there was widespread dissatisfaction with relationships with France. Edward III sought to exploit Philip's difficulties by forging an alliance with Louis of Bavaria, the Emperor of the Holy Roman Empire, and with the discontented lords in the Low Countries. Edward landed at Antwerp in July 1338 and made his way to Coblenz. Here he was appointed the Emperor's vicar, effectively vice-regent, in Western Europe for seven years and the Emperor's nobles gave Edward their homage. Edward summoned the nobles of the region to join his army in July 1339 with the objective of recovering the area around Cambrai from the French and restoring it to the Empire.

Edward's allies failed to arrive on time, and it was not until September that his army gathered. After a desultory attempt to take Cambrai by siege, the army moved into France and spread destruction in the hope of provoking Philip into coming to battle. By mid-October the allied lords were becoming restless and they were on the point of dispersing to return home when the prospect of battle persuaded them to stay. The French and English armies gathered near the town of La Capelle, with Edward in a strong defensive position. In the event, the French melted away and Edward's allies departed for home.

So far Flanders had remained neutral as the count had maintained a difficult balance between loyalty to the King of France and widespread internal opposition to his policy. However, Jacob van Artevelde, a powerful merchant from Ghent, had lent money to Edward and in return had secured the removal of restrictions on the import of English wool which was so important to Flanders. By late 1339 Artevelde had become *de facto* ruler of Flanders and the count had fled to France. A problem for Edward and Artevelde was that if the Flemish fought for Edward they would be in breach of their allegiance to their overlord, the King of France. The way around this problem was for Flanders to recognize Edward as King of France, and in Ghent in January 1340 Edward formally proclaimed his claim to the French crown.

English Successes in Flanders and Brittany – the Treaty of Malestroit
Edward returned to England to raise further subsidies, having expended huge sums during 1339 to pay and encourage his allies. In late June 1340 he set sail once again for Flanders. This was, on the face of it, a risky expedition. The French had had the upper hand at sea so far in the war, and a large fleet, including galleys furnished and crewed by the Genoese, had been assembled at Sluys in anticipation of Edward's return. Naval battles of the period were little different from combat ashore, with men boarding enemy ships to engage in hand-to-hand fighting. As on land, archers provided the English with a powerful weapon. The French chose to remain in harbour with their ships chained together to await the English. In doing so they sacrificed their ability to manoeuvre while Edward's ships were free to do so and optimize the use of their archers. The result was a crushing English victory in the first large-scale encounter of the war.

The success at Sluys brought in its train a treaty for Edward with Flanders, Hainault and Brabant. The main objective for the coming campaign was to be Tournai, with the goal of bringing King Philip to battle. The town was duly besieged while Philip watched events from a distance. He failed to come to the relief of the town and after six weeks it seemed close to surrender. However, Edward was faced with problems holding his allies together and he had little option but to agree to a one-year truce, the Truce of Esplechin, to run from September 1340. Early the next year Edward's appointment as the Emperor's vicar was withdrawn. The alliance collapsed, bringing to a close two years of war with little to show for the huge sums dispensed by the English exchequer.

In April 1341 the death of John III, Duke of Brittany, led to a disputed succession for the dukedom between John de Montfort and Charles de Blois. Initially, the struggle was a side-show but in early 1342 Edward III acceded to a request for help from Joan of Flanders on behalf of her husband John de Montfort, who was languishing in prison in Paris. An English force duly arrived in Brittany in May 1341, relieving the siege of Hennebout where Joan was holed up. A further English force, under the command of the Earl of Northampton who had been appointed Edward's lieutenant in Brittany, arrived in Brest in July. Northampton advanced to Morlaix and after an unsuccessful assault settled down to besiege the town. Charles de Blois came to its relief in late September, and in the first major land engagement of the war the Earl of Northampton drove off the relieving force. More English troops were to follow, with Edward arriving at Brest in person at the end of October 1342. The threat to the French was now such that it drew in both King Philip and his eldest son the Duke of Normandy, the future King John II. It looked in January 1343 as though there would be a set-piece battle between the French and the English, but once again this was not to be. Later that month the intervention of ambassadors of Pope Clement VI secured the Truce of Malestroit. The truce, which permitted the English and de Montfort's supporters to keep their gains, was intended to last for three years until September 1346.

A Return to War
In the next two years there were frequent outbreaks of fighting and finally in June 1345 Edward renounced the truce. With the resumption of war Edward conceived a three-pronged attack on France: the Earl of Northampton from Brittany, the Earl of Derby in the south-west and the king from Flanders. Edward crossed to Flanders, but here his plans came to nothing following the assassination of Artevelde during a riot in Ghent in July 1345. However, that month the Earl of Northampton, accompanied by John de Montfort who had escaped from France the month before,

returned to Brittany. The fighting continued through the winter and into 1346 with the English taking a number of towns, and in June 1346 Sir John Dagworth won a remarkable victory against superior numbers at St-Pol-de-Léon. Derby should have left for France at about the same time as Northampton left for Brittany but was delayed by the vagaries of weather in the Channel. He landed in Bordeaux on 9 August 1345 and embarked on an aggressive campaign from the outset, capturing a number of key towns, including Bergerac on the Dordogne, and La Réole and Aiguillon on the Garonne. In October 1345 he also defeated a substantially larger French army at Auberoche. Derby's success drew south the Duke of Normandy, who elected to attempt to retake Aiguillon and settled down to besiege the town in April 1346. The landing of Edward III in Normandy in July left Philip in a difficult position. John, Duke of Normandy, was in the south-west with a substantial force facing a relatively minor threat while the major challenge to the French developed in the north. The Duke of Normandy was recalled, but he was anxious to complete the siege of Aiguillon before he departed. In the event he left for the north without taking the town, but he did not leave until 20 August, too late to be able to join his father's army at the Battle of Crécy.

The Crécy Campaign
While Northampton and Derby continued with their operations during 1346, Edward revised his plans. Two further armies were now envisaged, one to be led by Edward III and a further army drawn from his Flemish allies and led by Sir Hugh Hastings. The destination of Edward's army was announced as Gascony, with the assumed aim being to assist in raising the siege of Aiguillon. However, this was disinformation intended to confuse the French, and once the army was at sea the true destination was revealed as Normandy. Godefroy d'Harcourt, a disaffected Norman noble in Edward's service, may have proposed the landing in his ancestral lands of the Cotentin peninsula, but another factor may have been the historical link between England and the duchy through its possession by English kings in the twelfth century. Whatever the reason, Edward's fleet made landfall off St-Vaast on 12 July 1346. Edward's subsequent march through France culminated in the Battle of Crécy, fought a little over six weeks later on 26 August 1346.

From Crécy to Brétigny
In the aftermath of Crécy Derby kept the pressure on the French in the south-west and in September and October 1346 struck north as far as Poitiers, but the main theatre of operations remained the north. From

Crécy-en-Ponthieu Edward III moved north with the objective of laying siege to Calais. On 4 September the first English troops approached the town. Over the next months considerable resources and determination were required to bring the siege to a successful conclusion. Late in July 1347 Philip approached with a large army to relieve the town, and issued a challenge to Edward. The English accepted the challenge but as so often in earlier years the French army faded away. The last hope for the garrison and the inhabitants had gone and the town surrendered. It was to remain an English town for more than 200 years until its surrender to the French in 1558 in the reign of Queen Mary.

In September 1347 a truce was agreed, initially until June of the following year. Although there was sporadic fighting in Brittany, the Calais Pale and Gascony during the formal respite in hostilities, the truce was extended several times until it finally collapsed in 1355. The focus now turned to Gascony, where the King of France's lieutenant, Jean I, Count of Armagnac, was making worrying incursions into English Aquitaine. Edward III despatched his eldest son Edward of Woodstock, the Black Prince, to Bordeaux, and between October and December 1355 he swept across the Languedoc as far as the Mediterranean before returning to Bordeaux. The following year he moved north and at the Battle of Poitiers in September 1356 won another great victory over the French. Poitiers was arguably the closest that the English came to winning a decisive battle during the Hundred Years War, with the King of France, since 1350 John II, captured and France thrown into chaos. John was taken to England in May 1357 and negotiations began to secure a lasting peace. It required a further English invasion, led once again by Edward III, in 1359 and 1360, marked by the unsuccessful siege of Reims, to finally compel the French to agree terms, enshrined in the Treaty of Brétigny which was ratified in Calais in October 1360.

The Peace of Brétigny

Under the Treaty of Brétigny, in addition to Edward and John trading sovereignty over Aquitaine for the English claim to the French crown, huge tracts of south-western France were ceded to Edward. Thus, the first phase of war left the English under Edward III in the ascendancy, but, due to the failure to implement all of its provisions, the Treaty of Brétigny, instead of providing the opportunity for a lasting peace, sowed the seeds for a renewal of war. On John's death in 1364 a substantial part of his ransom, agreed as part of the treaty, remained unpaid. The outstanding sum was to remain an issue between England and France, and its settlement was an objective in Henry V's negotiations with the French fifty years later.

The French Recovery, 1369–1389

Charles V succeeded John II in 1364. He had been a party to the Treaty of Brétigny. However, since the joint renunciations of sovereignty (over Aquitaine by John and by Edward of his claim to the French crown) had not been ratified he refused to be bound by them. From Charles' accession there was a steady deterioration in relations between France and England, and in 1367, at Nájera in Spain, an Anglo-Gascon army led by the Black Prince in support of Pedro the Cruel's claim to the throne of Castile defeated the other claimant, Henry of Trastámara and his Franco-Castilian army. Pedro reneged on his commitment to fund this campaign and the Black Prince, who since 1363 had been Prince of Aquitaine, had to resort to increased taxation on his subjects in Aquitaine. This resulted in considerable discontent, and in 1368 the Count of Armagnac, whose lands were within the newly expanded Aquitaine, appealed a dispute with the Black Prince to King Charles V. Charles was aware that hearing the appeal amounted to a rejection of English claims to sovereignty over Aquitaine, but nevertheless he issued a summons for the prince to appear in Paris in 1369. The prince failed to attend and the war was renewed.

Charles V was too astute to repeat the experiences of his grandfather and father at the battles of Crécy and Poitiers, and he generally avoided large-scale set-piece battles. His strategy was to harass English armies and gradually push back the boundaries of English-held territory by retaking towns and castles. He was aided by a shrewd and effective commander, Bertrand du Guesclin, Constable of France, and by the time of Charles V's death in 1380 the English possessions had been reduced to the Calais Pale and a coastal strip near Bordeaux.

An Uneasy Truce, 1389–1415

The war continued, with neither side making significant advances, until the Truce of Leulinghem in 1389. Negotiations to find a permanent peace dragged on but without success. In 1396, to forestall the risk of a return to war, an extension to the truce was agreed. The truce was cemented by the marriage of King Richard II to Charles VI's daughter Isabella. However, trouble was in the wind, and in 1399 Henry Bolingbroke, son of John of Gaunt, usurped his cousin Richard II to become Henry IV. The French would not recognize Henry as the lawful King of England, but they did agree that the truce of 1396 would remain in force. Henry had his hands full at home with rebellions and trouble in Scotland and Wales, and the French, while stopping short of formally reopening hostilities, missed no opportunity to create difficulties for the English, including incursions into Aquitaine, support for the Scots, recognition of Owen Glendower as Prince of Wales, and tacit support for acts of piracy against English shipping. From 1404 until early 1407 there were more determined, but unsuccessful, attempts to drive the English out of Aquitaine. Within the French camp Charles VI suffered from sporadic bouts of mental illness which, although never making him totally incapable of ruling, left a major weakness at the heart of French government. This weakness was exacerbated by the jockeying for power and feuding between Louis I, Duke of Orléans, and his supporters, later known as the Armagnacs, and the Burgundians led by Duke John the Fearless. The Duke of Orléans, an erstwhile friend of Henry Bolingbroke while he had been in exile in France during the latter years of the reign of Richard II, turned violently against Henry after his usurpation of Richard, and he was the leading protagonist in attempts to drive the English from Aquitaine. The assassination of the Duke of Orléans in 1407 at the instigation of John the Fearless, successor to Philip the Bold as Duke of Burgundy, relieved the pressure on the English in Aquitaine but also resulted in a period of political instability and complex diplomatic relationships that lasted for the rest of Henry IV's reign.

A triangular relationship emerged between the Armagnacs, the Burgundians and the English. Both French factions tried to gain English support as they manoeuvred for internal power, and the English attempted to exploit the weaknesses within France for their own ends. France descended into civil war during 1411 and 1412, with the English first of all intervening with an army led by the Earl of Arundel supporting the Duke of Burgundy and Charles VI against the rebel Armagnacs. In 1412 Henry IV, in response to a tempting offer from the Armagnacs which included recognition of English sovereignty over Aquitaine, sent an English army of 4,000 men led by the Duke of Clarence to support the rebels. However, by the time Clarence landed, the rebels, Charles VI and the Duke of Burgundy had come to terms and the competing factions were again at peace.

In March 1413 Henry V succeeded to the throne on the death of Henry IV. Because of his father's usurpation of Richard II and the history of rebellions during the reign of Henry IV, the new king could not feel entirely secure on his throne. However, the situation in France was even more precarious. In early 1414 the Duke of Burgundy had fallen from grace and been declared a traitor, and France once more descended into civil war with Charles VI, the dauphin and the Armagnacs launching a war against the Duke of Burgundy. Meanwhile, Henry had agreed a ten-year truce with John V, Duke of Brittany, declaring the duke to be an ally. Henry V had inherited from his father a campaign in Aquitaine being waged against the Armagnacs. This fighting came to a halt in early 1414, with a truce agreed to last for twelve months and applicable throughout France. Simultaneously Henry was putting out feelers for a lasting peace, with terms which included his marriage to Catherine de Valois, the daughter of Charles VI. With France in disarray due to internecine fighting Henry felt emboldened enough by May 1414 to start to press his territorial claims on the French king. At about the same time, in parallel with his negotiations with Charles VI, he also started trying to establish an alliance with the Duke of Burgundy to include mutual aid through the provision of men-at-arms and archers and a marriage to the duke's daughter. The Duke of Burgundy was prepared to help Henry conquer lands held by the Armagnac lords, but he would not go so far as to enter into an alliance against Charles VI or the dauphin.

The continuing part played by the causes of the war can be seen in Henry's demand for the restitution by Charles VI of lands granted under the Treaty of Brétigny, and the payment of the 1.6 million *écus* outstanding from the treaty for John II's ransom homage. He now went further, however, demanding lordship over Normandy, Touraine, Maine and Anjou, and the homage of Brittany and Flanders and marriage to Charles' daughter Catherine with a dowry of 2 million *écus*. Henry's hope was that with the danger of an Anglo-Burgundian alliance hanging over them Charles VI and his advisers could be pressurized into accepting these terms. The French were certainly concerned about the English negotiations with the Duke of Burgundy, but they were not prepared to go as far as Henry wanted. His ambassadors returned empty-handed to England in October.

A Return to War, 1415–1444

Meanwhile, Henry had begun to prepare for war. Parliament had agreed to grant taxes to support his policy, but it wanted Henry to continue to negotiate. In pursuit of a negotiated peace, the truce, due to expire in January 1415, had been extended until May, and English ambassadors crossed to France once more in February. By the time of the arrival of the English negotiating team Charles VI and the Duke of Burgundy had come to terms and agreed the Treaty of Arras. The treaty banned any alliances with the English which could be prejudicial to the interests of the French crown. When the negotiations reopened in March, Henry's ambassadors presented much reduced territorial demands and progress was being made on the marriage between Henry and Catherine. The French, although their position had been much strengthened by the Duke of Burgundy's accommodation with the king, were ready to move some way towards Henry's demand over territories in Aquitaine. However, they linked this concession to withdrawal of the English claim for the sum outstanding from John II's ransom. The English ambassadors withdrew from negotiations towards the end of March, declaring that they did not have the authority to agree the terms on offer. Henry had so far failed to exploit French divisions, but he continued to try to come to an accord with the Duke of Burgundy during the spring and summer and the French continued to harbour fears of an Anglo-Burgundian alliance. They also sought to delay Henry's preparation for war, and French ambassadors crossed to England in June. Negotiations, which were held with Henry in person, broke down acrimoniously and the ambassadors returned to France in early July.

As negotiations and preparations for war continued, Henry was acutely aware that his hold on the throne was insecure. There had been remarks by the French ambassadors that not only did he have no right to the French crown but also that they should be negotiating with the descendants of Richard II and not Henry, and there was an apparent plot against him on the eve of his departure from the Solent on 1 August 1415 (the Southampton Plot) which resulted in the summary execution of the Earl of Cambridge, Henry Lord Scrope and Sir Thomas Grey.

Henry had intended to assemble his army by 1 July, but delays in mustering troops and gathering enough shipping delayed departure until 11 August. The landing was to be made in Normandy, probably with the objective of taking the duchy to strengthen Henry's bargaining position. Harfleur was the initial target, a useful bridgehead in northern France which would also deny the French use of an important fortified naval base which had been used to launch attacks against the coast of England and on English shipping. Having besieged and taken Harfleur, Henry marched north-east towards Calais and safety. On reaching the Somme he found the ford at Blanchetaque too well defended by the French and he marched up-river until he was able to cross. He turned once again towards Calais and confronted and defeated the French at Agincourt. After his victory he continued to Calais and returned to England.

The Battle of Agincourt is popularly seen as the greatest English victory in the Middle Ages. However, despite the magnitude of the victory, it was not decisive. Edward III, Henry's great-grandfather, had been able to follow up his victory at Crécy with the siege and capture of Calais, and Edward's son the Black Prince had captured John II at Poitiers, thus giving his father perhaps the closest that the English were to come to a decisive victory during the Hundred Years War. After Agincourt Charles VI remained at large, and Henry V did not have the means to follow up his victory that year. However, it did secure Henry's position on the throne and he could pursue his obsession with France unchallenged at home. He could now return to England and capitalize on his success and plan for the future.

During 1416 the Holy Roman Emperor Sigismund, who had initially offered to mediate between the French and the English, recognized Henry's claim to the French throne. Later in the year Sigismund and Henry met the Duke of Burgundy at Calais. Henry was encouraged that, while the Duke of Burgundy would not go so far as to recognize him as King of France, he would not stand in his way, and in August 1417 Henry set off again for France. His aim was to conquer the Duchy of Normandy and use it to enforce his claims, and now sieges of major towns became a central element of Henry's strategy. By the end of September Caen was in English hands. Other towns, including Bayeux, fell soon after and the conquest continued with Rouen, the greatest Norman city, falling in January 1419 after being besieged for almost six months. The Duke of Burgundy was meanwhile taking advantage of the English operations to launch attacks against the Armagnacs. However, there was ambiguity in the Burgundian position and there were occasions when English and Burgundian troops clashed. The French were well aware that their disunity was playing into the hands of Henry V, and attempts were made to resolve the differences between the factions. In September the Duke of Burgundy met the dauphin. Heated discussions ensued and Duke John the Fearless was murdered by a member of the dauphin's party, thus precipitating the very event that the dauphin wished to avoid: pushing Burgundy, now ruled by the new duke, Philip the Good, into the arms of the English. In December 1419 Henry and Philip agreed to wage war together against the dauphin. They also agreed that if Henry succeeded in his pursuit of his claim to the French crown the Duke of Burgundy would be his lieutenant for his French domains.

Henry now turned his attention to King Charles VI with negotiations which concluded with the Treaty of Troyes in May 1420. Under the treaty

Henry was to be heir to Charles VI and to be regent of France during the remainder of Charles' life. He was to retain the Duchy of Normandy by right of conquest in the meantime, and his entitlement to hold Aquitaine without homage was recognized. Little more than a week after the treaty Henry married Charles' daughter Catherine.

The dauphin, who was by no means powerless, had been consolidating his position. In response to his invoking the 'auld alliance' with Scotland a number of Scots had entered his service, and at Easter 1421 the Duke of Clarence was killed when he was defeated at Baugé by a Franco-Scottish army. In June Henry V returned to France. In December Henry's heir, the future Henry VI, was born, but in August 1422, before a year had passed, Henry V died of dysentery contracted during the siege of Meaux. Less than two months later Charles VI followed him to the grave. The infant Henry VI was proclaimed King of England and France.

Henry V's untimely death at the age of thirty-five left his brother the Duke of Bedford as regent in France. Under his regency there were further English victories, but the duke was faced with a range of problems as he struggled to build on Henry's legacy and consolidate English rule in France. He and the Duke of Burgundy controlled large areas of France, but outside these areas France remained loyal to the dauphin, and Bedford struggled to make further inroads into this territory. He also faced growing discontent from Henry VI's subjects in France who were compelled to pay taxes to support the war and a similar reluctance at home to pay for the continuing fighting. Difficulties with his allies compounded his problems: the Duke of Brittany moved back and forth between the French and English causes, and the Duke of Burgundy was reluctant to pursue the war vigorously.

Then in 1429 Joan of Arc came on to the scene, bringing a change of fortune for the French. The siege of Orléans was broken in May, and the retreating English army was defeated at the Battle of Patay the following month. The dauphin, at Joan's urging, went to Reims and was crowned and anointed as Charles VII, giving a further boost to his standing and to French morale. The capture of Joan in 1430 and her subsequent trial and execution in 1431 offered the prospect of restored English fortunes, and the Duke of Bedford brought Henry VI to Paris to be crowned King of France in December. However, lack of funds from England to prosecute the war, and the continuing necessity of imposing taxes on the inhabitants of Normandy, led to increasing discontent among the population and an erosion of English control. The following year the Duke of Burgundy was beginning to look for ways to break with the English. In 1435 the Duke of

Bedford died, and only two weeks after his death Philip the Good finally made peace with Charles VII with the Treaty of Arras.

The Truce of Tours, 1444–1449, and the Defeat of the English

The war continued with the French making inroads into English-held lands and by 1444 the areas held by the English had been reduced to part of Aquitaine, the Calais Pale, the County of Maine and Lower Normandy, although Harfleur, lost to the French in 1435, had been recovered in 1440, as had some other parts of Normandy, and was in English hands again. But by now both sides were ready for peace, and the Truce of Tours was agreed. The truce collapsed in 1449, and the English were rapidly swept aside by a siege campaign and defeat in the field at the Battle of Formigny in April 1450. By August Cherbourg, the last of the English fortresses in Normandy, had fallen and all of Henry V's gains in northern France had gone. The French now turned their attention to Bordeaux and Aquitaine, and in July 1453 an Anglo-Gascon army was routed at Castillon, the last battle of the Hundred Years War. Three months later Bordeaux surrendered and the war was over.

At first sight it may seem strange that the English kings should win the three great battles of Crécy, Poitiers and Agincourt, as well as many less well known battles, and yet lose the war. However, with the benefit of hindsight it is difficult to see how English kings could have held on to power in France, a country significantly richer and more populous than England. Edward III overcame these imbalances in population and wealth through victories on the battlefield at Crécy and Poitiers, the exploitation of internal divisions in France, and his effective use of contracted armies. With the successive victories of Crécy and Poitiers, and the Treaty of Brétigny, he came close to bringing the war to a successful conclusion, but even if the treaty had held in the longer run the overall imbalance between the two countries would surely in due course have brought a renewal of war and the defeat of England. As it was, the inherent weakness of the English position became apparent after the collapse of the Treaty of Brétigny in 1369, when Edward now had to hold vastly expanded territories while Charles V with his larger resources in manpower and wealth avoided pitched battles and rapidly recovered towns and castles in the early 1370s. By Henry V's time the French internal divisions were even more acute than during Edward III's reign, and, in alliance with the Duke of Burgundy, Henry was able to take advantage of French weakness to conquer and hold wide swathes of territory and secure the French crown for himself and his successors. Who knows how events would have turned out if Henry had lived to take the throne and reign in France? However, in Henry VI's reign holding these lands imposed an intolerable burden of taxation both at home and in the English territories in France. In addition, French military reforms, some of which had been started in the reign of Charles V, came to fruition under Charles VII, resulting in a more professional army which made good use of its artillery to reduce the last English strongholds and bring Charles' army victory at Castillon. The internal divisions within France were also gradually mastered. Once this process had been completed and French resources could be effectively used, the expulsion of the English from France was probably inevitable. Within two years of the Battle of Castillon England became embroiled in the Wars of the Roses, and with the energies of English kings and the nobility turned inwards there was no way back to achieve the goals set by Edward III more than a century earlier.

Chapter 2

Siege Warfare

The Characteristics of a Siege

The popular image of a siege probably conjures up the picture of a long drawn-out confrontation between besiegers and besieged. The reality is that sieges could vary significantly in duration. The Black Prince's reduction of the castle at Romorantin in 1356 took only a few days, while eleven months were required to bring Calais to its knees in 1346–1347. Sometimes the arrival of an army intent on either a siege or an assault would be sufficient to induce the garrison to surrender. The end of the siege could result from the capitulation of the town, as happened at Calais, a successful assault, such as the Black Prince's notorious but much exaggerated sack of Limoges in 1370, by the relief of the town, as at Cosne in 1422, or by the withdrawal of the besiegers, as in the case of Edward III before Reims in 1360.

The withdrawal of a besieging force could be brought about by a number of factors. At Aiguillon in 1346 the Duke of Normandy reluctantly withdrew his force because he was ordered to do so by his father King Philip VI who had need of the men for his defence of the realm against Edward III's invading force. In the event the duke hesitated too long and arrived too late to affect the outcome of the Battle of Crécy. At Béthune, in the same year, the besieging force of Flemish and English troops under the command of Hugh Hastings was driven off after only ten days. In large part this was due to a vigorous defence which contributed to the collapse of the besiegers' morale and their dispersal. Edward III slipped away and abandoned his siege of Reims in January 1360 because the defence was well conducted and the town had been well provisioned, while the besiegers faced increasing penury in the depths of winter and could no longer sustain the siege.

The problem of feeding the men and horses of a besieging army was not limited to winter, however, and was a major challenge associated with maintaining a siege involving large numbers of men. At the siege of Bourges during the civil war between the Armagnacs and the Burgundians the problem of providing sufficient food and water was acute even in summer. A long heatwave dried up the streams and wells. After only a matter of days the army had exhausted the supply of cattle in the surrounding area, and crops and fruit had been stripped from an area for more than 30km around Bourges. As a consequence it was soon necessary to move the siege camp, and water and supplies had to be brought in from far afield by armed convoys.

Edward III had had to abandon the siege of Reims in 1360, having exhausted local supplies. Henry V learned the lesson from his great-grandfather's experience at Reims and for his siege of Rouen he made arrangements to secure access along the Seine for food to be shipped from England to Harfleur and then up-river to his siege camp.

Apart from the ever-present challenge of feeding the besiegers, maintaining an effective encirclement was no easy matter, especially of a large town. Admittedly the siege of Calais presented particular problems with the need to prevent access by sea as well as by land. The strength of the siege army varied over the period of the siege, and over the winter of 1346/7 probably numbered between 5,000 and 6,000 men. However, over the period of the siege Edward III deployed an estimated 32,000 men to maintain a secure cordon of a town with a population of around 8,000. It was impossible to contemplate a complete encirclement of a large city such as Paris, although, in view of the heavy demand for produce for such a populous city from the surrounding countryside, to some extent an effective blockade could be imposed by controlling major access routes. Between 1419 and 1422 there was a struggle between the Dauphinists and the English to control access to Burgundian-dominated Paris by taking and holding fortresses and towns around the capital. At its worst, for the English, the Dauphinists controlled strong places around Paris from Compiègne in the north in an arc to the east and as far round as Dreux to the west, leaving the English Mantes-la-Jolie, Meulan, Pontoise and Beaumont-sur-Oise protecting and permitting access from Normandy. Similarly, as we shall see later, the Anglo-Burgundians were unable to maintain a complete encirclement of Orléans in 1428–1429, leaving the Dauphinists free to come and go with ambassadors, messengers, reinforcements and supplies with relative ease.

To compound the problems of the besiegers, a well-organized defence could be maintained by a relatively small number of professional soldiers with the assistance of the town militia. At Harfleur Henry V had around 12,000 men and when the town surrendered 260 knights and men-at-arms, probably the sum total of men-at-arms holding the town, were allowed to leave. During 1403–1404, when Henry IV was attempting to counter Owen Glendower's rebellion in Wales, the mighty Caernarvon castle held out with a garrison of only forty men. In August 1403 Harlech had already been under siege for some months, but the garrison resisted until the following February with just twenty-one defenders.

Siege camps were notorious for their unhygienic conditions and Henry's army at Harfleur suffered badly from dysentery. The number of deaths was relatively small but at least 1,300 men had to be repatriated because they were unfit to take part in the march to Calais. In July 1412 the besieging army of the Duke of Burgundy is said to have lost 2,000 men to dysentery outside the walls of Bourges, a problem that was compounded by the corpses of many horses lost due to illness. In such circumstances it was not surprising that the numbers were further depleted by deserters as they saw their comrades succumb. Further perennial difficulties with medieval armies in general, and besiegers in particular, were discontent and desertions because of arrears of pay. This was another problem which occurred at Bourges, necessitating the provost of Paris, who was with the besieging army, being sent to the capital to raise funds. Similarly, during the siege of Orléans, bringing in money to pay the garrison was a high priority.

If the besiegers could cope with the problems of supply and sickness then, short of taking the town or castle by assault, they could expect to see the balance swing in their favour if their blockade proved effective. The length of the resistance would be linked to the preparedness of the defenders but also to the prospect of relief. A castle or town remote from friendly forces could be expected to surrender quite quickly, once honour had been satisfied, with token resistance. If there were a realistic hope of relief, however, resistance could be prolonged. Both Calais in 1347 and Harfleur in 1415 hung on until it became apparent that there was no possibility of relief. As we shall see, there were frequent examples of strong places making only token resistance. However, this could rebound on the commander. Jean Belon, the captain of La Roche-sur-Yon in 1370, was judged to have acted treasonably and was executed. Sir William Chamberlain, the English captain at Meaux in 1439, was tried for treason, but was more fortunate than Belon and was acquitted.

Another influence on the conduct and duration of the siege of a town could be the attitude of the inhabitants. Split loyalties among the inhabitants and differing interests between the townspeople and the professional soldiers charged with its defence could often prove fatal to successful resistance. For the inhabitants a desire to preserve property and wealth could often incline them to look for a peaceful solution, while the commander of the garrison would often be driven more by his sense of loyalty or duty. At Pontoise in 1417 the townspeople had become tired of the daily round of duty and, seeing the siege engines and artillery being put into place in front of the gates, feared for their lives. They decided that enough was enough and confronted the Armagnac garrison commanders to compel them to surrender to the Burgundians. In 1417 messengers bringing news of the surrender of Provins to Paris were asked why the town and castle, considered impregnable, had surrendered to the Burgundians. The reply was that 'After having at first refused to surrender and having been disposed to resist vigorously, the inhabitants allowed their resolve to be shaken by the prayers of the women shut up with them.' Faced with entreaties not to risk all being put to the sword, a treaty of surrender was negotiated on condition that the lives and goods of the townspeople would be spared. Unfortunately, the agreement was violated and the town was pillaged and sacked. Internal divisions could also manifest themselves in treachery. This might be for political reasons or simply a result of self-interest. In 1356 the rear-guard of the Black Prince's army did not have either the equipment or enough men for a siege of Bourges, but tried to enter the town with the help of a citizen, Perrot Monein, who had leased land close to the wall by one of the town gates and started to build a house. He offered to show the English a way into the town for an undisclosed sum of money. This came to naught, and the unfortunate Monein was discovered. His house was confiscated and sold for the profit of the king, and he was decapitated for treason. With perhaps more of a political motive, the Abbot of the Abbey of St Médard in the *bourg* of Soissons, despite its Burgundian garrison, opened the gates to the Armagnacs.

Divisions would be accentuated if the chance of relief seemed remote. As we shall see, the prospect of relief would also weigh in the calculations of the besiegers. The Bishop of Norwich's siege of Ypres in 1383 was abandoned in part due to the imminent arrival of a large French army.

The Strategic Context

At the start of the Hundred Years War, in the reign of Edward III, England had a population approximately one third the size of that of France. France was also wealthier than England, with the French king potentially able to raise three or four times as much in taxation as the English king. However, this is a little misleading since the English kings had the advantage of the parliamentary system which gave them, admittedly not always without difficulty, an almost constant flow of revenue. French kings were much more dependent upon emergency grants. The English also had the disadvantage of external lines of communication. They needed to use the sea for reinforcement of the Duchy of Aquitaine and logistic support from the home base for their armies in France. They faced the challenges of finding shipping and the vagaries of the weather, while the French enjoyed the inherent advantages of internal movement over land. Overall, the English did not have the capacity to wage a war of conquest and occupation. To achieve Edward's war aims he needed to defeat the French king on the battlefield. In the early years of the war he tried to achieve this through the recruitment of allies in the Low Countries, coupled with the exploitation of the *chevauchée*. The *chevauchée* was essentially a mounted expedition moving at speed, often across a broad front, which allowed the English to exert the maximum of pressure from the available resources, and to choose the area of operations.

Edward's allies in this phase of the war proved unreliable, since they were largely motivated by money rather than by a shared cause. The result was the expenditure of a good deal of effort and treasure to little effect. When Edward embarked on his invasion of France in 1346 his strategic goal remained the same: to defeat Philip VI in battle. He still hoped to enlist allies from the Low Countries, but the *chevauchée* took on greater emphasis as the primary instrument of his strategy. The objectives of the strategy at this stage of the war were encapsulated in a letter from Edward III to King Philip VI in 1346 in the days before Crécy: '... to punish rebels against us and to comfort our friends and those faithful to us ... to carry on the war as best we can, to our advantage and the loss of our enemies'. A secondary but important consideration was that the *chevauchée* kept the war away from home. As the fifteenth-century writer Christine de Pisan wrote, 'It is better to trample another country than to allow one's own to be trampled underfoot.'

In the right circumstances the *chevauchée* could encourage allies and entice the enemy to do battle, but a key aspect was, of course, pillaging. Some of this was necessary to supply the needs of the army, but in addition there would have been the looting of movable wealth by troops. A proportion of loot would be surrendered to the retinue commander of the man concerned and a proportion to the king. Nevertheless, there was still the prospect of considerable personal gain: a powerful recruiting incentive for the English. Looting also served to diminish the resources of the French king's subjects available for taxation. As was evident later in the war, troops engaged in garrison duty were often prone to (and indeed were sometimes encouraged to) raid in their surrounding area, which was supposed to be friendly territory, precisely because of the lack of opportunity for personal enrichment provided by a *chevauchée*. The preference for the *chevauchée* was essentially a pragmatic choice which reflected the imbalance of resources between the two kingdoms. This was not, of course, to the exclusion of sieges which complemented the overall strategy. Indeed, numerous sieges were conducted during Edward III's reign, but they were generally incompatible with the *chevauchée* since siege equipment, and later artillery, was heavy and could not be moved at the speed of the rest of the army. Of course, the exception proves the rule, and the Black Prince did, as we shall see later, conduct a successful siege at Romorantin during his *chevauchée* of 1356, although this did not include the use of siege equipment. It was through this strategy of the *chevauchée* that Edward came close to bringing the war to a successful conclusion with the Treaty of Brétigny in 1360 following the Black Prince's victory at Poitiers four years before.

With the return to war in 1369 King Charles V had drawn the appropriate lessons from the defeat of his grandfather at Crécy and his father at Poitiers, where he had also been present. Battle was a too unpredictable and high risk affair. He gave instructions to his commanders to avoid large-scale pitched battles with the English. His strategy was to defeat and drive the English out by taking towns and fortresses back under French control. The English simply did not have the resources to counter this strategy and hold on to the territory ceded to Edward III by the Treaty of Brétigny.

When war restarted in the reign of Henry V there was a change of emphasis. Henry's strategy, particularly from 1417 with his second campaign, was now focused on conquest and occupation. The underlying resource imbalance between England and France had not changed, but the political situation was very different. France was a divided country plunged into civil war between the Armagnac and Burgundian factions, raising taxes and armies was problematic and both sides in the civil war were constantly looking over their shoulders while ostensibly fighting the common enemy. In 1419 the assassination of John the Fearless, Duke of Burgundy, thrust the Burgundians into the arms of the English, creating a significant shift in the balance of power between the French and the Anglo-Burgundians.

Conquest and occupation of necessity required the taking and holding of towns and fortresses, and thus siege warfare became the predominant strategic tool for Henry. The defeats at Crécy, Poitiers and Agincourt had a profound impact on the French military psyche, and they also saw the holding of towns and castles as a more effective approach than facing the risk of battle. Of course, there were set-piece battles in this phase of the war, but the expansion of the English conquest was achieved largely through the taking and holding of towns.

When the tide finally turned for the French from 1449 until the final expulsion of the English in 1453 from all their French lands except Calais, there were major victories in the field for the French at Formigny in Normandy in 1450 and Castillon in Gascony in 1453. Nevertheless, the collapse of English power in Normandy largely resulted from the relentless return of towns and fortresses to French allegiance. Many of these surrendered without the need either for assault or the establishment of a siege, but there were numerous sieges, often of relatively short duration, most notably of Rouen, Caen and Cherbourg.

The Conventions of Siege Warfare

There were no codified rules of war during the Hundred Years War, but there were disciplinary ordinances issued to armies, chivalric customs and a widely held convention about the conduct of sieges. By the Middle Ages this had in Christendom acquired a religious context, but the practices went back well into antiquity with little if any change in the essential characteristics. The Old Testament Book of Deuteronomy encapsulates the approach in antiquity:

> When you advance on a town to take it, make an offer of peace. If the offer is accepted and the town opens its gates to you, then all the people therein are to be put to forced labour and work for you. If the town does not make peace with you but gives battle, you are to lay siege to it and, when the Lord your God delivers it into your hands, put every man in it to the sword; but you may take the women, the dependents, and the livestock for yourselves, and plunder everything else in the town. You may enjoy the use of the spoil from your enemies which the Lord your God gives you.

A chaplain with the army of Henry V at Harfleur in 1415, who gave a detailed account of the siege and the Agincourt campaign, remarked that Henry's conduct was in accordance with the Book of Deuteronomy: either peace in return for surrender or, if the town had to be taken by assault, no quarter for the male inhabitants with women and property liable to be carried off as spoils of war. This is the first known explicit link with Deuteronomy: the practice in the Hundred Years War was generally less extreme.

An offer normally led to negotiations for a treaty, often referred to as a composition, with the garrison or the citizens of the town. Often surrender was related to the prospect of relief with a date set by which, if relief had not arrived, the town or fortress would open its gates. It was in the interest of the besieger to give the relieving force as little time as possible to come to the rescue, while the defenders would want to maximize the time within the limits of their remaining victuals and supplies. At Harfleur it is not clear whether Henry V offered terms or if the town asked for them. It is also unclear whether or not the negotiations for terms followed an assault or simply the threat of the town being stormed. In any case Henry wanted the town to surrender the following day. In the event he conceded that five days could be allowed. The dauphin was 120km away at Vernon on the Seine, and by the time the messenger arrived the chance of an army of relief arriving by the given time was remote. As it happens the French had not yet mustered sufficient forces and relief was impossible. At Calais in 1347 Philip VI arrived with a relief army but stood by and then, judging the risks too great, turned away and left the town to its fate.

The treaties for the surrender of a town were often detailed and lengthy. They frequently permitted the professional soldiers to leave with their arms, stipulated what was to be done with weapons, military stores and valuables, and prohibited the demolition or repair of fortifications pending the surrender. Treaties also often stipulated those among the garrison who would not be granted safe conduct or pardons but would be subject to the king's mercy. Following the assassination of John the Fearless, Duke of Burgundy, in 1419 treaties drawn up by Anglo-Burgundian siege commanders commonly exempted those who may have been involved in the assassination from any right to pardon or safe conduct. There were instances of treaties being violated or ill-disciplined troops pillaging and raping contrary to the settlement reached between the besieging commander and the garrison, but in general the civilian population could expect mercy. At Harfleur, possibly in part perhaps because Henry wanted to turn the town into an English enclave on the pattern of Calais, those who swore allegiance to Henry were permitted to remain. Others were held for ransom. Women, children, the sick, poor and elderly were expelled. They were given money and an escort and handed over to the French.

A perennial problem for a town under siege was how to make supplies last as long as possible. There often came a point when those unable to contribute to the defence – women, children and the infirm – either left of their own free will or were expelled and abandoned to the mercy of the besiegers. The treatment of these *bouches inutiles* ('useless mouths') presented the besiegers with a dilemma. To allow them to starve was harsh even by the standards of the time, but to give them succour could encourage further expulsions and prolong the siege. At Calais around 500 people were reported as being expelled as the end of the town's endurance approached and one chronicler reported that they were refused re-entry and starved to death between the English lines and the walls of the town. Another report describes 500 men leaving the town earlier in the siege and throwing themselves on the mercy of Edward III, who fed them and sent them on their way with money. It may be that both accounts are true, since later in the siege the king's attitude certainly hardened as the enormous costs of the siege mounted. Calais also shows how convention could prevail over baser instincts. When the town finally surrendered Edward III was in no mood to be merciful after the loss of many lives and the expenditure of much treasure and was determined to show no mercy to the townspeople who had caused him so much trouble. The accounts of what followed vary in detail but it seems that one of the English negotiators, Sir Walter Manny, prevailed upon the king, reasoning that if he broke the conventions and put the inhabitants to the sword after they had surrendered the tables might be turned one day and the English given no quarter. The king relented and said that six prominent citizens must put themselves at his mercy and he would then spare the rest of the inhabitants. He was determined upon the execution of the six but Queen Philippa and other ladies pleaded with him on their knees to spare the celebrated six burghers of Calais. Edward relented and the convention was not breached.

If towns were taken by storm then the population certainly risked losing life and limb. When Henry V took Caen in 1417 he gave orders for women and priests to be spared, but even so a generation later one source claimed that around 2,000 of the inhabitants were killed. In general, contemporary chroniclers showed little if any concern for such loss of civilian life in the event of a town being stormed after refusing to surrender. However, the storming of the *cité* of Limoges in 1370 after a siege of five days has become notorious because of the account of Jean Froissart. Contrary to other chroniclers he showed sympathy for those who died, alleging that 3,000 people were killed. Froissart is not known to have visited Limoges and no other source refers to a massacre on such a scale. Recent analysis points towards Froissart's account as being fanciful at best and at worst black propaganda to sully the reputation of the Black Prince. Another contemporary account is more realistic, talking about 300 civilians being killed, and a letter written by the Black Prince has come to light which recounts that 200 of the garrison were captured; by extrapolation, it appears that some 100 men-at-arms and perhaps 200 civilians were killed.

Costs

Siege warfare entailed considerable economic and human costs for both the besiegers and the besieged alike. The ever-present threat of attack or siege brought recurring costs to the Crown and local government in towns in France in times of both peace and war. Fortifications had to be built, modernized and maintained. Weapons and equipment had to be provisioned and kept in good order, and garrisons paid. In times of war a well-prepared town or fortress would incur the costs associated with purchasing and storing supplies to enable a siege to be sustained. Often supplementary fortifications had to be constructed when a siege was expected and buildings outside the walls destroyed to remove shelter and cover for besiegers. The maintenance of fortifications and garrisons was to prove a tremendous burden for both the English and the Normans administering English-occupied Normandy, especially in the latter years of the war as the French established their supremacy.

At times of siege there were the obvious direct costs of paying for the besieging army and the garrison. Of course, these varied significantly with the size of the force and the duration of the siege. As an extreme example, the English siege of Calais in 1346–1347 absorbed an enormous proportion of the national resources at sea and on land for eleven months. At the other end of the scale, for example the Black Prince's short siege of Romorantin in 1356, the costs would be almost incidental to the overall costs of the two-month expedition. There would also be costs associated with moving large artillery pieces across country. At the Burgundian siege of Calais in 1436 just one of the ten great bombards deployed required eighty-four horses to move it to the siege. In addition to these more obvious costs there were other more minor costs; for example, at Romorantin in 1356 the Count of Blois paid a soldier in his service 40 *écus* to compensate him for lost armour. For many towns the end of a siege brought no relief from expenditure. There would often be buildings to be rebuilt, inside and outside the walls, and fortifications to be repaired, even if the place had neither surrendered nor been taken. For those towns which were subjected to a number of sieges, sometimes at relatively short intervals, the burden falling on the townspeople to rebuild their town and fortifications must have been both considerable and dispiriting to say the least.

Indirect, but unquantifiable, costs were those associated with the stripping of resources from often a very wide area of the countryside around besieged towns: resources taken by the garrison for their own purposes and to deny them to the enemy, and by the besiegers to sustain their operations. Of course, the exhaustion of these resources could lead to the fall of a town or fortress but equally it could compel besiegers to abandon their siege. If the local area was exhausted after the harvest then the inhabitants would be left in a parlous state as they attempted to survive the ensuing months before another harvest could be garnered.

The human costs for townspeople and garrisons were considerable during and after a siege. Inhabitants considered *bouches inutiles* could be expelled to die between the besiegers' lines and the town walls. Often, as we shall see elsewhere, insanitary conditions constituted a perennial scourge for besiegers, with dysentery often claiming lives and leaving other men so sick as to be unable to carry out their duties. The inhabitants also faced insanitary conditions and increasing shortage of supplies, leading to disease, famine and death within the walls. Measures would often be taken to impose price controls to try to avoid rising inflation for food supplies and keep essentials affordable for all inhabitants regardless of status. Of course, inhabitants also risked death and the destruction of their property and possessions if the place were taken by storm. Property and movable goods could also be lost by those who survived but were forced to surrender. Sometimes inhabitants were expelled from towns, or chose to leave rather than swear allegiance to the new ruler. In all cases lives, homes and businesses had to be rebuilt, often in the face of great adversity.

Chapter 3

Fortifications – Attack and Defence

Fortifications

The challenge for the besieger was to overcome the defences of towns and fortresses. From the eleventh century stone castles and town walls became increasingly common in France. Castles continued to be built beyond the end of the Hundred Years War and there were changes throughout the years preceding and during the war. With earlier castles the key defensive element was the keep, a usually rectangular tower surrounded by a perimeter wall enclosing one or several baileys or courtyards. By the early fourteenth century the emphasis was shifting towards the perimeter wall with interval towers exposing the flanks of assault troops close to the walls to attack. There was sometimes still a keep but this was often now either circular or multi-angular and frequently incorporated within the walls rather than standing alone. By the end of the Hundred Years War the effectiveness of gunpowder artillery was such that the design of fortresses would change fundamentally over the coming years.

Many towns in France had walls dating back to Roman times. In some cases these remained in use and indeed were enhanced. However, as medieval towns began to grow, it was necessary for the walls to enclose larger areas. The construction and maintenance of fortifications was a considerable burden on the inhabitants, and the crown on occasion granted tax exemptions to encourage townspeople to provide adequate defences. In the south-west of France English and French kings often paid for the construction of gates for newly built *bastide* towns in the thirteenth and fourteenth centuries, with the townspeople being responsible for the walls. The Hundred Years War brought an impetus for construction and maintenance of defences, although periods of peace sometimes resulted in defences being neglected or allowed to fall into disrepair. Indeed, where the risk seemed remote, such as in the early years of the war in the Languedoc beyond the river Garonne where the English had never ventured, defences were little more than earth walls, often in poor repair. Montgiscard, just to the east of the Garonne, was defended by earth walls with thatched gates. Judging by evidence from a town close to Montgiscard, these walls would only have been approximately 3m high. Such defences could be sufficient to counter a threat from small bands of brigands, but they were clearly inadequate when a substantial force was involved and the town was quickly taken and destroyed.

Throughout the Hundred Years War the ideal elements of town and castle fortification remained essentially the same: high stone walls, gates defended by towers, interval towers, often built forward from the wall to enable cross-fire, and a ditch or moat. Gates were clearly a potential weak spot, and a number of features were built into gates to enhance their defence: towers to allow cross-fire, draw-bridges, portcullises, murder holes above the entrance to allow liquids or projectiles to be dropped on intruders, and trap-doors with pits below. There could also be barbicans built forward of bridges and gates, either permanent in stone or brick or temporary in time of need built from wood, rubble and earth. The design of barbicans varied considerably, but the common purpose was to channel attackers into an easily defensible zone in front of the gate. Walls would usually be crenellated to give some protection for defenders on the ramparts, and further protection could be provided by embrasure covers, either rotating or in an overhanging box form. An extension of the concept of box covers was the hoarding. Hoardings were wooden constructions projecting from the wall to create an overhanging gallery. The gallery floors had openings to enable defenders to drop liquids and projectiles onto assailants. Wooden hoardings were, however, vulnerable to fire and an advance on this idea was the building of machicolations onto the stone walls serving the same purpose as hoardings. In some instances the base of the wall would project forward on a sloped plinth, and projectiles dropped from the hoardings above would then bounce forward into the ranks of the attackers. The splaying out of the base also enhanced the resistance of the walls to mining. Moats, whether water-filled or dry, were important elements of the defence. Water-filled moats, which ideally should be too deep for a man to wade across and too wide to be jumped, depended on a ready water supply. However, they could be drained by a besieger. Nevertheless, a dry ditch also had its value. It inhibited mining and made the use of siege towers, scaling ladders, battering rams and tonnelons (see below) more difficult. Ditches were not necessarily dug immediately below the walls. There are examples in the south-west where they were dug several metres from the wall. Palisades, sometimes no more than faggots of thorns, were placed between ditches and walls to slow the approach of attackers and make them more vulnerable to projectiles from the walls and towers.

The development of gunpowder artillery brought some modifications to defences, with the incorporation of gun-ports in walls and increased depth to walls, sometimes with earth used behind the stone walls. However, it was not until after the Hundred Years War that the vulnerability of high, comparatively thin walls became so evident that new designs for fortifications became common with low, thick walls and angular bastions to mount guns.

Siege Techniques

Little had changed in the siege techniques in use in Europe between antiquity and the start of the Hundred Years War. Gunpowder had come on the scene before the war, and there had been improvements in stone-throwing machines over recent centuries. However, the basics remained the same: a blockade to starve the target into submission, and the use of fire, mining, bombardment and assault to try to take the town or fortress.

Blockade

The blockade of a town or castle to prevent the passage of supplies and reinforcements was an essential tool of the besieger. However, it was demanding in men and a complete investment was not always possible. At the siege of Orléans in 1428–1429 reinforcements, messengers, commanders and ambassadors were able to come and go frequently and, of course, Joan of Arc was able to get into the town. There were also several examples of cattle and pigs being brought into the town despite the English blockade. However, an effective blockade did not simply rely on the cordon thrown around the town. Controlling the environs of the target castle or town was important not only to secure supplies for the besieging army but also to deny them to the inhabitants and garrison. Water was also of great importance and many castles had cisterns to collect and keep rainwater. Maintaining a blockade also had its problems. Disease due to unsanitary conditions was always a risk, and keeping the besieging army and its horses fed and watered was a major pre-occupation. Even when the blockade was complete a well-provisioned town with a well-organized defence could hold out with a small garrison for a considerable time.

Bombardment – Mechanical Machines

Gunpowder artillery was in use throughout the Hundred Years War and great strides were made in the development of cannon. Nevertheless, throughout and beyond the war, machines relying on mechanical means for launching projectiles played an important part in siege warfare for defender and besieger alike.

Mechanical machines had been in use for many centuries before the Hundred Years War. For much of this time there had been little change, but from the twelfth century onwards improvements in the design of stone-throwing machines brought more accurate and effective weapons. Machines used traction, torsion, tension and counterbalance systems to launch projectiles.

The ballista or springald was essentially a very large crossbow. It used either tension (with the string drawn back mechanically) or torsion (with twisted ropes) to propel a bolt of around 100g over a distance of up to 300m and was very accurate. Initially the bow was made of a composite of wood, sinew and tendons, but in the second half of the fifteenth century, towards the end of the Hundred Years War, steel bows were introduced. Some ballistae were mobile for use by besiegers. However, ballista projectiles could not penetrate stone defences, and it was better suited as a defensive weapon mounted on a post rather than for attacking fortifications.

There were numerous types of stone-throwing machines, varying at one end of the spectrum from those throwing relatively light stones and operated by simple traction by a team of men pulling on ropes, through to machines throwing heavy projectiles using torsion or counterweights. We cannot be certain about the precise nature of machines in use in any particular siege or indeed century, since chroniclers were rarely precise in their terminology. It is likely that the earlier Roman technique of using torsion to project stones was still in use, but by the time of the Hundred Years War the trebuchet, powered by an articulated counterweight at one end of a beam, seems to have become the most effective and accurate stone-throwing machine.

Mangonels and trebuchets were operated by means of raising a counterweight on the short end of a pivoted arm with a sling at the end of the long arm containing the projectile. The counterweight was raised mechanically and when it was released the weight descended and, with the mechanical advantage due to the projectile being held at the long end of the beam, the projectile was thrown forward. Mangonels had a fixed container for the weight, consisting of earth and stone. This design had its weaknesses, with vibration caused by the stone and earth moving in the counterweight container resulting in damage to the structure and inaccuracy. Subsequently trebuchets had articulated counterweights, in some cases with counterweight containers filled with metal, resulting in a more stable platform and consequently greater accuracy.

Work with reconstructed machines has given an idea of their capacity. At one end of the spectrum were bricoles, which could throw a stone of up to 20kg out to 80m simply through human traction. These weapons could achieve a relatively high rate of shooting, with one shot per minute. However, bricoles were more suited to defence than attack. They could not inflict significant damage on stone walls, but were able to project stones at up to 140kph, making them formidable anti-personnel weapons. At the other end of the spectrum were the large trebuchets, with a much reduced rate of shooting of around one to two shots per hour. However, they could throw stones of up to 140kg with remarkable accuracy at ranges in excess of 200m. A variation on the trebuchet was the couillard, throwing a lesser weight of 80kg out to around 200m but with the advantage of a significantly higher rate of shooting of up to ten shots per hour.

The construction and installation of a stone-throwing machine was a considerable enterprise. A trebuchet constructed at Martel required around 1,000 man-days of labour. It was important for a trebuchet to have a stable and solid platform, and at Martel this required a further thirty-three man-days of labour to clear and flatten the land and twenty-five days for a master mason to construct a stone platform. In this case the trebuchet was intended to be capable of being rotated through 360°. Evidently this capability, and the associated degree of engineering, would not be required for a weapon deployed to launch projectiles on a single axis of fire. Good engineering was also required to enable siege equipment to be easily broken down into its components for transport.

Bombardment – Cannon
Gunpowder was known in the West from the late thirteenth century. The first record of guns follows in the next century in a Florentine decree of 1326, with the first European image coming a year later in a manuscript presented to King Edward III of England on his accession in 1327. Guns appear to have been used during the siege of Berwick in 1336, but the first recorded use during the Hundred Years War came in 1339 with the French siege of the fortress of Puyguilhem in the Périgord. Gunpowder artillery may have been used by the English at the Battle of Crécy in 1346 and also at the subsequent siege of Calais in 1346–1347. Throughout the war cannon developed and their use became more prevalent and they played an increasingly important part in sieges, a step change for the English coming with their extensive use against a town for the first time at Harfleur in 1415.

The guns which may have been employed at Crécy were ribalds, small multi-barrelled guns firing lead shot. They were not powerful enough to damage fortifications and were essentially anti-personnel weapons. Ten cannon were deployed for the siege of Calais, but since only around 100g of powder was provided each day they seem to have been small and used infrequently. Within thirty years the situation had changed, with much larger and more effective guns coming into use. The development of gunpowder weapons was initially restricted by the high cost of gunpowder, that in turn dictated by the high cost of saltpetre which initially had to be imported. From the latter part of the fourteenth century, however, saltpetre was manufactured in Europe and the price decreased significantly. Somewhat surprisingly, early guns were cheap, with the price of a springald in the 1350s five times that of a cannon. Some guns were cast from bronze, but as technology progressed and larger guns were manufactured barrels were made from strips of wrought iron bound with iron hoops. Stone was predominantly used for cannon-balls through the Hundred Years War, with cast-iron shot sometimes used from the early fifteenth century onwards.

At Cherbourg in 1379 the English deployed guns which fired stones 60cm in diameter. In the late fourteenth century the size of guns and munitions grew rapidly. By the early fifteenth century the Prince of Wales, the future Henry V, deployed the Messenger, weighing 2 tonnes at the siege of Aberystwyth – but still failed to take the castle. There was a wide range of artillery pieces in common use, typically weighing between 150 and 5,000kg, firing balls of between 1kg and 50kg. There were also some huge guns, such as those recorded at the Paris Bastille weighing up to 15 tonnes during the period between 1428 and 1505. They were capable of firing stones of up to 450kg. Mons Meg, built in 1449 towards the end of the war by the Duke of Burgundy as a present for King James II of Scotland, is still on display at Edinburgh castle. It is recorded that with a charge of 50kg of powder, at optimum elevation of 45°, the gun could fire an iron ball 1,300m and a stone ball twice that distance. The increasing importance of guns can be seen in the logistic effort devoted to providing munitions, with 10,000 gun-stones provided for Henry V's expedition to France in 1415 and the siege of Harfleur. From 1423 the administration of artillery was placed on a more organized footing with the establishment of the office of Master of the King's Ordnance in Normandy.

Early guns were unwieldy and as they became larger the challenge of moving and deploying them became more acute. Moving men in response to an operational need was relatively easy; moving guns was more difficult – it was a slow business and required escorts to prevent their capture. Early cannons were attached to a wooden board or platform. Aiming was achieved by changing the elevation of the mount with wooden wedges.

The first record of trunnions and wheeled carriages dates from 1456 shortly after the end of the Hundred Years War. Cannon were inevitably within range of defensive weapons, whether stone-throwing machines, cannon or bows, and to reduce the vulnerability of the guns and their crews wooden shields were constructed which were raised for firing and then lowered once again during reloading. The development of artillery in France during the reign of Charles VII was a significant factor in the final expulsion of the English from Gascony and Normandy.

Assault

High walls, ditches, moats, flanking towers, barbicans, draw-bridges, the use of hot liquids, quicklime and sulphur to be thrown at attackers, and the shooting of projectiles all posed challenges for an assault. Sometimes direct assaults were made using belfries (mobile towers) or ladders, but if a breach could be made, either by bombardment or mining, so much the better for those making the assault. The technique for mining was to tunnel under the walls or a tower. Props were then set and fired to bring down the wall. The assault by the Earl of Lancaster on Meilhan-sur-Garonne in 1345 illustrates another technique for forcing a breach. The fortifications and the defenders of the town were very resilient, but Lancaster commandeered local labour to fill part of the ditches. He then brought up 300 archers to provide covering fire for a further 200 men to work with picks under cover of shields to make a breach in the wall. Once this was sufficiently wide to allow ten men abreast to enter, the town was taken by assault with a number of the garrison being killed, only those having retreated into the church before surrendering being spared. A footpath which climbs up from the river to the town bears the name La Brèche des Anglais.

Whether entry was to be effected through a breach, over the walls or by forcing an entry through the gates, protection was often provided for the attackers. Elaborate wheeled towers, known as belfries, were constructed of wood. Belfries had three main purposes: to provide cover for mining, to offer protection from the top of the tower for operations against the walls conducted from lower platforms including the use of battering rams, and to bring the attackers to the height of the top of the walls. There could be several internal platforms so that men could be sheltered prior to an assault across a drawbridge. Belfries could be very substantial affairs, up to 30m high and able to accommodate stone-throwing machines and substantial numbers of men. One used by King John II of France at the siege of Breteuil in 1356 housed 600 men. Sometimes belfries were constructed on site from local materials, but they could also be transported in pieces and then assembled for the siege. At the siege of Orléans in 1428–1429 the English deployed a prefabricated belfry which required twenty-six carts for its transport. Subsidiary purposes included providing cover for use of a battering ram at ground level or for mining. Deploying a belfry close to the wall was a dangerous affair, and often required a moat or ditch to be filled with stones, and considerable numbers of men were required to manhandle the tower into position. Towers were vulnerable to fire which could quickly spread with devastating consequences. As cannon developed and were deployed in defence of towns and castles, the belfry became increasingly vulnerable.

Another means to bring men to the height of the wall was the tonnelon, the name deriving from the French word for a barrel. Using counter-weights or winches, men could be lifted on platforms above the walls to shoot at defenders or to attempt to enter the town or castle. Of course, the simplest and most obvious way of scaling a wall is with a ladder, and these, made of wood, leather or rope, were widely used, but in the face of effective opposition they and those using them were particularly vulnerable.

Battering rams were used to attempt to break down gates or contribute to the demolition of walls. A variation of the battering ram was the trepan, which substituted a pointed iron pole for the ram and was designed to loosen and dislodge stones from the walls. Battering rams and trepans were protected by wooden shelters, but these, like belfries and tonnelons, were vulnerable to fire. Dung, earth, green vegetation, hurdles, animal hides and drenching with water were all means to reduce this risk.

Fire was an important weapon for both defenders and besiegers. Reference is often made to Greek Fire, a combustible material which was difficult to extinguish and stuck to wooden structures. There were numerous recipes for Greek Fire which could include resin, tar, fat, naphtha and oil. Of these naphtha seems to have been an essential ingredient. For the defenders Greek Fire could simply be dropped on attackers from jars, but both besiegers and defenders could also project jars of the burning material from stone-throwing machines. There are also cases of burning arrows being shot into towns, as at Ypres in 1383.

Countermeasures

Deliberate flooding of surrounding areas by defenders, such as at Harfleur in 1415, where the river Lézarde was diverted, could add to the difficulties of those seeking to enter the town by assault. It was also common practice to raze the suburbs outside the walls to remove cover and shelter for the besiegers. Within towns attempts were often made to keep a clear passage between the walls and housing to enable the garrison to move rapidly to a point under threat. In times of peace, however, buildings outside the walls often proliferated and inside towns houses were often built up to the walls. During the reconstruction of Carbonne in the Languedoc, after its destruction by the Black Prince in 1355, all buildings within the walls had to be at least 3m back from the ramparts, and external buildings at least 30m away from the wall.

Successful bombardment could, of course, breach walls and provide access for the attackers, but a well-organized defence could quickly fill breaches with temporary obstacles. At Harfleur in 1415 the defenders successfully used timber, tubs filled with earth, dung and stones. Walls were shored up with wooden faggots, earth and clay. As a countermeasure streets were strewn with sand and other materials to reduce the risk of cannon balls and stones splintering. Mining could be detected by listening or by placing jars of water on walls to detect the slightest movement. Defenders could be expected to undertake counter-mining, with men trying either to enter or undermine the opposing tunnel. The miners themselves seem to have been held in low regard, despite the importance and hazards of their work and the risks of hand-to-hand combat underground if the defenders broke through into the besiegers' tunnel. Attempts to disrupt assaults included pushing away assault ladders, lowering hooks to seize and overturn battering rams, the use of stone-throwing machines and springalds against assault troops, dropping projectiles and the pouring of liquids and quicklime onto the attackers.

Caltrops were also used to inhibit the approach of men and horses. These were small four-spiked objects, only about 5cm in height, in the shape of a tetrahedron so that however they fell there was always a spike pointing upwards. They could cause deep wounds to feet and horses' hooves. They were cheap to produce and widely used, often in combination with ditches. In Cahors in 1385 they were placed in fords to attempt to prevent the river being crossed. There is also an example of them being used as a precursor to the modern cluster bomb: at Villefranche-de-Roeurgue caltrops were placed in pots that could be dropped on assault troops, breaking open on contact with the ground and dispersing the obstacles.

We have already seen that Greek Fire could be used by defenders, but powdered lime was also widely used in defence. This could burn the skin and eyes of men. If mixed with boiling water there was a chemical reaction which increased the corrosive properties of the lime. Stones were a simple weapon, not only for use in cannon and stone-throwing machines. Larger stones were positioned to be dropped from ramparts, and smaller ones could be stockpiled to be thrown or projected from slings.

The Politics and Economics of Defence

Construction and maintenance of defences placed a heavy burden on citizens, either for the towns where they lived or for castles where they could take refuge in time of need. Taxation for defence was an unwelcome obligation, and in the circumstances it is hardly surprising that there were often disputes concerning payment for defences, and indeed even the need for fortifications. In 1356 during the Black Prince's *chevauchée* before the Battle of Poitiers the town of Issoudun and its defences were badly damaged, and repairs to the town stretched over many years. In 1358 nobles, ecclesiastics and townspeople assembled at the abbey of Notre-Dame to consider 'repairs and defence of the castle and the good people of the town and the surrounding area'. A tax of six *deniers* in the pound was agreed on the sale of goods in the castle, town and suburbs. However, in 1376 the remaining citizens of the town were still living within the castle, and around 1390 the repairs had still not been made. A further tax, this time on salt, was authorized in 1412, but in 1423 some work still remained outstanding.

Raising money for fortifications suffered from perennial problems. Memories could be short and short-term self-interest could quickly return. Less than two years after the Black Prince passed through the Languedoc in 1355, Thibaud de Lévis-Montbrun, Lord of Lapenne, felt the need to appeal to the seneschal of Carcassonne for help to persuade the inhabitants to repair the walls and ditches of his château on the grounds that it was there they would go with their families and possessions in the event of peril. The townspeople in turn appealed to *Parlement* in Paris who, somewhat surprisingly perhaps, did not summarily find in favour of Thibaud. Instead the seneschal was charged to arrange for expert inspection of the fortifications to verify the extent of the work required before *Parlement* concluded its deliberations. With the risk of abuses by those raising money ostensibly for the benefit of the local community, such appeals were not unusual. An example of the kind of problem that could arise comes a few years later in 1365, when the captain of the château of Loches was accused before *Parlement* of having raised taxes for the improvement of the fortifications, but having refused access to the local inhabitants. His case was probably not helped by the report that he had been heard to say he saw no great difference between the King of France and the King of

England, and they could both 'boil their pots for sixty years in front of the château before he would let either of them enter'.

There were also frequently differences of opinion between ecclesiastical and lay authorities over the importance to be attached to defence and payment for construction and maintenance of fortifications. In 1355 the citizens of Narbonne, as they watched the departure of the Black Prince and his army, may well have reflected upon, and given thanks for, the wisdom and resolution of their consuls a few years before. Construction of the cathedral of St-Just and St-Pasteur had started in 1272 and came to a halt in 1344. Completion of the transept and the nave would have required part of the walls of the *cité* to be demolished. The consuls, seizing on instructions from King Philip IV in 1344 to put the defences of the province in order, were adamant that they would not permit this demolition, and protracted discussions between the town government and the clergy ensued. The consuls petitioned the *viguier royal* of Béziers and, despite an appeal from the Archbishop of Narbonne, their case was upheld. The result was that the transept and nave were never completed and, most importantly for the people of Narbonne, the city walls remained intact in November 1355.

The financial burden for the defence of towns and fortresses, which could be very heavy, fell largely on the local population, both those who lived within and those who would seek refuge in time of need. The average share of town budgets allocated to defence between 1348 and 1409 in the Quercy in south-west France was around 40 per cent. On occasion in excess of 70 per cent was spent on defence. In these circumstances it is hardly surprising that in times of peace there was reluctance to spend on defence, and maintenance of fortifications was neglected, with walls falling into disrepair. Inhabitants made openings for windows if houses formed part of the walls, and unofficial gates were constructed to avoid long detours to leave the town. Materials were stolen for personal use. Ditches became overgrown and in some cases gardens were planted in them by townspeople.

The ownership of cannon brought with it, of course, the need to provide powder and balls, either of stone or iron. It is not surprising perhaps, in view of the burden of the cost of defence, that some towns seem to have been reluctant to spend the money to service their weapons. In 1346 the town of Cahors had nineteen cannon but had purchased only 40kg of powder. The same modest supply can be seen sometimes on the side of the besiegers, with only 104 projectiles being provided for five cannon for an attack on Chaliers in 1397. However, as cannon developed, calibres were increased and the quantity of pieces grew the situation changed and by the early fifteenth century French royal armies were being supplied with thousands of kilograms of powder. The reluctance to spend money on adequate quantities of munitions was not, however, restricted to gunpowder artillery. At Périgueux in 1339–1340, 1,000 shafts were bought for crossbow bolts and just 420 for springalds. These numbers are in stark contrast to the hundreds of thousands of arrows provisioned for English armies.

The Organization of Defence

Sophisticated measures were taken to optimize the defence. At times of crisis communications between towns to give early warning of enemy movements were commonplace. Look-outs could be placed at key points at some distance from towns. Not only would suburbs be cleared to remove cover and shelter for attackers, but also certain approaches to the town would be closed, roads degraded, fords obstructed and caltrops placed to canalize the approach to a town. In 1356 the consuls of Cajarc placed obstacles and degraded roads to drive an approaching enemy on to a ridge, making surveillance easier. Trees and other vegetation were also cleared from the side of roads to improve visibility and ditches were dug across roads to leave only a narrow passage for horses and men on foot. Bridges, as was seen at Périgueux in 1382, could also be partially obstructed to prevent passage by horses. Barriers constructed of wood and thorns would not be sufficient to stop an army, but they could bring men to a temporary halt and, if placed within range of defensive weapons, provided a stationary target while obstacles were cleared or crossed. Where measures were taken to canalize approaching troops, springalds, cannon and stone-throwing machines were sighted and ranges calculated for the most effective use of these weapons.

Plans were made for the deployment of men for defence. These could be in general terms just to indicate places to be manned, but in some cases were detailed, specifying the number of men to be deployed at key points and the weapons to be used. The fortifications would be divided into sectors and men nominated to command specific towers and gates. Much of the defence rested in the hands of the inhabitants, and measures were taken to equip and train these local militia to augment any professional troops available. They could never be expected to be as effective as professionally trained and equipped soldiers, but they could make a valuable contribution.

Chapter 4

The English Ascendancy, 1337–1360

The first phase of the war, which culminated in the peace enshrined in the Treaty of Brétigny signed at Calais in 1360, is marked in the English consciousness by the great victories of Edward III at Crécy in 1346 and of Edward the Black Prince at Poitiers ten years later. However, even with these victories the peace of 1360 was to last less than ten years before the two nations returned to war. Of much greater and lasting significance was the successful English siege of Calais in 1346–1347. The success at Calais gave the English a foothold in France that would be retained until 1558, more than a century after the loss of all other English possessions. There were other notable battles during this phase of the war but, as throughout the war, sieges were more numerous.

Cambrai, 1339

In the early years of the war both kings concentrated their main efforts in the north of France. Edward III, since 1338 acting as the vicar of the Holy Roman Emperor, had expended much effort and a good deal of treasure in trying to hold together an uneasy alliance of discontented lords in the Low Countries. Ostensibly, his objective was to recover the Cambrésis, the region around Cambrai, from France and return it to the rule of the Emperor. However, Edward also hoped to provoke Philip VI into giving battle.

Cambrai, held by the Bishop of Cambrai, who was a staunch supporter of Philip despite the town lying within the Holy Roman Empire, was an obvious target for Edward and his allies. Edward arrived before Cambrai on 20 September 1339, but found that it was well prepared to resist attack. The fortifications had recently been repaired and in anticipation of an attack the garrison had been strengthened. Edward III appears to have seen Cambrai as bait to attract the French rather than as a town he wished to seize as a prize. Philip VI is often portrayed as being excessively timid in his approach to warfare. However, he can also be seen as astute in his judgement on this occasion. He advanced towards the frontier between

France and the Empire, halting initially at Noyons while the bulk of his army moved on to Péronne, 35km to the south-west of Cambrai. Edward and his allies had the usual problem of sustaining their men and their horses. In addition, Philip appreciated that Edward had the problem of holding together a coalition of fickle and largely mercenary allies. With winter approaching and supplies dwindling, despite wide-ranging raids of pillage throughout the Cambrésis, the lack of response by Philip was causing increasing frustration for Edward who wanted battle before his coalition started to fall apart. In the last days of September the siege was pursued with greater determination, and towards the end of the month an assault came close to success. However, this was not a sign of growing weakness on the part of the defenders. The defences had not been breached. Entry was made by bribing the captain of a fortified gate to the north of the city to lower the drawbridge to allow the besiegers to enter. However, before sufficient men could pass through the fortified gate, known as the Château de Selles, the alarm was sounded by the cathedral bells and the attack repulsed.

By early October it was becoming increasingly obvious to Edward that the siege was not going to bring the result he was looking for as Philip resolutely refused to be drawn into battle. On 9 October the siege was raised and Edward and his allies marched away to the south to cross the border into France in the hope of provoking Philip with this new threat to his territory.

Tournai, 1340

In late October 1339 there seemed to be the prospect that Edward would have the battle he was looking for near the small town of La Capelle. However, Philip refused to be drawn into the trap of attacking a well-prepared English position and Edward in his turn was certainly not going to attack a larger army also in well-prepared positions. Edward now turned his attention to strengthening his coalition and in particular persuading the Flemish to join him. A problem for them was that they owed allegiance to the King of France. There was an easy solution to this hindrance and on 26 July 1340 Edward was proclaimed King of France to relieve the Flemish of their obligations to Philip. A treaty with the Flemish followed, which included the cession to them of the Tournaisis, the area around Tournai.

Edward, however, while waging war in the Low Countries and trying to consolidate and expand his coalition, had lost touch with public opinion and the concerns of Parliament at home. He returned to England in

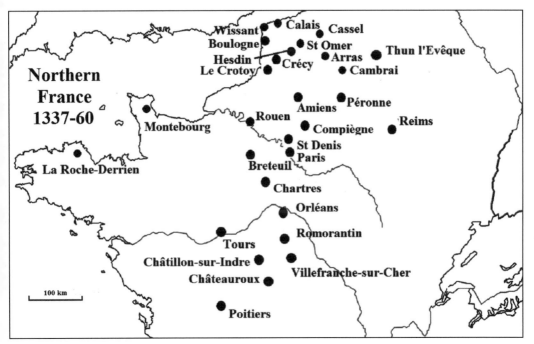

Northern France, 1337–1360.

February 1340. The fighting continued inconclusively and on about 20 June 1340 there was another fruitless stand-off near Thun-l'Évêque. On 24 June Edward arrived at Sluys on the estuary of the Zwin with reinforcements from England. A large French fleet was waiting for him, but in the ensuing Battle of Sluys the English secured an overwhelming victory. A setback followed on 26 July when an Anglo-Flemish army commanded by Robert of Artois was defeated at St-Omer. The army had been predominantly made up of unenthusiastic Flemish levies, and its defeat was of no great significance for Edward, in particular since the majority of the English archers with Robert of Artois managed to rejoin the main English army. The problem was more of a strategic nature: the French success opened up the Tournaisis and the main army of the coalition to a concentrated French attack. It also disconcertingly damaged the cohesion of the coalition. Edward's response was to attack Tournai, the most important French fortress close to the Flemish border. Once again the objective was to bring the French to battle.

On 18 July 1340 Edward III left Ghent for Tournai. He stopped five days later at the village of Chin, about 5km north of Tournai, and waited for reinforcements from his allies. Men from Hainault and his German allies joined him, but he was still without the Duke of Brabant's force when he issued a challenge to Philip, whom he addressed as Philip de Valois rather than as King of France. He offered to resolve matters with either single combat between Philip and Edward, or a combat between

100 selected men from each side. Failing that, he would take what was rightfully his by force. Philip refused to respond to the challenges but said that he would throw the English out of his realm. Edward received Philip's response on 31 July and invested Tournai on the same day.

Tournai was a substantial town with a population of around 20,000. The walls, completing a perimeter of around 5km and incorporating seventy-four towers and ten gates (eight other gates having been walled up earlier in the fourteenth century for reasons of security), were relatively modern, having been constructed in the thirteenth and early fourteenth centuries. The permanent garrison had been supplemented by the contingents of the constable and two marshals of France, and on 23 July the Count of Foix arrived with more men. The garrison was now very substantial. On the negative side the town was not as well provisioned as Cambrai had been the year before. The presence of such a large garrison together with several thousand horses clearly exacerbated the problem of food supplies, and early on in the siege old men, women, children and the poor and weak were expelled to stretch supplies among those who could contribute to the defence of the city. The townsmen were allocated the watch and defence of the walls, with the trained troops kept in reserve to

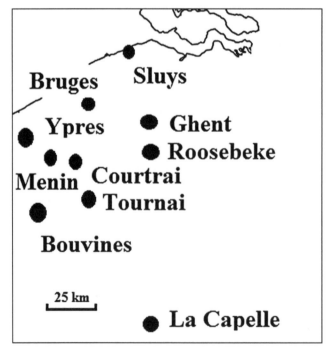

Flanders.

move quickly to points under threat and to make sorties out of the gates to disrupt the besiegers. The town was also equipped with stone-throwing machines. These were used to good effect during the siege, with projectiles destroying the belfry of the convent church of Pré-aux-Nonnains to the north which was being used as an observation post by the Flemish, beheading the Count of Hainault's chief engineer, and destroying a Flemish siege engine.

The English took up station to the west of the city, covering the likely direction of advance by the French. The Flemish and the men from Hainault were positioned to the north and east. The Germans and the contingent of the Duke of Brabant, who finally joined Edward's army on 8 August, covered the south. The English element of the army comprised around 1,300 men-at-arms and 3,000 archers. The overall strength of the coalition army was probably around 8,000 men-at-arms and perhaps 18,000 infantry. The river Scheldt flowed roughly from south-east to north-west through the city. Temporary bridges were built over the river to ensure communications between the different contingents of the besieging army. Siege engines were constructed on site on higher ground, but the walls were solid and well designed and the projectiles from these machines had little effect. There may also have been a small number of cannon. Only six defenders are recorded as being killed by the siege engines. The Count of Hainault planned to hurl explosive projectiles into the town, but the engineer appointed to put this scheme into effect ran off with his advance of pay and was never seen again.

While the garrison faced an increasingly acute situation with regard to supplies, the besiegers had a rich area to pillage and plunder. In addition to plundering store houses and fields for food, the besiegers systematically set about destroying everything within 25km of Tournai. In part this was to attempt once again to provoke the French into trying to relieve the city and in part to satisfy the desire for plunder for the soldiery and to allow the Count of Hainault to exact revenge on the French. The inhabitants of the city conducted a spirited defence, and frequent sorties were made to disrupt the siege and seize supplies. Notable examples of the success of such sorties include the seizure of part of the booty taken by the Count of Hainault in a raid on a local town and an attack on the English camp which, but for the courage of a squire, could well have resulted in Bishop Burghersh being run through with a lance. Such activities were good for the morale of the defenders but carried the risk of pursuing besiegers forcing an entry through open gates. This almost happened after the attack on the English camp and strict controls were subsequently put in place to minimize the risk.

With its modern fortifications in good repair, a very large garrison and a resolute citizenry, Tournai was going to be a difficult nut to crack by assault. The weak link for Tournai was its precarious food situation, and in time, if the French did not come to its relief, the city must inevitably have fallen. However, Edward did not have time to wait. The parties to his coalition all had different interests, and the mercenary elements from the German states became increasingly impatient with Edward's financial difficulties and inability to meet his commitments to them. On top of this, although the besiegers were well provided for with victuals from the surrounding countryside, the inevitable boredom and demoralization associated with a long siege were setting in.

The difficulties of holding the coalition together were becoming more acute by the third week of August and it was decided that the city should be taken by assault. On 26 August an attack was launched by Flemish and English troops near the Porte Ste-Fontaine on the Courtrai road to the north-west of the city. This attack was repulsed with heavy loss. A second assault was made a week later at the same place. This time an attempt was made to force the gates, which were set alight with large quantities of brushwood and battered by projectiles from siege engines. Despite these more thorough preparations and fighting that lasted throughout the day, the assault was again unsuccessful. The defenders were granted a barrel of wine in recognition of their courage.

The failure of these assaults only served to exacerbate the divisions between the parties to the coalition. The English and the Flemish had fought alone in the assaults. The men of the Count of Hainault had also been vigorous in pursuing the siege in their sector, but the Brabanters and the Germans had done nothing. In view of the lack of money coming from Edward to pay the mercenaries, the inactivity of the Duke of Brabant and the Germans was unsurprising, but it resulted in a serious dispute between the leaders which became violent, with the Flemish leader Van Artevelde running a knight of the Duke of Brabant through with his sword.

On 7 September the garrison must have felt that the prospect of relief was at hand when Philip advanced to Bouvines, 15km to the west of Tournai on the river Marcq, with 21,000 men-at-arms and 2,700 infantry. The French position was well protected, with marsh spreading out to both north and south along the banks of the river, and there they stayed. It seems that Edward had recognized for some weeks that, despite his efforts to raise money at home, he faced the risk of his coalition falling apart before he could either take Tournai or, more importantly, since the city was only a means to an end, bring Philip to battle. By the time the French arrived at Bouvines, it was apparent that little time was left to him to achieve his objective.

The arrival of the French raised hope both in the city and in the coalition camp that the decisive battle was at hand. Edward redeployed his army. Covering forces remained to guard the gates but the bulk of the army moved to the west of the Scheldt to face the expected line of approach of the French. Edward took the centre with the Count of Hainault to the north and the Duke of Brabant to the south. Within the city the leaders of the garrison planned a mass sortie to fall on the rear of the coalition army during the anticipated battle. They asked the citizenry to provide volunteers to reinforce the garrison, but the town leaders were more interested in ensuring that those sallying forth settled their bills before doing so. Meanwhile the coalition continued to exert pressure on the citizens to surrender. On 14 August English archers shot messages into the city, promising friendship if they surrendered or if they would not, then the destruction of the town and the death of its inhabitants, including women and children. To prove that they meant business a large siege tower was constructed by the Flemish. It is perhaps unsurprising that, with relief apparently close at hand, none of these efforts had any effect on the resolve of the inhabitants. As for the French at Bouvines, they remained behind their natural defences, contenting themselves with parties of volunteers passing through the siege lines to take food to the garrison. There was to be no battle, with the French resisting the temptation to respond to skirmishes.

The prospect of the long-awaited battle might have been expected to help the coalition leaders to put their differences to one side. However, on the contrary, for the mercenaries in particular, the forthcoming combat focused the minds of the troops on their lack of pay. Exploratory talks started between members of the coalition and the French. Edward was aware of the discussions, but he did not take part, although he had first sent out feelers for talks in mid-August. Philip's attitude was ambivalent. The two armies were more or less balanced numerically, although the preponderance of men-at-arms in the French army gave Philip the edge. In addition, the substantial friendly garrison to the rear of the coalition gave Philip a significant advantage. Even so, he still saw the risks of battle as too great. Equally he was reluctant to negotiate with the coalition, and in particular with Edward, while they remained on his territory.

Eventually his advisers prevailed upon him to relent and on 24 September 1340 a nine-month truce was signed at Esplechin. The siege was lifted, Edward having failed in his objective of provoking Philip to join battle.

Aquitaine, 1345–1346

Although Edward III's preferred method of waging war was the wide-ranging *chevauchée*, as we have seen already sieges played an important part in trying to achieve his objective of bringing the French to battle. In addition, he had to secure the borders of his lands in Aquitaine in the south-west and this meant holding towns and fortresses. Indeed, the borders had been progressively pushed back and if the duchy were to survive, it was necessary to bring places back into the allegiance of Edward III. The Seneschal of Gascony, Ralph, Lord Stafford, started the campaign with local forces. In June 1345 Henry of Grosmont, Earl of Derby, was despatched to Bordeaux with reinforcements, 500 men-at-arms, 500 Welsh infantry, and 1,000 archers. He arrived on 9 August 1345.

Stafford began the campaign by besieging both Blaye and Langon with the Anglo-Gascon forces already in Gascony. Derby took a different view and decided that it was better to concentrate his forces. This would avoid giving the initiative to the French and allowing them to concentrate their forces while the Anglo-Gascons became immobilized by sieges. A truce was negotiated with the commander at Blaye and the siege lifted. Derby now joined forces with Stafford at Langon. He abandoned this siege and decided instead to attack Bergerac which was of greater strategic importance, controlling an important crossing of the Dordogne and well placed to serve as a forward base for raids into French territory. Bergerac was poorly fortified with an eleventh-century castle, a ditch and a perimeter made up of houses with fill-in walls between them. Bergerac fell to assault. Just to the south of Bergerac was the castle of Montcuq, under siege by the French. Derby had moved so rapidly as to catch the French by surprise and the besiegers fled, crossing the bridge over the Dordogne to enter the town. The Anglo-Gascons were in close pursuit. In the pandemonium on the bridge as the fleeing Frenchmen tried to enter the town, the Anglo-Gascons were able to force their way past the barbican at the south end of the bridge, across the bridge and past the portcullis on the north side to take the town. There was no need for a siege.

From Bergerac Derby moved north, and from Mussidan followed the Isle upstream to Périgueux. The town, as was so often the case in the south and west of France, consisted of two fortified parts: the *cité*, still relying largely on Roman walls from the third century, and the *bourg*, protected by walls about 1.5km in length built in the twelfth and thirteenth centuries. Fortunately for the inhabitants the Count of Armagnac had fled there with survivors from the fall of Bergerac, thus enabling an effective defence of the walls to be mounted. Derby did not have the resources to besiege the town closely and elected instead to take a number of fortified places in the vicinity of the town and so cut off supplies. It seems that Derby did not have either the inclination or the forces to take the town. The blockade did not have time to become effective before Louis of Poitiers, despatched by the Duke of Normandy, the future King John II who was now the king's lieutenant in the Languedoc, relieved the town and set about retaking the surrounding fortresses which had fallen to Derby. One such fortress was Auberoche, but here the tables were turned when on 21 October 1345 Derby fell upon and defeated the besiegers. Although the Duke of Normandy still had under his command an army larger than that defeated at Auberoche, he decided to abandon the campaign and disbanded his troops at Angoulême on 4 November. This decision had far-reaching consequences as Henry of Grosmont, who on 22 September 1345 had

South-west France, 1337–1360.

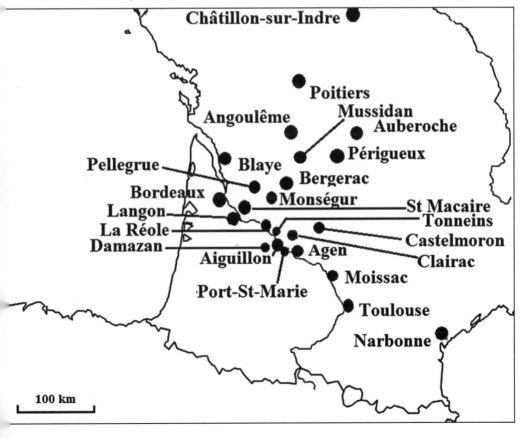

succeeded to the Earldom of Lancaster and become the most powerful and wealthy of Edward III's vassals, turned his attention to the Bordelais.

La Réole, 1345–1346

As the new Earl of Lancaster moved towards the Garonne valley the *bastide* of Pellegrue surrendered and Monségur was taken by storm. At the beginning of November the English force arrived before La Réole. La Réole had strong fortifications with three circuits of walls. At the western end on high ground overlooking the Garonne and built on rock was a strong castle with four towers. It had originally been constructed by Richard the Lionheart but it had been strengthened over the intervening years. There was a large French garrison, but the town had a weak link: the population's lack of loyalty to the French. A plan was hatched between the inhabitants and the besiegers. On 8 November a diversionary attack was launched at one end of the town which drew off the garrison, while the gates at the other end of La Réole were opened to allow Lancaster's men to enter the town. The men of the garrison managed to avoid being trapped on the ramparts and withdrew into the castle. On their way they rounded up some pigs to take with them to sustain them over the weeks ahead.

Attempts to breach the walls with siege weapons proved ineffective and efforts to scale the ramparts were repulsed. Lancaster now changed tactics and started work undermining the castle walls from inside the town. The earl led from the front, working underground as the tunnel was slowly advanced. After three weeks of tunnelling the garrison commander could see the way things were going and negotiated terms. A truce would be maintained for five weeks and he would surrender if relief did not come within that period. The garrison would be allowed to depart with safe conduct. Notice of the terms was sent to the Duke of Normandy with a request for a relief force to be sent. However, Duke John, having disbanded his army, was 350km away in his winter quarters to the north at Châtillon-sur-Indre and could not help. The Duke of Bourbon and the Count of Armagnac were closer at hand and tried to raise men. We do not know how successful these recruiting efforts were, but in the event relief did not arrive and the garrison surrendered early in January 1346 and marched away under safe conduct.

Following his success at La Réole the Earl of Lancaster took up winter quarters in the town. Part of the English army returned home, and the Gascons dispersed and returned to their homes until the start of campaigning the next spring. The English who remained set about raiding and taking towns and fortresses, mainly in the Garonne valley and to the north. In the Agenais many lords who had been uncertain about where their best interests lay came across to the English side, and in December the English opened a campaign in the area to extend their influence. By March 1346 the English were predominant in the region through a combination of conquest and defections. The French had been reduced to a handful of strongholds at Port-Ste-Marie, Agen, Moissac and Castelmoron. Among the places to fall was Aiguillon, a strategically important town at the confluence of the Garonne and the Lot. The surrender was probably the result of secret arrangements made in advance, the inhabitants turning on the garrison when Lancaster arrived. The importance of Aiguillon passing to the English was not lost on the French and during 1346 they attempted to retake it.

Aiguillon, 1346

With the approach of the spring of 1346 came fresh energy on the part of John, Duke of Normandy. He left his winter quarters at Châtillon-sur-Indre and moved south for a campaign planned to restore French fortunes in Aquitaine. With him as he marched south were the Count of Burgundy and Duke of Athens and numerous other nobles, as well as the great military officers of state: the constable, both marshals and the Master of the Royal Archers. Meanwhile the Duke of Bourbon and the Bishop of Beauvais were gathering an army at Toulouse drawn from the Languedoc. The two armies came together in the Quercy, 120km or so to the east of Aiguillon, during March.

On 1 April 1346 the vanguard of the French army arrived before Aiguillon and the *arrière-ban* was proclaimed in the south the following day to rally more men for the campaign. The peak strength of the army that Duke John of Normandy had at his disposal was possibly the largest ever gathered by the French for war in the south-west and has been estimated as being between 15,000 and 20,000 strong. It included 1,400 Genoese mercenaries and a siege train with five cannon. It was not until the middle of the month that the Duke of Normandy arrived with his principal advisers. The duke's declared objective was to retake La Réole downstream on the Garonne. However, the French would need the rivers for resupply and the English held Aiguillon upstream and St-Macaire downstream of La Réole. Duke John had bitter experience of trying to take towns without securing the rivers for communication, and Aiguillon was the key to freeing up use of the Lot and the Garonne to enable a successful move against La Réole.

Despite its strategic importance, Aiguillon was a small town with defences which left something to be desired. It had been formed over the years by two communities growing together. To the north was Lunac-d'Aiguillon, an ancient Gallo-Romain town surrounded on a rectangular pattern by crumbling brick walls. In the north of Lunac, overlooking the confluence of the Garonne and the Lot, was the seigneurial castle. This had brick and stone walls about 10m high. There were gates in the northern, eastern and southern walls. To the west, where the Garonne flowed against the walls, there was a postern gate. The castle had the rivers Garonne and Lot to protect the northern and western walls. A moat, fed by the rivers, protected the south and east. A short distance to the south was Le Fossat-d'Aiguillon, another seigneurial castle, and a small village which had developed around the fortress. The two parts of the town had grown together and work had started on modern walls in a rectangular form to enclose the town in its entirety. Unfortunately the work had never been completed and the gaps had to be filled with barrels full of stones. There was a bridge over the Lot terminating in a barbican gate on the north bank.

Within the town were some 600 archers and 300 men-at-arms, led by the seneschal, Ralph Stafford, and Hugh Menil. Among the garrison were also two distinguished soldiers: Walter Mauny from Hainault and the Gascon Alexander de Caumont. Lancaster, who had been at La Réole for the winter, withdrew to Bordeaux initially to reassemble his army and muster companies assembled by the Gascon lords. Reinforcements from England were promised, mainly archers, and some men arrived during the summer. Conscious of the importance of Aiguillon, Lancaster had strongly garrisoned the town of Damazan, 6km to the west of the town and the Garonne, and Tonneins, 11km to the north. Aiguillon had fallen to the Anglo-Gascons the year before in a matter of hours. The scene was now set for a siege that would last throughout the summer, to the increasing frustration of the Duke of Normandy, who at one point swore that he would not withdraw until the town had fallen.

Initially the French took up position on the plain to the east of the town. They set about digging trenches and constructing earthworks in their rear to protect against a surprise attack and a recurrence of the disaster at Auberoche the year before. This left access to the town open across the bridge to the north and the Garonne to the west. To deploy troops to the west and north without ensuring rapid communications between the three elements would be to risk attack and defeat in detail of parts of the army without the means to concentrate all of the besieging forces. The English garrisons of Tonneins and Damazan close to hand made this threat more acute. One of the first actions of the French was to take control of the bridge at Clairac, 8km upstream on the Lot. They also built a wooden bridge over the Garonne downstream of Aiguillon. This work was carried out over several weeks by some 300 men defended by Genoese crossbowmen. Despite this protection the garrison made determined efforts to prevent the construction of the bridge with frequent sorties and attacks launched from barges to attack the bridge and its builders. The bridge was destroyed twice before it was finally completed late in May. The French then stretched a chain across the Garonne to prevent river-borne communications from the west. With the French holding Port-Ste-Marie upstream on the Garonne and Clairac upstream on the Lot then, in theory at least, the town was cut off from reinforcement and resupply by river. This should, in turn, have given the French free use of the rivers for their own ends, but that proved to be far from the case.

On 16 June 1346 two large barges coming down the Garonne from Toulouse laden with supplies for the besiegers were intercepted and captured by the garrison. Two raiding parties set out from the town: one in small boats from close to the castle of Lunac and the other across the bridge over the Lot. The second of these comprised around 100 men-at-arms led by Alexander de Caumont. Although they succeeded in passing through the French lines and achieving their objective, the withdrawal of the raiding party to the town proved to be a disaster. The French reacted vigorously and both sides threw reinforcements into the fighting developing on the bridge. The French took the barbican and advanced across the bridge. To prevent them entering the town the portcullis was dropped, with the result that the raiding party was trapped outside. There were numerous casualties and Alexander de Caumont was captured. It seems strange by modern standards that the French should release such a celebrated soldier. However, the ransom of prisoners was first and foremost a commercial transaction and in return for a large sum, much of which was advanced by the Earl of Lancaster, de Caumont was back with the Anglo-Gascons in a matter of days.

Meanwhile Edward III was planning his great expedition that would culminate in the battle of Crécy in August. When news of the advance of the Duke of Normandy towards the Garonne reached England, it seems that Edward was considering taking his army to Aquitaine. The indenture between Edward and Lancaster stated that 'the king has agreed that if it shall happen that the said earl is besieged or beset by so great a force that he cannot help himself unless he is rescued by the king's power, then the king is bound to rescue him in one way or another, provided that he can be rescued easily'. Of course, Lancaster was not in Aiguillon, moving initially from La Réole to Bordeaux and then returning to La Réole to direct support of the besieged town. However, there can be no doubt that if Aiguillon were to fall Lancaster would be beset by a great force and the terms of his indenture would apply. It is possible that Edward was initially planning to go to Gascony to bring relief directly to Lancaster, even though the terms of the indenture would not require the king's personal presence. However, he kept his cards very close to his chest and it may be that his eventual landing in Normandy was his objective from the start. The landing in Normandy had the primary objective of bringing Philip to battle. However, it is possible that there was a deliberate strategy of the indirect approach with the secondary objective of the landing in the north being to relieve the pressure on Lancaster, judging correctly that his invasion would compel Philip to recall the Duke of Normandy to join the royal army gathering to counter the English *chevauchée*.

Despite the success in taking the barbican gate in mid-June the French were making no progress in bringing the siege to a successful conclusion. At some point Lancaster had returned to La Réole with his army. He kept the pressure on the besiegers by harrying French lines of communication, foragers and messengers. Notwithstanding their vastly superior numbers, fieldworks and barriers, the French were unable to seal off the town and there were numerous examples of supplies reaching the town by stealth, and at least one case of a detachment from Lancaster's army fighting through the French lines with victuals. As was so often the case with a prolonged siege, the besiegers, perhaps ten times more numerous than those within the walls, found obtaining food an increasing problem. The strong English presence in the Périgord and downstream of Aiguillon on the Garonne restricted the scope for foraging. Purveyors were sent as far afield as Béarn, 160km to the south, and to the hills of the Aubrac, more than 300km away to the east, to requisition cattle. The area around Toulouse was also stripped of food and wine for the besieging army.

The besiegers tried to break the deadlock with an assault on the castle of Lunac. The plan was to make the attack from three siege towers mounted on barges. The attack was a complete failure. One of the barges carrying a tower was struck by a stone thrown from a trebuchet; it capsized and sank, taking with it the tower and all the crew of the barge. The attack was abandoned and the other towers withdrawn.

With the arrival of Edward in Normandy on 12 July 1346, and a further Anglo-Flemish army in Flanders under the command of Sir Hugh

Hastings, it was apparent to Philip VI that the most serious threat he faced was now in the north. It seems that elements of John's besieging force were withdrawn early in the summer, since shortly after the landings of Edward III the French constable and at least one of the marshals were in the north involved with countering the English landings. Indeed, it appears that the constable was recalled to take command of the defence of Harfleur on the Seine estuary when the English fleet was believed to be on the point of departure. John was reluctant to leave before he had brought the siege to a successful conclusion and he quarrelled with his advisers and dragged his feet. He was more concerned, it seems, about his loss of honour than the threat to the realm, and with the hope of saving his dignity he sent a mission to Lancaster, now in Bergerac, to offer a truce and suspension of the siege of Aiguillon. The earl was every bit as well informed of events in the north and saw no incentive to agree to the French proposals. John had no option but to obey his father's orders and lifted the siege a few days later on 20 August. The French departed in haste and left their camp, equipment and horses in the safe-keeping of some local men who were quickly overwhelmed by men of the garrison. The Duke of Normandy could not cover the 780km to Crécy-en-Ponthieu before the battle six days later and Philip VI was deprived of a valuable contingent of men largely because of the resilience of the garrison in Aiguillon, Lancaster's shrewd management of his forces, and the pride of the Duke of Normandy.

Calais, 1346–1347

Edward and the English army left the Crécy battlefield on 28 August 1346 and arrived in front of Calais a week later on 4 September. Their arrival was not unexpected. During July and August, although King Philip did not personally give much credence to the reports, local commanders were growing concerned that the Flemish were attempting to persuade Edward to attack the town. The Flemish, who had coveted the town for some years, were also reported to be preparing for a siege. The town was reinforced with men, supplies, munitions and weapons.

The historian Clifford Rogers has described the siege of Calais as 'probably the largest single military operation undertaken by England until the modern period'. It has been estimated that 32,000 troops in the service of Edward III served for part or all of the eleven months of the siege. However, the figures varied over the duration of the siege. It is probable that the army was scaled down as a holding operation over the winter of 1346/7, with perhaps 5,000 to 6,000 combatants serving at the siege. In

June 1347 these numbers were increased with the arrival of Henry Gros-mont, Earl of Lancaster, from Gascony, together with retinues from England, which had been sent home after Crécy and led, *inter alia*, by the Earl of Oxford, the Earl of Pembroke and Walter Mauny. The scale of the English effort in terms of finance, manpower and logistical support was extraordinary. To this must also be added the not inconsiderable com-mitment of the Flemish allied to the English. The potential impact on the French crown of the loss of Calais after the disastrous defeat of Crécy was such that efforts to support and relieve the besieged inhabitants and garrison also became almost all-consuming.

Edward III's motives for moving against Calais were probably two-fold: a continuation of his policy of trying to draw Philip into battle and to secure a permanent base in the north of France for further operations. Indeed, it may well have been the objective of his campaign from the outset. He certainly did not set out with the intent of using Calais as a port of embarkation to return to England, for to attempt to take a well-defended town simply to return home would have been foolhardy and an unnecessary risk. If he had just wanted to find a convenient port to return home there were better options. Going back to Normandy would have seemed too much like a withdrawal, and would have involved a long march across countryside that had already been stripped of food supplies for both armies. Closer at hand were Le Crotoy, which had been earmarked for use for the disembarkation of supplies and was already in English hands, and Wissant, about 80km from the battlefield and 20km south-west of Calais, which had long been used as a port for travellers from England.

The choice of Calais as both bait for Philip and as a forward base for the future was sound. Calais was strongly fortified and surrounded by marsh-land that was susceptible to flooding and could only be crossed by cause-ways. This meant that the siege army could easily defend its position with field works, and in the longer term the extended marshland and the out-lying fortresses which were to be on the border of the Calais pale would make the town relatively easy to hold – although the costs of maintaining the numerous garrisons necessary for defence in depth were considerable. Other ports taken by the English during the war, notably Harfleur, which surrendered to Henry V in 1415, proved impossible to hold in the longer term largely because they did not have this defence in depth. The strength of Calais' position is borne out by the fact that it remained an English possession for more than a century after all other territory held by the kings of England had passed into French hands.

Of course, the strengths which made Calais an attractive proposition for Edward in the longer term also presented him with a great challenge in the short term. The town was less than 200 years old, having been founded in 1165. It was a good-sized town with a population probably of around 7,000 or 8,000. It owed its wealth to fishing, processing of fish, piracy, and the importation and distribution of wine from Bordeaux and English wool. The walls, built in 1228, enclosed between 40ha and 50ha with streets laid out in an ordered manner. The walls were surrounded by double ditches filled with water by the sea and streams. There was a castle in the north-west corner with a circular keep and a large rectangular bailey protected by its own curtain walls and moat. The harbour was to the west, with entry passing between the northern walls and a spit of land known as the Rysbank, where a tower controlled entry to the port.

The walls were in good repair and the ditches had been dredged of drifting sand. The command of the town was in the hands of the Burgundian knight Jean de Vienne and a local knight, Enguerrand de Beaulo. Jean du Fosseux, one of two lieutenant-governors of Artois, arrived on 14 August to take command of the castle. The English were not, however, presented just with a town and garrison well prepared for a siege but also with very unusual conditions. The nature of the land meant that mining was out of the question, since with the high water table tunnels would flood immediately, and the marshland would not support siege engines. Also, with the high walls and double ditches launching an assault was extremely problematic. Edward, with the primary objective in mind of drawing Philip into battle, would also have been conscious that taking the town by storm would cost him heavily in casualties. Although vain attempts were made later in the siege to enter the town by assault, the success of the operation would depend ultimately upon ensuring an effective blockade. This would require the English to establish control at sea and prevent shipping gaining access to the harbour.

With a long siege clearly in view, the English started to prepare thoroughly. Their initial camp was set up on firmer ground about 800m south of the town. On the first day the first English ships arrived, bringing reinforcements who disembarked across the beaches. The strength of the army at this point was probably around 10,000 to 12,000 men. The available troops invested the three landward sides of the town. They dug trenches across causeways and built fortifications beside bridges to protect themselves from attack from the rear. The camp lay alongside the causeway to Gravelines to the east and, using this as the central axis, a town was built which became known as Villeneuve-la-Hardie. It was an elaborate affair with wooden housing for the king, officials and nobility, market halls, brushwood and thatch housing for members of the besieging forces of lesser rank, and a market square. Supporting a population larger than an English provincial town, it was the centre of an enormous and complex logistic effort which was maintained throughout the siege. The men who had marched from the landings in Normandy almost two months before were short of clothing and footwear and in urgent need of rations. Once the initial resupply was achieved, attention turned to sustaining the siege. Supplies were brought in by land from Flanders and by sea from England. The call went out to wholesalers in eastern and south-eastern England to bring their goods to Calais. Grain for export was reserved for the besieging force and purveyors ranged far and wide in England to secure supplies. Throughout the siege English raiding parties also took food from the local countryside. On one occasion late in the siege, on 18 July 1347, the Earl of Lancaster was despatched to ravage the local countryside out to a radius of 50km. He returned two days later with 2,000 cattle and 5,000 sheep. These raids served both to spread the war to the surrounding area and to supplement supplies from England and Flanders.

Even after the arrival of the English before Calais, Philip was reluctant to believe that Edward would embark on a prolonged siege. He preferred to think that he would flee towards Flanders. Thus, the day after the start of the siege he disbanded the greater part of the army. A few days later he met his son John, the Duke of Normandy, who recounted the failure of his campaign in Aquitaine and the recent dispersal of his army. As news came in of the scale and nature of the English preparations at Calais it became clear to the French that they needed to reverse the demobilization and muster a new army to relieve the town. On 9 September 1346 a summons went out to muster at Compiègne on 1 October, an optimistic timescale in the circumstances.

Control of access to the port was going to be essential for the English if they were to reduce Calais. Equally, if the French could disrupt the re-supply of the besiegers by sea they could weaken the position of Edward and his army. The Genoese galleys which were in the service of the French had arrived at the mouth of the Seine around the beginning of August. However, they had been decommissioned and their crews used to supplement the French infantry. At the beginning of September the galleys were recommissioned and on 17 September struck a serious blow against the English. Twenty-five ships bound for Calais were intercepted approaching the town. All were taken and their crews killed. The immediate impact was a blow to the morale of the besiegers, but the longer-term effect was one of higher cost, with a requirement to provide escorts for convoys and to crew all ships with men-at-arms and archers for their defence.

It is easy to overlook the maritime aspect of this siege, but the effort put into providing shipping and men was prodigious. Some 853 ships and almost 24,000 men were involved in naval operations in support of the siege. In May, June and July 1347, 107 ships were stationed in the harbour at Calais and a further 20 employed in ferrying men to and from England.

The destruction of English shipping on 17 September was the one glimmer of light for Philip in an otherwise disastrous situation. He was concentrating his resources around Calais and along the Flemish border, but could do nothing to prevent the English and Flemish ranging widely in the County of Artois. Although the Flemish decided they had had enough by the end of September and abandoned a siege which they had established at St-Omer, much damage had already been done. Thérouanne had been sacked, and considerable plunder taken, on 19 September. Encouraged by this success, the English and Flemish spread terror as far as Boulogne. Philip was helpless to intervene, let alone relieve Calais. In the south-west the Earl of Lancaster had taken advantage of the vacuum created by the withdrawal of the Duke of Normandy in the days before Crécy and had continued to extend English influence. Philip had no more luck elsewhere. He had for some while been trying to persuade the Scots to invade England to divert English manpower and money from sustaining the war in France. At last on 7 October a Scottish army crossed into England. Only ten days later the Scots were defeated and King David captured at the battle of Neville's Cross near Durham.

The muster of the new French army at Compiègne was going badly. When news came that Lancaster had reached as far north as Poitiers, plans were laid to draw off some of the men gathered in the north to go south with the Duke of Normandy. Orders were also issued to divert men answering the king's summons to Orléans to join the duke. The news that Lancaster had turned south again led to the reversal of the decisions to send Normandy south and to muster men at Orléans. Philip was also having great financial problems funding his army, and to add to his woes the military class was not responding as he had hoped and the numbers gathering were disappointing. Finally, on 27 October 1346 Philip abandoned hopes of a campaign that year. Troops were left in main garrisons but apart from that the army and maritime forces were disbanded. The Genoese and French galleys were laid up.

At Calais itself stalemate set in. The French managed to continue to get supplies and men in by sea, and in early November they inflicted a major blow by succeeding in getting through with sufficient ships to resupply the town with food until the spring. Over the winter Edward made an attempt to take the town by assault. An elaborate plan was hatched using small craft in the moat to support ladders to scale the walls. Reinforcements were sent over, scaling ladders were manufactured and stone-throwing machines and at least ten cannon were deployed. Repeated attempts were made over the winter to carry the town by assault. All failed and the last recorded attempt was made on 27 February 1347. Despite the construction of Villeneuve-la-Hardie and effective resupply from Flanders and England, the usual problems of a long siege were present: poor morale during periods of inactivity, disease due to insanitary conditions and desertions. For the French the prospect of the return of better weather in the spring meant that evading the English blockade would be increasingly difficult. This required ships or galleys. The Genoese, however, were not retained in French service and were paid off in November. Those galleys which were still seaworthy were purchased by the French, but laid up without crews. Philip turned to the Castilians, who were contracted to provide 200 large ships with crews, men-at-arms and crossbowmen. However, for reasons which are not clear, but may have been financial, the Castilian fleet never arrived and the French had to fall back on their own resources. The available French shipping had been much diminished by English operations, but the Admiral of France, Pierre Flote de Revel, made effective use of what remained. Supplies were brought to Dieppe and St-Valéry and sent north in ships to Boulogne where they were formed into convoys, filled with troops and provided with escorts. Two convoys got through successfully in March and April with the loss of only one ship, which sank in a storm.

On 18 March, at the cathedral of St-Denis, Philip took the *oriflamme*, the banner carried into battle when the king was present and raised to signal that no quarter would be given. Philip planned to have his army ready by the end of April and to march against the English early the following month. The problems of the previous autumn were present once again, with men coming more slowly and in smaller numbers than had been hoped. It was not until July that the army was in any shape for operations, and then only on a reduced scale. In March and April there were operations in the north of France with the French trying to cut the English supply lines north of Calais, and English and Flemish raiding parties penetrating into France. Although the French could not cut the English supply lines they had the best of a number of minor engagements.

After the arrival of the second French resupply fleet in April Edward finally succeeded in surrounding Calais on all sides. This was achieved by seizing the Rysbank and constructing a wooden fortification at the end opposite the town. Cannon were sited here and a garrison of 40 men-at-arms and 200 archers installed. A block ship was also sunk in the channel to restrict access. At about the same time around eighty large ships arrived to give the English control of the Channel in the vicinity of Calais. Just as Philip was experiencing problems mustering his army, Edward was finding that the arrival of reinforcements and resupply was not meeting his expectations. He was unaware of the difficulties being faced by the French king and there was alarm in England and in the siege camp during May as Philip advanced first to Amiens and then to Arras. The Earl of Lancaster, who had returned to England from Gascony, was despatched to Calais at the end of May with those reinforcements that had been mustered, several thousand of them, but by no means all of those expected.

Despite their setbacks in April and May the Flemish had not been discouraged and this presented Philip with problems. Ideally he would have liked to strip garrison troops from towns and castles to swell his field army, invade south-west Flanders, cut the English supply lines along the coast, and attack the English at Calais from the north. The problem was that this would expose his own supply lines to attack and leave towns and fortresses stripped of their garrisons vulnerable to attack by the Flemish. If this plan were to succeed the Flemish troops in the border regions would have to be dispersed. Two large contingents were formed to achieve this: one under Edward de Beaujeu with Charles of Spain and another under Robert de Waurin and Jacques de Bourbon. The first tried to take Cassel on 8 June 1347 but was driven off and withdrew to St-Omer. The second force, reinforced with elements from the first, attacked the Flemish who had occupied much of the area around Béthune, which itself remained in French hands. An engagement which by and large favoured the French ended with the bulk of the Flemish slipping back into Flanders. Overall, the results were inconclusive. The approach to Calais from the north would be too risky in these circumstances, and the more direct approach from the south became the preferred option. The army was reassembled, and Philip set off north for the coast, establishing his headquarters at Hesdin, 80km south of Calais, on 23 June.

While Philip was moving towards Hesdin the civil war in Brittany, in effect a proxy war with the French and English supporting the different parties, took a turn for the worst for the French. Their protégé Charles de Blois was defeated at La Roche-Derrien on 20 June and captured by the

English. The English supported the war in Brittany through independent captains who were not state-funded. Similarly, the French had given support to Charles de Blois but not committed troops. The timing of the defeat at La Roche-Derrien could not have been worse, since now Philip was obliged to give direct support. This was not on a large scale, fewer than 100 men-at-arms and 600 Genoese crossbowmen, plus six recommissioned galleys and ships and their crews, but it was an unwelcome diversion of resources from the main objective of relieving Calais.

By the time Philip arrived at Hesdin the situation in Calais was becoming desperate. There had been no successful resupply since April. In May a French convoy had turned back when it reached Boulogne and its commander saw the strength of the English fleet waiting for him. A more determined attempt had been made in June. Ten sailing ships and a barge loaded with food had assembled at the mouth of the Seine. They set off escorted by ten galleys and twenty-one armed merchantmen. Two days after Philip's arrival at Hesdin the convoy met with disaster when it was intercepted by a much larger English fleet. The French fleet dispersed, the galleys fled and the crews of the supply ships threw their cargos overboard to reduce weight before leaping into the sea to let their ships drift onto the shore.

Writing to Philip following the failure of the latest convoy Jean de Vienne described the situation clearly:

> But, right dear and dread lord, know that, although the people be all well and of good cheer, yet the town is in sore need of corn, wine and meat. For know that there is nothing therein which hath not been eaten, both dogs and cats and horses, so that victuals we can no more find in the town, except we eat men's flesh. For formerly you wrote that I should hold the town so long as there should be food. And now we are at that point that we have not wherewithal to live. So we have resolved amongst us that, if we have not succour quickly, we shall sally forth from the town into the open field, to fight for life or death. For it were better to die with honour in the field than to eat one another. Wherefore, right dear and dread lord, apply what remedy shall seem fitting; for, if remedy and counsel be not briefly found, never more will you have letters from me, and the town will be lost and we that are therein. Our Lord grant you a good life and long, and give you the will, if we die for you, to requite it to our heirs.

The letter was smuggled out of the town by a Genoese officer who set off at first light with companions in two small boats. They were pursued by the English and the Genoese jettisoned the letter attached to an axe. This was retrieved by the English at low tide and taken to King Edward. He read it, attached his seal and forwarded it to Philip. Both sides were now well aware of the situation and the urgency of relief.

Philip responded with another attempt to get supplies to the town by sea. Eight barges set out from Dieppe, with armed men aboard but un-escorted, in an attempt to creep in unseen. The convoy was captured. This latest failure led to desperate measures. Around 500 *bouches inutiles* were turned out to preserve the remaining resources for those who could fight. These women, children, the old and infirm, and the wounded could expect no mercy and there was no obligation for the besiegers to bring them succour. There are differing accounts of this episode, with one chronicler placing the expulsion earlier in the siege and recording that the refugees were brought before King Edward, given food, drink and money, and sent on their way. The other account places this event in the last days of the siege and says that those expelled were left to die below the walls in sight of both the besiegers and the garrison. The latter account seems more probable, although these may have been two separate incidents.

Reinforcements had been arriving from England since May and by the end of July Edward's army had likely reached its maximum. To these men could be added probably large numbers of Flemish troops beyond the Aa, a little over 20km away. Philip moved towards Calais from Hesdin on 17 July, travelling slowly and gathering troops as he went. On 27 July they arrived on the relatively high ground south of Sangatte, about 10km south-west of Calais. The situation was not encouraging for Philip. He faced an army much larger than his own. The approaches were either along the beaches or along two paths across the marsh. Between the two armies was the river Ham, with only one bridge across it at Nieulay. There were palisades on the beaches, ships moored offshore with archers, a tower defending the approach to the bridge over the Ham, and behind the bridge a strong force under Lancaster in prepared positions. In addi-tion, the encampments of the besiegers were protected by earthworks and trenches.

On the day of their arrival the French set about a reconnaissance of the English positions. They took the tower protecting the bridge at Nieulay and killed the men therein. The results of the reconnaissance were dis-couraging: there was not a single approach which could be forced without the risk of heavy losses, and the terrain was judged to be completely unsuitable for cavalry. It was clear to Philip that it would be impossible to relieve Calais. He now turned to thoughts of a diplomatic solution to save face. Two cardinals, the Italian Annibale Ceccano, Cardinal-Archbishop of Naples, and Étienne Aubert, the French Cardinal-Archbishop of Ostia, had been dogging the campaign since early after the English landing in Normandy the year before. At Philip's request they went forward to the bridge at Nieulay to ask to speak to senior representatives of the English king. The Earls of Lancaster and Northampton went forward with officials to meet the cardinals, who said that Philip wished to discuss peace and had some reasonable proposals. After some hesitation, since the cardinals were widely mistrusted in the English camp, a three-day truce was agreed for discussions which were held in pavilions within the English lines. It was obvious that the French regarded the siege as a lost cause and their principal objective was to secure the best possible terms for those remaining within Calais. They were also prepared to discuss a broader peace but the terms were unattractive, leaving Aquitaine as a fief of the French king. Nothing had changed since the same terms had been offered before Crécy, save that Edward was now in an immeasurably stronger position. On 31 July, after four days of fruitless talks, Philip issued a challenge to Edward to come and fight at a suitable place for battle to be selected by a joint commission. To give up a position of such strength would have been foolhardy in the extreme, but the concept of honour at the time meant that Edward could not reject the challenge out of hand. It was not clear exactly what happened, although Edward's later claim that he had accepted the challenge was denied by the French.

In any case the challenge was overtaken by events. The garrison had found encouragement in the arrival of Philip's army but they did not know what was going on at Nieulay. They could hold out no longer and on 1 August 1347, the day after the challenge was issued, they signalled to the French on the heights above the marsh that they were going to surrender. Philip broke camp that night, with the French burning their tents and equipment and destroying their supplies.

Edward's response to the decision to surrender was initially uncompromising. After eleven months of siege, with its extraordinary expenditure and loss of life, he was not inclined to be generous. He declared that he would not offer terms and would take everything in the town and do as he pleased with the occupants. There was unease in the English camp, with the king's advisers arguing that the boot could be on the other foot one day and he should show clemency. The king agreed to compromise. The defenders would be allowed their lives but neither their liberty nor their possessions. There was a sting in the tale. Six prominent citizens were to come before the king in shirtsleeves with nooses around their necks and bearing the keys of the town for him to dispose of as he wished.

A good deal of myth has grown around what followed, but a near-contemporary account by the chronicler Jean le Bel tells us that the king decided that the six would be beheaded in front of the army. The king's advisers were aghast but could not prevail upon the king to change his mind. It was only the queen's intervention that resulted in the lives of the men being spared. The town was rich and all movable goods were taken as plunder. With a few exceptions, the townspeople were expelled without their possessions and sent on their way to fend for themselves as best they could, having been given wine and bread from the English stores. Some of the most prominent people within the town, including the garrison commander Jean de Vienne, were held for ransom and sent to England. The rest were allowed to go. Edward now set about turning Calais into an English town. Philip expected Edward to return home but the English king wanted to pursue the war. In the end this proved beyond the capacity of the English and in September a truce was negotiated which was favourable to the English, who could remain in their positions throughout France proper, Aquitaine and Brittany.

Breteuil, 1356

There was sporadic fighting in the years after the post-Calais truce, particularly between 1349 and 1353. However, it was in 1355 that the truce finally collapsed and full-scale war resumed. In September 1355 the Black Prince landed in Bordeaux and set out on a *chevauchée* which took him as far as Narbonne on the Mediterranean and then back to La Réole, spreading destruction and terror in the Languedoc. The following year he struck north on a campaign which was to result in the great English victory at Poitiers in September 1356.

Meanwhile a long-running quarrel between Charles, King of Navarre, and King John II, the former Duke of Normandy who had succeeded to the throne in 1350, came to a head in April 1356 when Charles was arrested by the king and imprisoned. Charles, who was also Count of Évreux in Normandy, had been negotiating with the English for several years and following his arrest his son Philip turned to England for help. The Duke of Lancaster arrived in Normandy in June and together with English troops already in Brittany and a small number of Navarrese mustered around 2,400 men. This small force caused disproportionate problems for the French with a limited campaign which diverted resources and effort from the recruitment of the army destined to fight the Black Prince at Poitiers in

September. As Lancaster returned to his headquarters at Montebourg, King John decided to take the Navarrese fortress of Breteuil, 80km south of Rouen, laying siege around 12 July. This was an unimportant castle and the siege itself of no consequence for the events which were to follow the Black Prince's departure from Bordeaux. The interest is largely that once again we see John, much as at Aiguillon ten years before, become fixated on a siege as a point of honour to the detriment of the more important task of raising his army to confront the Black Prince.

Breteuil was well provisioned with food and water, and its garrison proved resolute. It had been built by William the Conqueror and its square construction and high towers should, in theory, have rendered it vulnerable to mining. The besiegers filled the ditches around the castle and set about undermining the walls. These efforts failed and an assault made in August using a siege tower also failed, with heavy French casualties. As the siege dragged on fruitlessly the Black Prince continued to move north. It eventually became clear even to John that the priority must be to counter the prince. On 20 August, with the Black Prince some 320km away and only 130km from Tours, John paid the garrison a large sum of money to surrender the castle. They were allowed to march away to rejoin the Navarrese forces in the Cotentin.

Romorantin, 1356

On 28 August King John had arrived at Chartres, 160km to the north of the Black Prince, and was gathering his army. There was contact between reconnaissance parties sent out by King John and an Anglo-Gascon detachment. The latter was considerably less numerous than the French force, but it had much the better of the encounter. The French were routed with many killed and eighteen knights and men-at-arms captured.

On 29 August, in the vicinity of Villefranche-sur-Cher, there was further contact with the French. Fortunes ebbed and flowed as the day progressed, but in the end the prince proved victorious. The start of the events was a clash between the Lord of Caumont for the prince and some of the French force, resulting in the capture of eight French knights and men-at-arms. From these prisoners the prince learnt that a French army was assembling and moving towards Orléans with the intention of doing battle with the prince. He was also able to confirm that the party encountered the day before had been sent to gather intelligence. Similarly, it became apparent that the prisoners were part of a second scouting party in the vicinity, possibly amounting to 300 men-at-arms. Later in the day this party ambushed and captured a small Anglo-Gascon foraging party, together with their booty. However, reinforcements quickly came to their relief, and some 150 of the French were captured and the English prisoners released. The remaining French fled and, finding the drawbridge down and the gates open, took refuge in the castle at Romorantin, 8km to the north.

On the next day, Tuesday, 30 August, the prince's army converged on Romorantin. The modern town sprawls out across the river Sauldre, with suburban housing and light industry, but in 1356 as the army approached from Villefranche it would have come first to the unprotected suburb of Le Bourgeau on the south of the river. Beyond that was an island in the river with a twelfth-century church, and beyond that again on the other bank was the walled town with the castle and its substantial keep. The town fell with little if any resistance. The following day the army attacked the castle where the French commanders had holed up. The outer walls were scaled and the gates forced with little difficulty, and the French withdrew further to the keep. The prince and his council decided that they would remain until they had taken the castle.

To date the prince had avoided sieges, largely to conserve his forces for his primary objective: battle with King John. At first sight his departure from this policy seems strange, but it accounts for the importance of this otherwise minor siege. Why would the prince now take the risks associated with a siege of losing valuable resources and remaining static? Only a week earlier at Châteauroux he had rejected a siege precisely because he wished to conserve his resources for battle with the French main army. The answer seems to be that the situation had changed to the extent that he now knew that King John was approaching with a view to battle. Since he wished to do battle with the French, if he remained at Romorantin and laid siege to the castle this might provoke the French into an ill-timed attack. In this context, it seems that the prince thought the enemy forces were about 60km away, much closer than was in fact the case.

The keep proved to be a very tough nut to crack. On 31 August there were two notable casualties among the prince's forces, with Bernadet d'Albret and a knight in the company of the Captal de Buch both killed. The next day three successive assaults were made by the Earl of Suffolk, Bartholomew de Burghersh and an unnamed Gascon knight. The keep still held. A change of tactics was required, and the emphasis was placed on undermining and setting fire to the keep. This was achieved over the next two days to the extent that by Saturday, 3 September the keep was burning so severely that the garrison had no hope of extinguishing the fire with their remaining stocks of water and wine. Their choice was between losing their lives to the fire and surrender. They opted for surrender.

Among the defenders was Robert de Gien, a soldier-cleric from the Maison-Dieu in Romorantin, who received forty *écus* as compensation for the armour he had lost in the service of his master, the Count of Blois, in defence of the keep. The siege did not draw John close to the prince at this stage. It was some two weeks later near Poitiers that the two armies finally joined in battle.

Reims, 1359–1360

Following his capture at the Battle of Poitiers King John was taken to England in May 1357. Over the next two years Edward III attempted to negotiate a peace settlement with John. In June the Cardinal of Périgord and the Cardinal of San Vitale arrived in England to join the discussions. These dragged on until eventually, in May 1358 at Windsor, King John agreed to the peace treaty known as the First Treaty of London. The terms of the treaty set the ransom for the French king at the enormous sum of 4,000,000 gold *écus*, of which the first instalment of 600,000 was to be paid before his release. Edward agreed to drop his claim to the French crown in return for the transfer to the English crown of great swathes of France in full sovereignty. The territories to be ceded, which amounted to almost one-third of France, comprised: Aquitaine, Saintonge, Poitou, Angoumois, Périgord, Agenais, Limousin, Rouergue, Quercy, Bigorre and Gaure in the south and west, and Calais, Guînes and the County of Ponthieu in the north. The first payment of the ransom was due by November 1358, but despite strenuous efforts on the part of King John the money could not be raised.

With the expiration of the truce of Bordeaux, signed in 1357 in the aftermath of the Battle of Poitiers, fast approaching Edward increased the pressure. In December 1358 arrangements were made for John to be moved from the comfort of the Savoy Palace to the more austere Somerton castle in Lincolnshire. This transfer was put in abeyance until July 1359, but nevertheless John was now held in the Savoy Palace without the freedom of movement that he had enjoyed hitherto. On 18 March 1359 it was agreed to extend the truce of Bordeaux until 24 June 1359. John was presented with a revised treaty, the Second Treaty of London, the terms of which were much more severe than those of the preceding year. He signed the draft on 24 March. In addition to the territories in the earlier treaty, John also now agreed to cede Touraine, Maine, Anjou and Normandy. In effect, the Angevin Empire of Henry II would be restored and the west of France would pass to the English crown. In addition the English king would have sovereignty over Brittany. As for the ransom, the sum was reduced to 3,000,000 *écus*, but with a bond of 1,000,000 which would be forfeit if payment was not made by 24 June 1360. A first payment of 600,000 *écus* was due on 1 August 1359. The Estates General were summoned to consider the treaty. They met on 25 May 1359. They judged that the terms were displeasing to all the people of France, and that they were neither feasible nor acceptable. They advised the regent, the dauphin Charles, to make war on England.

The renewal of the war was now inevitable, and in 1359 King Edward mustered the largest army that ever went to France during his reign. It was 12,000 strong and organized in three divisions led by the king, the Black Prince and the Duke of Lancaster. By the end of October the army had crossed the Channel. They set out from Calais on 4 November. The objectives were clear. The king would go to Reims and be crowned and anointed as King of France and then go on to occupy Paris.

The three divisions marched separately to maximize the opportunities for foraging. They converged and came together at the end of November about 50km west of Reims. They moved towards the town and arrived before the walls on 4 December. Reims, in common with many cities, had had perennial problems between the civil community and the church concerning the construction of and payment for fortifications. It was only a little more than a year before the arrival of Edward III and his army that the circuit of the wall had largely been completed. Even so there remained one section near the episcopal garden and the château de Porte-Mars which was protected only by a low wall in poor repair. The current archbishop, Jean de Craon, had a poor relationship with the citizens of the town, partly because he claimed kinship with Edward III and partly because of quarrels over guard duty and money. However, despite this enmity the citizens and the archbishop had jointly appointed a determined commander: Gaucher de Châtillon. An energetic and determined man, he constructed a wall with towers between the cathedral and the weak point on the perimeter wall near the château de Porte-Mars. He walled up three of the eight gates and dismantled their drawbridges, and dug a second ditch around the town. Buildings outside the town which could provide cover for besiegers were razed, and an entire forest was felled for the construction of defences. Supplies were requisitioned throughout the local area and brought into the town. Chains were positioned to disrupt any besiegers who entered the city, and artillery brought within the walls. The citizens were organized and rostered for round-the-clock watch and guard duties. No one was exempt from defending the town, even an ageing poet, a cathedral canon, was compelled to don armour and stand duty.

Initially the blockade was loose, with the English encampments some way back from the walls. Edward's headquarters lay 15km away to the south-east in the Benedictine monastery of St Basle near Verzy. The Black Prince's division was at the monastery of St-Thierry, 10km to the north-west, with the marshal and the Duke of Lancaster at Bétheney, 5km to the north-east. Despite the blockade being maintained at a distance it seems that it was effective, with patrols making crossing the siege lines a hazardous business. Talks were held with the leaders of the defenders in the hope of persuading them to surrender. During this period, since Edward hoped to be admitted to Reims to be crowned King of France by the archbishop, orders were given for the English soldiery to refrain from looting. After two weeks it was clear that the defenders were resolute and there was no hope of them surrendering, despite the intelligence gained from prisoners that Edward was prepared to maintain a long siege and the knowledge that the dauphin did not have the means to raise an army to relieve the town. The English moved forwards on or about 18 December to enforce a close blockade.

Shortly afterwards a determined attempt was made to take the town by storm. Three divisions attacked the walls at the same time: one in the south-west near a fortified bridge, the others from the east. English archers provided cover while the ditches were filled with trees and timber and two wooden siege-towers were brought forwards. The defenders responded with stones thrown by machines within the walls and by sending men to set fire to the wood in the ditches, despite the shooting of the English archers. The Black Prince's men, after a day's fighting, succeeded in laying a causeway across the ditch to the west but were unable to reach the walls. The men on the east could not achieve even this and the attack was called off, not to be repeated.

The siege had started late in the year and the besiegers were at a great disadvantage in comparison with those within the walls. The inhabitants were well supplied and had the benefit of shelter in the town. The besiegers were for the most part encamped in the winter conditions and were becoming increasingly short of food. Raiding parties now had to range further and further afield to find supplies. By the second week of January 1360 supplies in the local area had been exhausted and there was no alternative but to lift the siege. During the night of 11 January the army slipped away, leaving the morning watch to discover that they had successfully defied the English king.

After leaving Reims Edward's army moved south and east and then eventually looped west and north to approach Paris. The army needed to keep moving to find food, which was in short supply since the French had moved reserves into towns to deny them to the English. Paris was far too tough a nut to crack, despite the size of the English army. Also, the English continued to face the problem of a lack of victuals, the surrounding area having been stripped by the French. On 7 April Edward came before Paris hoping to provoke the dauphin into coming out to do battle but the future Charles V was too canny to fall into that trap. On 12 April Edward withdrew and the following day, which came to be known as Black Monday, disaster struck in the form of extraordinary weather conditions. Ferocious storms resulted in wagons sinking into pools of mud and being abandoned with their contents; men and horses died of exposure, while others were killed by huge hailstones. It has been argued that although Edward's military position was by no means desperate, he interpreted these events as a sign from God that it was time to settle, and he decided to resume negotiations for peace. Talks started on 1 May 1360 in the small village of Brétigny near Chartres. Within a few days terms had been agreed for the Treaty of Brétigny which was ratified at Calais in October. At last a peace settlement had been agreed. Large swathes of territory in the south-west were ceded to the English in full sovereignty. In return Edward agreed to renounce his claim to the French crown. As we shall see in the next chapter this peace was to be short-lived.

Chapter 5

The French Recovery, 1369–1389

The death of John II and the succession of Charles V in 1364 left an awkward situation to say the least. The joint renunciations of the English claim to the French crown and the French claim to sovereignty over lands held by the kings of England in France, key terms of the Treaty of Brétigny, had not been signed by Edward III and John II. In these circumstances Charles V did not feel bound by these provisions, and a return to war was to be expected.

In 1367 the Black Prince fought and won the battle of Nájera in Castile. He was fighting to support Pedro the Cruel's claim to the throne of Castile. Against him had been the French, with the future Constable of France, Bertrand du Guesclin, in support of the rival claimant to be King of Castile, Henry of Trastámara. The sequel to the victory, however, was less than happy. The prince contracted a debilitating disease from which he was never to recover. More importantly for the prospects of continuing peace was Pedro's refusal to meet his obligation to pay for the expedition to Castile. On his return to Bordeaux the prince had to resort to exceptional taxation to pay the cost of the war. There was considerable discontent among the Gascon lords, and in 1369 the Count of Armagnac appealed his case to the Parlement in Paris. If the provisions relating to sovereignty had been implemented then this would have been impossible, but Charles V elected to hear the case and the Black Prince was summoned to appear in Paris. He refused and the result was war once again, with the formal breach coming in May 1369.

Charles V had been a boy of eight when his grandfather was defeated at Crécy, and he had been present at Poitiers when his father was captured. He was determined that he would not suffer the same fate and gave strict instructions that set-piece battles with the English, save in the most exceptionally favourable conditions, were to be avoided. This renewed phase of the war would be about places: taking them by guile, persuasion, siege or assault. The principal commander to implement his policy was Bertrand

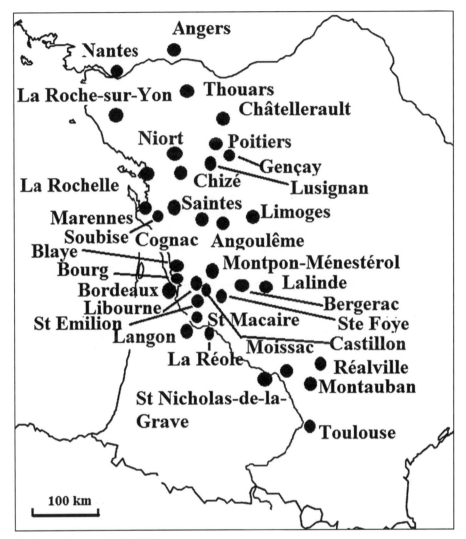

Southern France, 1369–1389.

du Guesclin, a thoroughly professional, determined and effective Breton commander, who from 1370 served as Constable of France.

As the storm clouds of war gathered again Charles V made his plans: the Duke of Anjou was to take responsibility for the war in Aquitaine, which bordered on his lieutenancy of the Languedoc, and the Duke of Berry was assigned the Loire river basin. The Duke of Burgundy was charged with a seaborne invasion of England. In the event the invasion did not materialize, but war broke out across the south-west as the French sought to push back the frontiers of English Aquitaine and retake territory ceded by the Treaty of Brétigny. There was also fighting in Brittany and in the north in the English County of Ponthieu and around the Calais Pale.

Réalville, 1369

Fighting had started before the formal return to war. A first objective for the Duke of Anjou in the south-west was to detach provinces which had passed to the expanded Principality of Aquitaine after Brétigny, but which had no tradition of loyalty to the English crown. Key among these were Quercy and the Rouergue.

Montauban, standing on the Tarn, was the most important English fortress in Quercy. It was ill-prepared for a siege, and Sir John Chandos elected to protect the town from a distance. He secured Moissac on the Tarn and the castle St-Nicholas-de-la-Grave on the Garonne. He also put a garrison into the *bastide* town of Réalville on the Aveyron, about 15km from Montauban. Holding these places prevented the French taking supplies by river for a siege of Montauban.

Towards the end of March or in early April the French laid siege to Réalville. The seneschal of Quercy had prepared for such an event, laying in supplies. It was evident that the garrison would not yield easily. The French brought four stone-throwing machines from Toulouse and set about bombarding the walls by day and night. Tunnelling also started to undermine the walls. The English attempted to foil this by counter-mining, but in the end a large stretch of wall came down as a result of the mining and bombardment. The garrison had resisted for more than a fortnight but in the end was overwhelmed by an assault through the breach. The defenders were massacred to a man, which was no more than they could expect, not having come to terms.

Duravel, 1369

The sacrifice of the garrison of Réalville was not in vain. The French abandoned the siege of Montauban, which had been reinforced by Chandos in the interim with 200 men-at-arms, and marched north towards the Lot.

Sir Robert Knolles had come from Brittany with sixty men-at-arms and a similar number of archers. He had arrived by sea at La Rochelle and then made his way to Angoulême to see the Black Prince. From there he set out, accompanied by other Gascon and English captains, to join the Anglo-Gascon forces in Quercy. He is reported to have had with him 500 men-at-arms, 500 archers and 500 infantry. He began to move up the valley of the Lot. The news of the approach of Knolles and the defection of some Gascon lords to the English cause had caused concern in Cahors. Five French *routier* captains had been sent down the river with their men to occupy the small town of Duravel, 30km to the east of Cahors, to stop English supplies and reinforcements passing up the river and Knolles found his way blocked.

The fortifications of the village were in a poor state, but on their arrival the French set about improving the situation. They brought in supplies of grain and wine, installed artillery and prepared for the inevitable attack. They had also stripped the countryside around of victuals, either destroying them or bringing them into the village. On his arrival Knolles besieged the town and after two weeks or so attempted to take the place by assault, but his men were driven off by artillery fire and a resolute defence. Knolles settled down to starve the garrison. When the news of the siege reached Montauban, Chandos marched north-west for 60km to join the besiegers. There were numerous skirmishes between besiegers and besieged, but in the end the decisive factors were logistics and the weather. It rained day and night and, due to the thorough preparations of the French, supplies of food were in short supply for the Anglo-Gascons. The cost of bread rocketed, if it could be found. The only comfort was that stocks of wine were plentiful. After around five weeks the besiegers could continue no longer and marched away.

La Roche-sur-Yon, 1370

The ensuing months saw the Anglo-Gascon effort, largely through a shortage of supplies, split into small companies trying to hold back concentrated, larger French forces. The result was a series of failures of small-scale attacks on towns and strongholds. Further north the French were making inroads into the Vendée and Poitou. The town of La Roche-sur-Yon was held by the French. The captain was Jean Belon, who held the town for his lord the Duke of Anjou. It was strategically important, standing on the line of advance for any invasion force approaching Aquitaine from Nantes. In March 1369 the Earls of Cambridge and Pembroke had landed at St-Malo along with between 800 and 1,000 men. In mid-July Cambridge started to besiege La Roche. He was joined by Sir James Audley, a veteran of the Battle of Poitiers, who brought more men from Poitiers.

The English transported siege engines from Poitiers and Thouars to supplement the cannon and springalds already with the besiegers and began a bombardment. The fortifications were in good repair and the garrison well provisioned, but this time the besiegers were also well supplied. Within days Belon entered into negotiations for the surrender of the fortress. Although he had ample stores he could see no relief in prospect and did not relish the thought of an assault with all that would entail for him and his men if they were defeated. Belon agreed to surrender La Roche if relief did not come within one month and to sell his remaining stores for 6,000 francs. Armaury de Craon was charged with going to the relief of Belon and his men. Time was short and Craon had too few men initially. By the time he had assembled sufficient forces it was too late and Belon had opened the gates. The garrison were allowed to go free but were escorted by the English as far as Angers.

Belon was arrested when he arrived in Angers and charged with treason. His misfortune was that, although he could argue that he had acted within the code of conduct for sieges, he had surrendered after a very short time and with plentiful supplies remaining – sufficient, it was said, to hold La Roche for a year. He paid for his conduct with his life in a barbaric fashion, sewn in a bag and drowned in the Loire on the order of his lord the Duke of Anjou.

Limoges, 1370

Operations in the north of the Principality of Aquitaine drew English forces away from Quercy and the Rouergue and in effect these provinces passed into French hands. In July 1369 around 4,000 reinforcements arrived in Calais led by John of Gaunt and the Earl of Hereford and in September the Earl of Warwick joined them with a further 2,000 men. Operations in Normandy succeeded in finally putting paid to the plan for an invasion of England, but brought little else in the way of success. In early 1370 the French continued to push back the frontiers of Aquitaine, moving into the Agenais and taking control of much of Périgord and the valleys of the Lot and Garonne.

Edward III's plans for 1370 were to send limited reinforcements to Aquitaine and land a larger force in the Cotentin peninsula in Normandy. The hope was that this army would be allied with that of Charles, King of Navarre, who had significant interests in Normandy. For Aquitaine 300 reinforcements recruited on behalf of the Earl of Pembroke were sent out to the Principality in the spring with a further 500 men in June. The plan for Normandy was for Sir Robert Knolles to take 2,000 men-at-arms and 2,000 archers and join forces with the King of Navarre. The king was a duplicitous character, always trying to keep his options open and playing Edward III off against Charles V. The French, meanwhile, intended to concentrate on driving the English out of Aquitaine. The Duke of Anjou would lead one army into Aquitaine along the Garonne with La Réole and Bergerac as their objectives. The Duke of Berry would invade from the east through the Limousin. A third invasion force would move south from the region of the Loire and Creuse. It was at this time that du Guesclin was appointed constable.

The thrust from the north brought an early success with the capture of Châtellerault. Anjou made limited progress with his campaign along the Garonne, but success came through the arrival of du Guesclin to join Anjou. He had been recalled from Castile to take his office of constable and crossed the Pyrenees with perhaps 4,000 men. He operated far and wide, taking Moissac, the last English stronghold in Quercy, establishing control of the Dordogne from Lalinde, only 20km to the east of the major English possession of Bergerac, eastwards. Little had been done to prepare the defence of the Limousin in the face of the threat from the Duke of Berry. Berry struck south, encountering little opposition, and reached Limoges on 21 August 1370.

Limoges comprised, as was often the case in French medieval episcopal cities, effectively two towns with suburbs between them. The larger and older of these, known as the Château, was grouped around the château of the viscount and an abbey on high ground about 800m from the river Vienne. It was the main commercial centre of the town of Limoges, had a population of around 10,000 and was well defended by strong thirteenth-century walls about 2,500m in circumference with numerous towers and fortified gates. The smaller of the two parts was the *cité*. It covered about 10ha and was surrounded by walls with a circumference of 1,500m with six gates. The fortifications were in a poor state of repair. It was under the jurisdiction of the Bishop of Limoges. The Château had a strong English garrison, with a small number of men detached to the *cité* who could be withdrawn to the Château in case of trouble. The Château held out against Berry and remained loyal to the Black Prince. In the *cité*, however, the bishop, an erstwhile supporter of the Black Prince, presumably taking the view that the English cause was on the wane, decided that he would surrender and on 24 August submitted to the Duke of Berry. Perhaps for financial reasons, the French campaigns suddenly came to an end at the end of August, and only three days after he had accepted the submission of the *cité*, Berry marched away leaving Roger de Beaufort, Hugh de la Roche, and John de Villemur to hold the *cité* with 140 men. Berry made no attempt on the Château before his withdrawal, leaving the *cité* with its small garrison isolated and vulnerable.

Retribution was not long in coming. John of Gaunt's army had been moved by sea from Calais during July, arriving in Bordeaux probably in mid-August. In early September he arrived at Cognac and joined forces with the Black Prince and the Earls of Pembroke and Cambridge. Less than three weeks after Berry's departure the Anglo-Gascon army arrived before the *cité* of Limoges. The Black Prince summoned the inhabitants to surrender with the customary warnings of the consequences of the town being taken by assault: the destruction of their homes by fire and sword, and implicitly the risk of their lives being lost.

The citizens may now have been regretting their submission to Berry, but with his garrison installed in the *cité* there could be no question of immediate surrender. The Anglo-Gascons did not seem inclined to settle down to starve the population and the garrison into surrender. Thus the inhabitants faced the unenviable prospect of the consequences of the town being taken by assault. John of Gaunt took charge of the ensuing siege. Reconnaissance showed that a section of the perimeter wall was built on soft limestone rather than rock. Mining started to exploit this weakness. The defenders detected the work of the miners and dug a countermine, breaking into the besiegers' tunnel. The French were driven back in fierce hand-to-hand fighting in which John of Gaunt was said to have been involved personally. The mining continued and by 19 September all was ready. The timbers supporting the mine were set alight and about 30m of wall collapsed to the north-east of the *cité*.

Waiting for this moment was the assembled Anglo-Gascon army. They surged towards the breach but were initially driven back by the garrison, some 500 strong if we add the likely numbers of town militia to the 140 men-at-arms installed by the Duke of Berry. However, a second assault was successful. Sixty of the garrison lost their lives as the Anglo-Gascons stormed the *cité*. The surviving eighty men of those left by the Duke of Berry formed up in a hollow square outside a monastery in the *cité* and fought to a standstill, before surrendering.

Thanks largely to the account of the chronicler Jean Froissart, the sack of Limoges has gone down in history as an infamous day in the life of the Black Prince. Froissart alleged that in the mayhem of looting, killing and burning that followed the assault more than 3,000 people were killed and the whole *cité* was stripped of its goods and then left in flames. The casualty figures are improbable; even if refugees from outlying places are added in this would have equated to almost the total population. It seems that Froissart's numbers are much exaggerated and another contemporary source put the figure at 300. Whatever the casualty figure, the damage to property was extensive and severe. Traces of the sack of the *cité* were visible for many years and the bishop's palace remained uninhabitable until the sixteenth century. The bishop and the three captains left behind by Berry to defend the *cité* were all captured. The Black Prince threatened to behead the bishop for his treachery, but in the event his life was spared and he was ransomed the following year.

Montpon-Ménestérol, 1370–1371

Despite the Anglo-Gascons retaking the *cité* of Limoges, the tide of war was running inexorably in favour of the French. In late summer 1370 Sir Robert Knolles arrived in Calais. He had brought with him several companies of men amounting to around 4,000 in total. He had initially struck towards Paris, arriving in late September, hoping to tempt the French out from behind the walls to fight. However, Charles V, who was present in the capital, was having none of it and ordered his men to remain behind the security of the ramparts. Knolles did not have the men, equipment or time to besiege Paris and his forces moved off into Normandy and the Beauce in separate columns. They came together in mid-October in the Vendômois and Touraine. The captains had quarrelled over winter quarters and had decided to split the army and go their separate ways. However, before they could do so they were caught by du Guesclin, newly appointed Constable of France, and the English army was destroyed in a series of engagements at Pontvallain, 30km south of Le Mans, at Vaas 10km to the south-west and during the subsequent pursuit of the routed soldiers.

The defeat of Knolles' companies was serious not only because of the destruction of a substantial army but also because it destroyed the myth of the invincibility of English arms on the battlefield and ended all hope of an alliance between the King of Navarre and Edward III. At the end of 1370 the Black Prince embarked for England, unable due to his illness to continue as Prince of Aquitaine. His brother John of Gaunt assumed his responsibilities. Gaunt's priority was to try to reverse losses in Aquitaine, or at least to stem further French inroads being made into English-held territory. However, once the *cité* of Limoges had been retaken the Black Prince and his men had withdrawn, leaving the town isolated in increasingly hostile territory. To all intents and purposes the Limousin was lost, and in November 1371 the Château of Limoges submitted to the French crown. However, all was not lost elsewhere and in the autumn of 1371 Sir Thomas Percy took the castle of Moncontour 45km north-west of Poitiers. Defence of the Dordogne, with its ancient alliances and proximity to both the Atlantic coast and the base of English power in Aquitaine, was also a more practicable proposition than had been the case for the Limousin, the Rouergue and Quercy.

Montpon-Ménestérol on the river Isle, little more than 30km to the east of Libourne, had been taken by du Guesclin in August 1370. Its position and its control of a bridge over the Isle made its recapture an obvious objective for John of Gaunt in his defence of Aquitaine and in early December he and the Earl of Cambridge laid siege to the town and castle with an Anglo-Gascon force.

The town was walled and dominated by a strong castle protecting the bridge. The captain of the castle, Guillaume de Montpon, who had surrendered to du Guesclin, feared English reprisals and fled to Périgueux, leaving the defence in the hands of Breton men-at-arms. Jean de Malestroit and Sylvester Budes, two Breton squires in command of the garrison of St-Macaire, drew lots to see who should go with help to Montpon. Budes, a cousin of du Guesclin, set out with a dozen men-at-arms to take command of the garrison.

Gaunt had brought with him some 700 men-at-arms and 500 archers. The first task was to fill the ditches with brushwood and earth, work which was to take almost three weeks. A series of assaults were then launched which were repulsed on each occasion. Once the ditches had been successfully filled, however, men could approach the foot of the walls under the cover of shelters with the archers forcing the defenders back from the ramparts. Eventually, men working with picks brought down a section of wall, creating a breach 12m wide. The Anglo-Gascons entered through the breach with the archers driving the defenders back with a hail of arrows. The defenders sought to negotiate terms. John of Gaunt, extremely irritated by the stubborn resistance over eleven weeks, was not inclined to be merciful and demanded that Guillaume de Montpon should be given up to be judged as a traitor and that the rest of the garrison should surrender unconditionally. The garrison argued that they had done no more than their duty and had a right to be treated by the rules of war. Guillaume de Montpon had long since gone, and Gaunt relented for the rest: they surrendered as prisoners of war with their lives spared.

Soubise, 1372

During 1372 du Guesclin continued to make progress in driving the Anglo-Gascons out of towns and fortresses across Aquitaine. By 7 August he had entered Poitiers. Shortly thereafter Owen of Wales, with a mixed force of Castilian and Welsh, landed near the estuary of the Charente. His planned destination had been Wales, but Henry of Trastámara, once more King of Castile, got cold feet on hearing rumours of a large English naval build-up in the Channel. The destination was changed to La Rochelle, but in the event the troops disembarked in the small port of Marennes. On hearing the news du Guesclin, still about 150km away, despatched 300 men-at-arms to reinforce Owen and the French naval commander with him, Morelet de Montmor. In the third week of August the combined French, Castilian and Welsh force besieged Soubise, about 13km from Marennes, on the banks of the Charente.

The castle was held by the Lady of Soubise, with the garrison commanded by Sir Walter Hewitt. She appealed to the Captal de Buch, a Gascon lord faithful to the English cause throughout his life, for help. He was at St-Jean-d'Angely and was concerned about this second front and so set out to nip the problem in the bud. He drew men from the garrisons of Saintes, Angoulême, Niort and Lusignan. During the night of 22 August he took the siege lines totally by surprise as Sir Walter Hewitt led a sortie of thirty men-at-arms out of the castle to join the attack. Initially the attack was a complete success, but the besiegers rallied and eventually overwhelmed the Captal's men and took him prisoner. Hewitt managed to make his way back into the castle, but with all hope of relief gone after the defeat of the Captal he surrendered and opened the gates next morning. The siege had been of short duration and few men had been involved. However, several prominent and experienced Anglo-Gascon captains were taken and around half of the troops available for the defence of Aquitaine were lost. Its impact was out of all proportion to the strategic importance of the fortress. The Duke of Anjou prepared to take his army down the Garonne, and two weeks after the surrender of Soubise the great port town of La Rochelle opened its gates to the French.

Chizé, 1373

The French campaign to retake Poitou continued unabated and by December 1372 the Anglo-Gascons held only around ten places of any military importance in Poitou. Of these the most important was Niort. Sir John Devereux, based at Niort, was in overall command of the remaining strongholds with perhaps 1,000 men spread throughout the garrisons. About 25km south of Niort the English held the small town and castle of Chizé. Robert Morton and Martin Scott commanded the garrison with sixty men. During March 1373 du Guesclin laid siege to Chizé with around 500 men. Morton and Scott appealed to Devereux for help. He assembled possibly as many as 700 men drawn from a number of garrisons.

When Devereux arrived at Chizé the garrison sallied out to join the attack on the besiegers. Although outnumbered by the Anglo-Gascons, du Guesclin's men prevailed, killing most of the relief army, and Devereux was captured. Niort surrendered six days later. There is another version of the story of the attempted relief of Chizé, which relates how du Guesclin, concerned about the strength of Devereux's force, decided to lay a trap. It seems that even in those days the English had a reputation for liking a drink. Du Guesclin, knowing his enemy well, placed two carts laden with wine from Montreuil-Bellay on the route that the reinforcements would follow. Devereux's men fell upon the carts and settled down to enjoy the wine. They were set upon and killed or captured by du Guesclin's men. Whatever the true circumstances, the defeat before Chizé was the beginning of the end for English-held Poitou and Saintonge. The final stronghold, the castle of Gençay, fell in February 1375.

Brest and Derval, 1373

While du Guesclin was busy recovering Poitou, events were unfolding in Brittany. John IV de Montfort, Duke of Brittany, had been treading a difficult path between the English and the French. In February 1373 he assured Charles V that the English would be gone from his duchy as soon as the weather permitted them to set sail. Despite the duke's assurances, he was preparing to welcome an English landing of troops at St-Malo. Charles seems to have had little faith in John and he decided to occupy Brittany. In mid-April the Earl of Salisbury landed with 1,700 men and several companies of Genoese crossbowmen. His force was intended to be an advance guard for a larger army to come under the command of John of Gaunt, due to arrive the following month. It was important that the French did not allow the English to re-establish control across the duchy. The French entered Brittany about the same date as Salisbury landed. They brought around 3,000 men and marched in three columns. The Duke of Bourbon, in overall command, marched towards Salisbury to contain his landing, the constable, du Guesclin, headed for Rennes, and the Viscount of Rohan moved towards John de Montfort at Vannes. Support for de Montfort was fading, and he fled to England at the end of April. The departure of the duke accelerated the erosion of his support, and in these adverse circumstances the plan to land Gaunt's army in Brittany was abandoned. In late May Salisbury's force was recalled. By the end of June only four places continued to be held for John de Montfort: Derval, Auray, held by the Duchess of Brittany, Bécherel and Brest, held by Sir John Neville with Sir Robert Knolles, who had assumed *de facto* command of the remaining English forces in Brittany. On 1 June 1373 du Guesclin arrived to besiege Brest. Around the same date Olivier de Clisson was sent by du Guesclin to besiege the fortress of Derval, held by *routiers* on behalf of Robert Knolles.

In England plans were put in hand to relieve Neville and Knolles, holed up in Brest. De Montfort had hoped to raise an army in England to restore his fortunes in Brittany, but instead his efforts were diverted and he subsequently sailed for Calais with Gaunt. Nevertheless, it was decided that Salisbury should return to Brittany with 3,000 men with the specific objective of bringing support to the garrison in Brest.

The English in Brest knew nothing of these plans and their situation quickly deteriorated. After five weeks of siege, with no obvious hope of relief and their supplies exhausted, they sued for a treaty to surrender to du Guesclin. The terms were generous. The fortress was to be handed over one month later, on 6 August 1373, if John de Montfort had not brought a relief force in person and arrayed in sufficient strength on open ground outside Brest to hold his own against the besiegers. Meanwhile there was to be a truce in the surrounding area within which the garrison could go to find supplies. Bretons in the garrison would be pardoned and allowed to keep their lands, and the English would be free to leave under safe conduct with all their possessions. Six hostages were delivered up to

Northern France, 1369–1389.

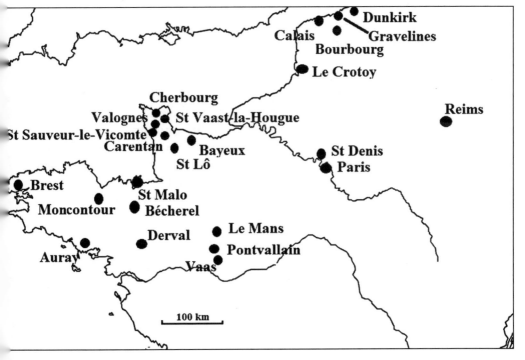

guarantee the agreement, with a further six more nominated for surrender later if required.

Confident that his mission was accomplished, du Guesclin left Brest to raid the Channel Islands, returning on the appointed day of 6 August with the entire French army in Brittany, about 3,000 men. Not only had the garrison in Brest been ignorant of the relief planned by Salisbury, but so was du Guesclin. Late in July Salisbury set out from Southampton, arriving off Brest with shiploads of stores and 3,000 men a few days later. The garrison was, of course, delighted but there was a problem. The composition for surrender required the presence of de Montfort in person. The English, justifying their action with the claim that the French had failed to respond satisfactorily to complaints of minor breaches of the truce, reneged on the agreement. The French were furious but could do little other than draw up their army and see what would transpire. The two armies, roughly equivalent in numbers, were arrayed outside the town, but neither side wanted to leave their defensive positions. After a few days du Guesclin marched away and Salisbury returned to England in mid-August leaving a garrison of 200 men. The town was periodically resupplied by sea and remained in English hands until its return to the Duke of Brittany in June 1397.

While events had been unfolding at Brest, the siege of Derval had continued. Towards the end of August Charles V had decided to withdraw du Guesclin and his army to confront the threat posed by John of Gaunt and the Duke of Brittany, who had set out from Calais on 10 August. The garrison of Derval were unaware of the pressure on the French to redeploy men from Brittany, and seeing no sign of relief entered into a treaty to surrender if they were not relieved by 29 September 1373. Hostages were delivered up to guarantee the agreed terms. However, fresh from his repudiation of the terms for the surrender of Brest, Knolles went to Derval and reneged on the agreement made by the garrison commanders on the grounds that they had acted without his authority.

On the appointed day the Duke of Anjou and Olivier de Clisson arrived at Derval to find that the castle would not surrender. The six hostages were executed in full view of the garrison. Although harsh, this action was consistent with the conventions of war. Knolles' response – to behead four French prisoners and throw their bodies into the moat – was not.

La Réole, 1374

Much of the military activity on both sides in the latter months of 1373 was taken up with John of Gaunt's great *chevauchée* from Calais to

Bordeaux. From the French perspective likely objectives for Gaunt's army were Brittany and Paris, but in the event he set out south and then south-west for Bordeaux. The march was marked by frustration and failure as the French refused battle, but engaged in harassing and skirmishing. Late in the year the army crossed the Massif Central in appalling weather conditions. The bedraggled army which entered Bordeaux at the end of December had lost around half of its 30,000 horses, and many knights entered on foot, to all intents and purposes a defeated army even though there had been no significant combat.

In the early months of 1374 the French and English both had designs on drawing the kingdoms of Spain into the war to further their aims. The English hoped to invade Castile in alliance with Aragon, while the French hoped to obtain a Castilian army to augment their forces in the south-west of France. By the spring of 1374 these efforts had come to nothing and both French and English attention turned once again to the war in Aquitaine.

At the beginning of August 1374 the Dukes of Bourbon and Anjou gathered a force of 4,000 men at Toulouse. Their first target was La Réole, an important strategic fortress town on the Garonne which protected the approach to Bordeaux down the Garonne valley. We have already seen that when La Réole was taken by Lancaster in 1345–1346 it fell because of a weakness in the defences of the castle and the loyalty of the inhabitants to the English cause. Both of these factors were again to play a part in the fate of the town almost thirty years later.

By the middle of August the town was besieged. The Anglo-Gascons had had time to prepare for this eventuality and the castle was strongly garrisoned, equipped with artillery and well provisioned under the command of Sir Hugh Calveley. A sortie by the garrison to disrupt the Duke of Bourbon's encampment turned to disaster. The raiding party was driven back with the French in such close pursuit that they entered the outer of the three circuits of town walls before the gates could be closed. A change of sentiment among the population now came into play, as Calveley did not benefit from the support that Lancaster had had. The townspeople entered into discussions with the besieging army and opened the gates of the town to the Duke of Anjou on 21 August.

The weakness of the castle on the town side was recognized by the French just as easily as it had been by Lancaster. This time, however, the French did not need to undermine the walls. Calveley was aware of this inherent weakness. Furthermore, having lost the town and with the castle overlooked by the tower of the church of St Pierre less than 150m from the castle walls, he concluded that his position was indefensible. A week after the French had entered the town Calveley negotiated to surrender if King Edward III or one of his sons did not arrive with sufficient force to raise the siege by 8 September. It was impossible for the English to raise such a force in time, even if there had been the will to do so, and on the due date the castle was surrendered.

St-Sauveur-le-Vicomte, 1374–1375

The return of John of Gaunt to England in the spring of 1374 marked the start of a period of neglect of Aquitaine by the English. The next major expeditionary force to arrive from England would not come until 1412. By the spring of 1374 there was a desire for peace, or at least a truce, in both France and England. However, as is so often the case in such situations, both governments wanted to freeze the situation with the most favourable military aspect that they could obtain. For the English this meant supporting a joint expedition to Brittany led by John de Montfort and the Earl of Cambridge. The French wanted to tie up some loose ends and eradicate the remaining English strongholds outside the traditional heartland of Gascony. In what remained of Aquitaine this meant the castle of Gençay south of Poitiers, and the walled town of Cognac. In the north the key surviving strongholds were Brest, Auray and St-Sauveur-le-Vicomte in the Cotentin peninsula.

St-Sauveur was the first priority. This was to be the fourth attempt on the fortress since 1369. The three previous failures had at least shown that considerable resources would be required if the place were to be taken. King Charles had been told that a successful siege would require 600 crossbowmen, 3,000 men-at-arms, artillery and large numbers of labourers. In the event Charles went ahead, disregarding the advice on the resources needed. Jean de Vienne, who was charged with the siege, arrived in the Cotentin in mid-August with only a few hundred men. Nevertheless, he methodically set about the task of isolating the fortress, constructing bastilles 8km to the east at Pont-l'Abbé near the village of Picauville, a second 4km further south-east at Beuzeville-la-Bastille, controlling the river Douve which flowed through St-Sauveur, and a third at St-Sauveur-de-Pierrepont 8km to the south-west. St-Sauveur was only 16km from the coast, and to prevent the prospect of English relief or resupply by sea Castilian galleys were stationed off the coast. A loose siege of this type could in principle limit the opportunities of the garrison to launch sorties in the surrounding countryside to forage for supplies, but it was unlikely to bring a well-supplied and garrisoned fortress to surrender.

St-Sauveur was garrisoned by about 300 men commanded by Thomas Catterton assisted by Sir Thomas Trivet and a Breton, Hennequin Vallebreton. They were well supplied with wine and food. Catterton and his lieutenants conducted a vigorous defence from the outset. They demolished buildings outside the walls within bow-shot and a nearby abbey to prevent their use by the French. Stones from the abbey were taken into the castle for use as projectiles. Raids were also launched to disrupt the siege army as far afield as St-Lô and Bayeux, 45km and 60km distant respectively. The English were able to take advantage of the weakness of the besieging army and the loose blockade to bring in as reinforcements the garrison from Bécherel, which had surrendered to du Guesclin and been granted safe-conduct to go where they wished. It was clear that the loose siege would not succeed. In October the besieging army was reinforced, but numbers were still inadequate. In January 1375, with no progress having been made to force a surrender, it was decided that the force should be increased to 2,000 men and workmen sent to build the siege works needed for a close siege. Stone-throwing machines were already in use, but cannon were brought from Paris along the Seine and then along the roads of Normandy. Foundries were set up in the region to manufacture further guns. What had started as a low-cost, undermanned operation was turning into a major enterprise.

In England it had been hoped that deployment of de Montfort's and Cambridge's army would draw off some of the besieging army, but due to a series of problems the army had still not sailed by March 1375. Meanwhile, by the end of February the siege was starting to become effective. A fourth bastille had been constructed, 500m from the walls in the ruins of the abbey destroyed by the garrison. Some at least of the guns were operational and were proving effective: the keep had to be abandoned. The garrison ventured elsewhere in the town at their peril and were sheltering in towers on the wall.

Negotiations had been progressing at Bruges which made, *inter alia*, provision for the siege of St-Sauveur to be frozen for the duration of a truce proposed by papal legates towards the end of May 1375. It was too late to save St-Sauveur. In the face of relentless and effective bombardment day and night, and with their supplies exhausted, the garrison had reached the limits of endurance. Perhaps a close shave for Thomas Catterton when he was almost killed by a cannon ball passing through the window of the tower in which he was sleeping, rolling around the walls and then crashing through the floor had an influence on the decision to agree to surrender the fortress. More probably mining, which brought down a tower and opened a breach in the wall, was the final incentive to agree terms.

A treaty of surrender was agreed on 21 May whereby the castle would be surrendered on 3 July 1375 if not relieved by the Duke of Brittany in person by the previous day. Eight hostages were to be handed over as surety, including Sir Thomas Trivet. The garrison would be allowed to leave under safe-conduct with transport supplied by the French to take away the men, their possessions and booty. The garrison would also be allowed to collect ransoms for their prisoners. In addition to these generous terms, substantial payments were promised to the commanders of the garrison and their men.

Peace negotiations were still under way in Bruges, and the papal legates had secured agreement that the castle would pass into the hands of the legates in the name of the Pope. The French, however, ignored this provision and mustered a large force of more than 6,000 men to forestall any attempt at relief. Perhaps Catterton, aware that at last de Montfort and Cambridge had landed in Brittany in April, believed that the six weeks of truce provided for in the surrender agreement would give de Montfort plenty of time to come to his relief, but in the event he was too preoccupied with his own priorities. The garrison was confused about the relationship between their surrender agreement and the truce negotiations. They started to prevaricate, until it was made clear that, if they did not honour the agreement to surrender, the hostages would be executed. The castle duly surrendered on the appointed date.

Bergerac, 1377

In Bruges the peace talks ground on, and a truce was finally agreed a few days before St-Sauveur-le-Vicomte surrendered. It was initially to run until June 1376, but was later extended until June 1377. Before the truce Gençay had fallen to du Guesclin in April 1375 and Cognac had followed suit on 1 June. With the resumption of war the French made a somewhat desultory attempt to take Calais. However, in the face of terrible weather, which made resupply and the siting of siege equipment extremely problematic and forced the dispersal of his fleet, the Duke of Burgundy withdrew his force after only ten days. The principal focus of efforts now was to be what remained of English Gascony.

The Duke of Anjou took command of the campaign. He marched south from Poitiers at the beginning of August with about 2,000 men. He entered Périgord, moving down the Dronne and driving all before him as small garrisons either fled from their castles or surrendered after token resistance. During the month the Seneschal of Beaucaire joined Anjou with a further 1,000 men. Anjou's objective was first of all Bergerac on the Dordogne, and thereafter to descend the river valley to Bordeaux. He arrived before the town on 22 August 1377.

The threat to Bergerac came as no surprise to the English. It was the most important English-held town on the Dordogne, and an obvious objective. By early July intelligence confirmed that the town was indeed the next target for the French. To face the threat posed by Anjou the Seneschal of Gascony, Sir Thomas Felton, ideally needed to reinforce garrisons and raise a substantial field army. He simply did not have the resources to do so. No reinforcements were forthcoming from England, although £5,755 was sent out in the spring to pay for troops. This was too little to do other than settle existing commitments for pay. Nevertheless, Felton raised a small field army by pulling men from garrisons. He also put more men in to defend Bergerac.

Bergerac's strategic importance was due to its control of the only bridge over the Dordogne in Périgord. Unfortunately, despite its importance its defences were in a poor state, with little having been done to improve them since Derby had taken the town more than thirty years before. The perimeter, protected by a wet moat and earthworks, still consisted of no more than buildings with the gaps between filled by insubstantial brick walls. There were fortified gates, some free-standing towers and an eleventh-century citadel. On the positive side, the citadel was well manned and equipped with stone-throwing machines and guns. The defence was in the hands of Bertucat d'Albret, a *routier* captain. He probably had 300 or so men under his command.

There was an early attempt to assault the town which was driven off with heavy French losses. However, the fate of Bergerac would be decided close to the *bastide* town of Eymet about 20km to the south. Anjou had decided that siege equipment would be required, and trebuchets and covered battering rams were brought from La Réole, about 55km distant. The equipment needed to pass via Eymet to use the nearby bridge to cross the Dropt. The Seneschal de Beaucaire was given 400 men-at-arms to escort the convoy. Sir Thomas Felton gathered around 400 men and set an ambush near Eymet. After a hard-fought combat, the French prevailed and Felton, among others, was captured.

The news of the Anglo-Gascon defeat reached Bergerac on 1 September, and two days later the inhabitants were faced with the prospect of bombardment from the siege engines and a renewed assault. Du Guesclin sent a messenger into the town to impress upon the inhabitants the consequences if they did not surrender and the town was taken by assault: the town would be totally destroyed and no mercy shown to the people. The inhabitants needed little persuading and decided to surrender without seeking the opinion of Bertucat d'Albret. Nevertheless, he saw the way the wind was blowing and did not wait to negotiate a surrender but rode out with his men to take refuge in the castle of Montcuq in the village of Pomport, 9km south-west of Bergerac.

St-Macaire, 1377

The forfeiture of Bergerac, the capture of the seneschal Sir Thomas Felton and the loss of most of his army caused great consternation in Bordeaux. Sir William Elmham, governor of Bayonne, appears to have taken the initiative to step into Felton's shoes. He organized what few forces he had to defend Bordeaux. He would hold the fortified towns of Libourne and St-Émilion on the Dordogne. A second force, under the command of Edmund Cresswell and William Chandler, would hold Bourg and Blaye on the north shore of the Gironde.

The Duke of Anjou moved down the Dordogne as expected, taking Ste-Foye and Castillon. However, rather than trying to force his way past Elmham's men at St-Émilion and Libourne, he turned south-west, marching 35km across country to the Garonne. The only remaining strong places on the Garonne held by the Anglo-Gascons were St-Macaire and Langon on opposite banks of the river, about 50km from Bordeaux. Cresswell and Chandler were redeployed up-river by ship to garrison St-Macaire. Langon was left undefended.

The Duke of Anjou arrived at St-Macaire during the third week of September. The citizens entered into negotiations immediately, and four days later opened the gates to the town. The garrison looted the town and then withdrew into the thirteenth-century keep. The French started a bombardment of the keep with eight trebuchets. The keep was strong, with walls 3m thick, but after two weeks the garrison had had enough. They surrendered at the end of the first week in October. Fortunately for Bordeaux the Duke of Anjou decided to call a halt to campaigning shortly after the fall of St-Macaire. The approach of winter and increasing problems in finding supplies for men and horses had brought the army to the point of exhaustion.

Cherbourg, 1378

The Black Prince had died in June 1376 and his father one year later, leaving the twelve-year-old Richard II as King of England. With the change of reign came a new strategy. The government, seeing the continuing French progress against English Gascony and faced by the perennial problems of resupply and reinforcement from England, decided to try to establish further enclaves on the French coast modelled on Calais. Not only would such ports create bases for resupply, they would also provide alternative points of entry for expeditionary forces. Initially it was decided that these ports should be Le Crotoy, St-Malo, Brest and Cherbourg. In the event no attempt was made to capture Le Crotoy, and two attempts to take St-Malo failed. At the end of 1377 Brest was reinforced.

In 1378 Cherbourg was occupied by the King of Navarre's men, but the garrison was too small to expect to be able to hold for long against a substantial French force. An agreement was reached with the Navarrese for the town to be garrisoned by the English, and the town was handed over on 27 June 1378.

Preparations for a French attack on Cherbourg began in April 1378, and the siege started in July. However, an attempt by John of Gaunt to take St-Malo during August and October had diverted French efforts. By mid-September the last of Gaunt's force had left for home and du Guesclin could turn his attention once again to Cherbourg.

Cherbourg was well fortified. The walls had only recently been rebuilt. There was a large castle, a dozen interval towers and ditches. After taking control of the town the English had brought the garrison strength to 760 men and stocked the town with supplies and armaments. In early December 200 reinforcements arrived. The storehouses were stocked with dried vegetables, wine and salted meat and fish, crossbows, longbows, crossbow bolts and arrows. Ten cannon were forged in a foundry created in the town and stocks of stone cannon balls and powder provisioned. Ships were stationed to head off any attempt by the French to blockade the town from the sea. Early in November 1378 John, the brother of the Earl of Arundel, arrived and took command of the defence of the town.

Du Guesclin appreciated that taking Cherbourg would be a challenging task and set about his preparations methodically. Depots for supplies and war material were set up at the port of St-Vaast-la-Hougue, used thirty-two years before for Edward III's landing at the start of his Crécy campaign, and the town of Carentan, 25km and 55km distant respectively from Cherbourg. In addition to men-at-arms and crossbowmen, du Guesclin recruited large numbers of carpenters, masons and miners. Twenty or more cannon were produced in Normandy and transported across land to join the siege army. Large wooden mobile shelters were constructed to shelter troops during assaults. By 20 November du Guesclin had assembled an army at Valognes, 17km south-west of Cherbourg.

There was an inauspicious start for du Guesclin when the vanguard of his army was ambushed as it advanced to the siege. Sixty or so men-at-arms were captured, including a cousin of du Guesclin and his brother Olivier. The constable set up his headquarters in the ruins of an abbey defended by field works and ditches. The rest of the French encampments, however, were less well protected and frequent sorties by the garrison caused extensive damage to equipment and shelters. We do not know the precise size of the besieging force, but the demands for food were beyond the capacity of the supply train. To the problem of hunger was added severe weather with intense cold and high winds which made horses and men alike suffer. Less than three weeks after the start du Guesclin decided that enough was enough and raised the siege. He took measures to try to contain the garrison, but these proved ineffective. The initial agreement with the King of Navarre had been that the English would hold Cherbourg for three years in return for the recruitment of 500 men-at-arms and 500 archers to serve with Charles for four months each year. The town was to remain in English hands for the next fifteen years.

Nantes, 1380–1381

In 1378 Charles V summoned the Duke of Brittany, John de Montfort, to appear in Paris to answer charges of treason. He failed to attend and he was tried in his absence and his duchy forfeited. The campaign against Gascony, abandoned by the Duke of Anjou in 1377, was not renewed and the focus of war now shifted to Brittany. In April 1379 Charles V decided to take possession of Brittany. A small force led by the Duke of Bourbon approached Brittany but found that they would face unexpected and widespread opposition from the newly formed Breton League. The League brought together disparate interests in the duchy united by a desire to maintain its independence. Bourbon withdrew to think again. Meanwhile the English planned to send de Montfort back to Brittany with a substantial army to support the Breton League. By the autumn Charles V had abandoned thoughts of taking Brittany by force. Negotiations to resolve the differences between de Montfort and Charles V were opened in the autumn of 1379. A potential settlement between Brittany and France threatened to throw English plans for operations from Brittany into disarray. Nevertheless, an army was despatched in October but the fleet was wrecked and dispersed by storms.

In early 1380 de Montfort, frustrated by the lack of progress in his negotiations with the French, turned once again to the English. In March a treaty of perpetual alliance was agreed between Brittany and England.

The English would be permitted to transit Breton territory en route to France and Gascony. In return the English would come to de Montfort's aid if the French were to invade his duchy.

The English planned to take advantage of the treaty to send 5,000 men directly to Brittany under the command of the Duke of Buckingham. However, the threat of a Castilian fleet coming north in support of the French resulted in a hurried change of plan. Instead of sailing for a Breton port the army was ferried across from Sandwich to Calais. The English left Calais in late July and made their way to Brittany, pillaging and burning as they went, arriving in early October. By 4 November 1380 the English vanguard was in front of the gates of Nantes, whose citizens had refused to open its gates to John de Montfort.

News of the English arrival before Nantes reached King Charles VI at Reims during his coronation celebrations. Nantes had only a small garrison, and a hastily convened council despatched two lords with orders to bring men from other garrisons in the vicinity of Angers. By the time the remainder of Buckingham's army had arrived, the French had boosted the garrison with 600 men. The town was walled and stood on the north bank of the Loire, which was wide, fast-flowing and divided into several branches separated by islands. The river Erdre flowed under the walls to the north and west. Nantes was compact, with a perimeter of around 1,000m. These factors aided the defence and made a siege more than usually challenging. The besieging army had to be deployed in three divisions. Communications between them were difficult and none would be able to come quickly to the aid of another. Furthermore, 5,000 men were insufficient to seal off the town. Buckingham called for another 2,000 men from England and sent numerous messages to call on John de Montfort to send reinforcements. However, after the death of Charles V in September de Montfort had been looking for a chance to be reconciled with the French crown. Unbeknown to Buckingham, the Duke of Brittany's ambassadors had been busy shortly after the siege started and by mid-November an indefinite truce had been agreed between the Duke and the new king's council. Secret negotiations were under way for a permanent settlement, and in the circumstances John de Montfort kept his distance.

Sustaining the war presented both governments with significant financial difficulties. As a consequence, the French were slow to respond to the presence of the large English force besieging Nantes. Nevertheless, in December the new Constable of France, Olivier de Clisson, who had been appointed after the death in July 1380 of that scourge of the English, Bertrand du Guesclin, arrived in the vicinity with fresh troops. The

English meanwhile had finally agreed to finance the 2,000 additional men requested by Buckingham. Sir Thomas Felton was to sail to the Loire with armed barges to prevent river access to Nantes. It was too late.

Buckingham's men had made numerous assaults on the town. All had been repulsed. For their part the garrison had launched frequent sorties right from the outset of the siege to harass the besiegers. On one occasion the French took advantage of the rivers and the divided deployment of the besieging army to launch a daring attack with 200 men-at-arms and 100 crossbowmen in boats. The English were initially taken by surprise but rallied and drove the French back to their boats. The town continued to receive supplies by river while the besiegers faced hunger during a bitterly cold winter. Local men had already been attacking English foragers and ambushing messengers passing between the Dukes of Buckingham and Brittany. With the arrival of Clisson the pressure on the besiegers was stepped up. He started raiding the siege lines from outside and his men also fell upon foraging parties, exacerbating the problems of feeding Buckingham's army. Night raids, including one in some strength on Christmas Eve, deprived men of sleep, and to add to the problems of hunger and falling morale, dysentery started to spread among the besiegers during December. By the beginning of January 1381 Buckingham had lost almost all his horses and 1,000 men, through sickness, desertion and battle casualties. He had no choice but to abandon the siege and did so on 6 January 1381. A little over a week later de Montfort reached an agreement with the French government and in the spring the remnants of Buckingham's army sailed for home from Breton ports.

Ypres, 1383

Both realms suffered from internal dissent between 1380 and 1382, largely due to poor economic conditions. In England the most important rising was the Peasants' Revolt of 1381. In the following year there were revolts in Rouen and Paris. These revolts were suppressed, but they diverted attention in both countries from the prosecution of the war. Much of the inspiration for revolt, at least in France, had been the rebellion of the towns of Ghent, Bruges and Ypres in Flanders against the Count of Flanders, Louis de Mâle, which began in 1379. The situation degenerated into civil war. Trade with Flanders was important to England, and hitherto the English had been content to maintain good relations with the count.

However, in January 1382 Philip van Artevelde became Captain of Ghent. In February van Artevelde sent ambassadors to England carrying proposals to recognize King Richard II as Count of Flanders and King of France in return for weapons and an English fleet and army. The intervention was well timed. In England war weariness was growing, Parliament was reluctant to raise taxes and there was a desire to negotiate peace with France at talks planned for early 1382. However, it was appreciated that a satisfactory peace settlement required negotiation from a position of strength. The situation in Flanders gave King Richard's council an opportunity to carry the war to France in the north with the support of the Flemish and thus strengthen the hands of the English ambassadors for the peace talks. Plans were made to send 6,000 men to Flanders but, paradoxically, by the end of March Richard's council's enthusiasm for settling with France had started to cool.

During May and June Louis de Mâle's authority in Flanders collapsed. The planned peace talks started in June and continued until early 1382. Peace could not be agreed and the only result was an extension of the truce between England and France until October 1382. With the breakdown in the talks the French immediately set about marshalling an army to invade the Duchy of Aquitaine once the truce expired. Meanwhile in England the king's council wrestled between two alternative strategies: sending John of Gaunt to Bordeaux and then on to Castile, and despatching an army under command of the king to Flanders. The potential expedition to Castile was seen by some as furthering John of Gaunt's personal interests rather than the prosecution of the war with France. Funding either expedition, let alone both, was problematic. A solution came from an unexpected quarter against the background of the Papal Schism which divided the Catholic Church between 1378 and 1417. Since 1381 Henry Despenser, the Bishop of Norwich, had been hatching a plan, under the authority of Pope Urban VI, to crusade against the supporters of Clement VII, the Avignon Pope who had been elected by French cardinals in 1378 in opposition to Urban, wherever they might be. He sensed that parliamentary support for his crusade would be more likely if he went to Flanders. The fact that the Count of Flanders was a supporter of Urban doesn't seem to have come into the calculations.

Despenser proposed to take an army to Flanders and then onwards to France. The costs would be less than those of a conventional army. Some crusaders could be expected to serve without pay and others could be sold indulgences to help finance the expedition. When intelligence reached France of the negotiations between the Flemish and the English, the muster of the army to invade Aquitaine was postponed. The French tried to negotiate a settlement with the Flemish but their overtures were rejected. The invasion of Aquitaine was cancelled and attention turned to Flanders. During November the French moved into Flanders, taking the surrender of Ypres as they advanced. On 27 November the French routed the Flemish at the Battle of Roosebeke. Van Artevelde was among the dead. Although the town of Ghent held out for a further three years, to all intents and purposes the Flemish rebellion was over.

The plan for sending Gaunt to Castile had been wrecked by a reconciliation between Portugal and Castile. The English government therefore turned again to plans for an expedition to Flanders, but there was little enthusiasm for sending a largely amateur army led by Despenser with limited military experience. The government's preference was for a professional army led by the king. This ambition foundered on Richard's reluctance to go to war personally and the improbability of persuading Parliament to grant the money. In the end Despenser led an army, paid for in part by money which had been held over from a previous parliamentary grant and partly from the sale of indulgences. By mid-May 1383, 8,000 men had reached Calais with a further 3,000 or more being assembled in England.

Despenser set out from Calais on 19 May and achieved some notable successes: the fortress of Bourbourg surrendered without resistance, the town of Gravelines was taken on the first assault, and a locally raised French army was soundly defeated at Dunkirk. On 9 June 1383 the English army arrived outside Ypres, joining forces with men sent from Ghent led by Peter van den Bosche. Ypres was of strategic importance, standing on the route between Ghent and Calais and blocking the most convenient entry route into Flanders for the French. Immediate attempts were made by the English to storm two of the town gates. The defenders were ready and well prepared and drove back both assaults, in one case using gunfire. The following day the men of Ghent joined the English and attacked several gates. They were again unsuccessful and the English and men of Ghent settled down to besiege the town.

Ypres had a circuit of walls with towers and two concentric ditches which had been flooded in preparation for the siege. Despenser believed that the garrison was weak and that victuals were in short supply. However, not only had the ditches been flooded but a range of other measures had been taken in anticipation of a siege. The population, which might normally have been expected to be sympathetic to the cause of England and Ghent, had rallied to the defence of their town – no doubt influenced by the disasters that had recently befallen the revolt led by Ghent. They were led by a Flemish lord, Peter van der Zype, who had the support of a number of retainers of the Duke of Burgundy, local lords and a willing population. People from the countryside had come into the town bringing livestock with them. Grain had been stockpiled and rules to prevent profiteering imposed. Inhabitants were ordered to arm themselves and set aside four months of rations. Suburbs had been demolished to deny cover to the besiegers. Wooden hoardings had been constructed protruding from the ramparts to allow projectiles to be dropped on assault troops, and the walls, towers and gates repaired. Guns had been forged and gates equipped with cannon, and, most importantly, citizens had been trained.

Despenser had contributed most of the men, but it was the men of Ghent who led the siege operations. They were better equipped than the English and were used to conducting sieges in the marshy land of eastern Flanders. They fortified those few buildings outside the walls which remained standing and installed artillery. Trenches were dug and wooden field fortifications constructed. Work started on draining the ditches, and after two weeks they had been drained and filled with faggots of wood. Pontoons were built to enable besieging troops to cross the ditches and reach the base of the walls. Stone-throwers battered the towers and damaged houses within the town. Mines were dug towards the walls. The defenders made sorties to harass the work of the besiegers, destroying one night some of the pontoons which had been laid across the ditches, worked through the nights to repair damage to fortifications, and captured and destroyed mine tunnels. To hamper repair work in the town English archers shot flaming arrows into the town at night.

After two weeks the flow of supplies into the town had been cut. At dawn on 24 June an assault was launched between two gates to the north of the town across seven pontoons against the walls. On reaching the base of the walls the attackers tried to enter the town using scaling ladders. They came under cross-fire from cannon on both gates and were driven back with heavy casualties.

At one stage the Count of Flanders became concerned that the monastery at Menin, standing on the Lys 17km south-east of Ypres, might be captured and fortified by the English. He despatched forty men-at-arms and sixty crossbowmen to demolish the monastery. A substantial English foraging party of 200 men-at-arms came upon them as they were working. The English had the better of the ensuing fight and returned to Ypres with prisoners for ransom, including the captains of the Count of Flanders' force.

Later in the month the besiegers tried again. This time they attacked from north and south simultaneously and were protected by four large,

wheeled, wooden shelters. Seeing that the assault troops were well protected, the defenders made a sortie and attacked the shelters before the
English could reach the base of the wall. Once again the attack failed, and
this time 500 men are said to have been lost.

To add to the failed assaults and the heavy casualties, supplies were running short and dysentery set in, with many succumbing to the disease over
the coming weeks. To compound the problem of the shortage of supplies,
men started to arrive from England who, having heard of Despenser's
earlier successes, wanted to share in the spoils of Ypres. The majority
added nothing of value to the fighting capacity of the army, and instead
were simply a drain on already scarce supplies. Morale deteriorated and
there were quarrels between Despenser and his men. The newcomers
quickly assessed the situation and started to desert in droves, taking many
of the original army with them.

The French had not been standing idly by as Despenser's army fell apart.
They recruited throughout June and at the end of the month summoned
men to muster during the last week in July with a view to striking into
Flanders. Despenser was aware of the French preparations and wanted to
conclude the siege rapidly. During the last week of July he declared a truce
and offered terms to the inhabitants. They could choose between surrender, saving their lives and possessions, or the destruction of their town
and the death of all within. Despite the stubborn resistance of the garrison
and the inhabitants, there was a shortage of supplies and the remaining
streams running into the town had become polluted and so there was a
willingness to seek a peaceful solution. Provisional agreement was reached
for the surrender of the town on 20 August 1383. However, on 30 July
negotiations were broken off for reasons which remain obscure. The truce
ended with Despenser unfurling his banners and excommunicating the
townspeople in his capacity as a Legate of Pope Urban. The irony of
excommunicating those who were also supporters of the Pope in Rome
seems to have escaped him.

King Charles VI, having taken the *oriflamme* at the abbey of St-Denis the
day before, left Paris four days after the breakdown in talks. An advanced
guard was sent ahead to secure crossings of the Lys, while the remainder
of the army was summoned to assemble at Arras, just 65km south of Ypres,
on 22 August. Time was running out for Despenser and on 3 August,
the day Charles left Paris, the English launched a final desperate assault.
The assault had been in preparation throughout the previous month and
involved the entire army. In an unusual prelude to the assault, letters
calling on the population to 'kill your captains and think of the future.

Certainly we shall come to your aid and we shall forever be loyal and good friends' were projected into the town by a stone-throwing machine. The appeal did not have the desired effect and the assault began with simultaneous attacks on five gates. Men-at-arms approached with ladders, protected by massed archers and wheeled shelters. Wagons loaded with faggots of wood were pushed against the gates and set on fire. Defenders sallied forth and drove back the teams positioning the fire-wagons. The contents of the wagons were tipped into the ditches. A narrow ramp constructed to carry men to the ramparts was destroyed by a gun-stone, with several knights killed. The defenders fought the attackers with arrow, sword, lance, axe and Greek fire. Once again men were caught in the crossfire from cannon and suffered heavy casualties. The attack was repulsed.

Despite the failure and the casualties, the attacks were repeated for a further six days. At one point the besiegers managed to get a siege tower and bombard up against one of the gate towers but they could not exploit this advantage to cross the walls. On 8 August the final assault was abandoned as news arrived that the French vanguard was now on the Lys only 25km to the south. There was now disharmony between the English and their Flemish allies, and dissent between captains within the English army. The men of Ghent wanted to continue with the assault, believing that the defenders were at the end of their resistance. They may well have been right since on the eve of the siege being raised the captains of Ypres had been preparing to expel married women whose husbands were elsewhere, telling them to find and join their men. The English disagreed that the town was on the point of surrender, and refused to continue. On 10 August the army broke up in disorder, abandoning siege works, artillery and booty. Stores were burned. Despenser's captains had been unable to agree what to do next, and the army split into two parts: one withdrawing to the fortress of Bourbourg 50km away near the coast and the other, led by Despenser, heading initially towards the French vanguard before also withdrawing towards the coast.

At the end of August the French army advanced into Flanders. The English withdrew progressively from Bourbourg, Dunkirk and Gravelines, and during October the remnants of Despenser's army returned to England from Calais.

The Truce of Leulinghem, 1389

War fatigue was widespread in both England and France, and both countries suffered from internal dissensions. England's king was young and weak and his policies were divisive, while France's problems were aggravated by a king who passed in and out of periods of madness. The next few years after the ill-fated Flanders campaign of 1383 saw only desultory campaigning in France. The French made elaborate preparations for an invasion of England which came to nothing, but for the main part they were concerned with growing rivalries between the royal princes, the increasing power of the Duke of Burgundy who had inherited the County of Flanders from Louis de Mâle in 1384, and the widespread operations of *routier* companies in the south. The English were preoccupied with the threat of invasion from France, renewed war with Scotland between 1383 and 1385, an expedition to the Iberian Peninsula by John of Gaunt between 1386 and 1387, largely in pursuit of his own interests, and a rebellion of nobles against Richard II in 1387. Talks for a truce started in Leulinghem church, 32km south-east of Calais, in March 1386. In July 1389 a truce was agreed for an initial period of three years during which the parties would negotiate a permanent peace. The permanent peace was beyond reach, but the truce was extended and lasted for thirteen years.

Chapter 6

From Harfleur to the Death of Henry V, 1415–1422

Harfleur, 1415

Although the Truce of Leulinghem collapsed, in 1402 and 1403 an uneasy peace with sporadic fighting had survived the strong French disapproval of Henry Bolingbroke's usurpation of Richard II to take the English crown as Henry IV. From the moment of the succession of his son as Henry V in 1413 the path to a reopening of the war seemed almost inevitable, and by early 1415 Henry was well advanced with his preparations.

During the summer of 1415 Henry V gathered his army in and around Southampton. The army was around 12,000 strong. In round figures 2,500 were men-at-arms and the remainder archers. There were also gunners, with thirty or so recruited from outside England. In addition to the combatants there are known to have been 560 men employed as miners, stonemasons, carpenters, labourers, smiths and wagoners. As well as guns, for which 10,000 stones were provided, Henry brought siege towers, ladders, rams, chains and coal. Apart from these military stores he brought bread, dried fish, salt, meat, flour, beans, cheese, ale, clothes, shoes, cattle, sheep and pigs. Some 600 casks of wine were brought from Bordeaux. There would certainly have been many more non-combatants than combatants, with the personal households of the king and his great lords, pages for the men-at-arms, and tradesmen and artisans of all sorts including fletchers, armourers and bowyers. The numbers cannot be quantified with any certainty but an estimate of an overall total of 15,000 combatants and non-combatants is probably on the conservative side. There would also have been wagons to carry supplies, the personal baggage of the king and the senior members of the army, and spare arrows, bows and bowstrings. In addition, there was the artillery train to be used at the siege of Harfleur. And of course there were horses. The number of horses would certainly have exceeded the number of men, with knights taking typically four horses on campaign, esquires three, men-at-arms two and mounted archers one. To carry this army a fleet of around 700 ships of varying sizes and types, 258 of which were foreign, had assembled in the Solent off Southampton.

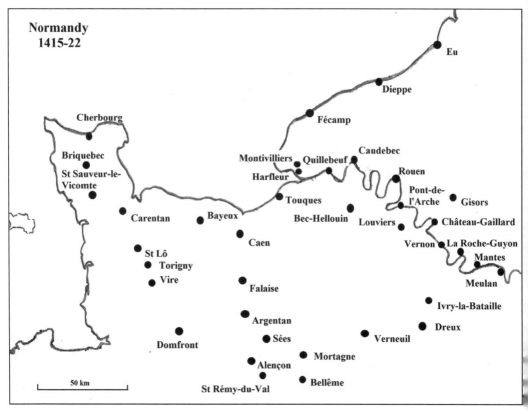

Normandy, 1415–1422.

Henry's fleet entered the mouth of the Seine on 13 August 1415, drop-ping anchor at around 5.00pm on 13 August off St-Denis-Chef-de-Caux. Behind the shore were deep, water-filled ditches, and beyond these thick earth walls with ramparts. There was also a marshy area down the Seine towards Harfleur, and on the high ground stood the castle of Vitanval. Thus the area was readily defensible, and yet there were no French troops to hinder the landing.

This was perhaps not surprising. The garrison of Harfleur was num-bered in hundreds, and to have sallied out to oppose thousands of men would have been foolhardy in the extreme. The French had taken some preliminary measures to counter the anticipated English landing, and in June the French nobility, and those others accustomed to bearing arms, had been given notice to prepare themselves to rally to the defence of France. However, Charles VI could not realistically have mobilized a sufficiently large army before Henry arrived.

The king gave strict instructions for the disembarkation and ordered that no one was to land before he did so. This instruction was probably given to ensure that the landing was controlled and that troops did not disperse in search of plunder. Nevertheless, the king prudently sent a

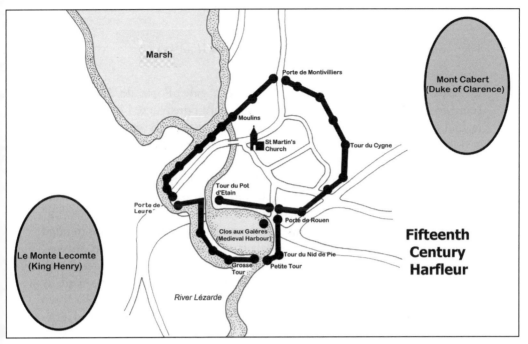

Harfleur in the fifteenth century.

small reconnaissance party ashore early on the morning of 14 August to ensure that the area immediately inland from the landing beaches was clear of enemy forces. The main disembarkation began in the afternoon, and was completed three days later on 17 August. The king immediately made his way towards high ground, and spent his first night ashore on the heights between the coast and Harfleur, possibly lodging in the priory of Graville, with the Dukes of Clarence and Gloucester nearby.

Harfleur lies in the valley of the river Lézarde, between high ground close by to the west and east. There is further high ground just over 1km to the north towards Montivilliers. To the south, towards the Seine, the ground has long since been drained and developed, but in 1415 this was marshland. The river Lézarde runs south through the town from Montivilliers. By damming the river where it entered Harfleur the townspeople were able to cause it to burst its banks and flood the area between the western walls and the high ground. The sluice gates had been closed when news of the English landings reached the town, and by the time Henry reached Harfleur the water was already thigh deep. As a consequence, Clarence's deployment to the east of the town required his men to skirt round well to the north, covering a distance of about 16km. The town was defended by walls 2,900m long with twenty-two interval towers, water-filled ditches perhaps 4.5m deep with steep banks, and three gates. To the west was the Porte de Leure, to the north the Porte de Montivilliers and to the south-east the Porte de Rouen. All of the gates were well protected by outworks. Those protecting the western gate, Porte de Leure, were recorded by a witness to the siege. They were constructed of tree trunks lashed together and driven into the ground, with earth and further wood inside to add strength. There were embrasures for small guns and cross-bows.

The walls were relatively modern, having been built between 1344 and 1361, and they appear to have been kept in repair. The defences were further enhanced by the fortified port, Le Clos des Galées or Clos aux Galères, to the south of the town. The entrance to the port was defended with chains drawn across the entrance channel between two towers. A Spanish sailor reported in 1405 that the defences included a good wall with strong towers, town gates all protected by drawbridges flanked by towers, and water-filled ditches with steep sides built of stone. The town was equipped with artillery, and no doubt had stocks of catapults and large crossbows. The town had also prepared for a possible attack by stocking wood and stones, and it seems that the inhabitants may have torn up the paving slabs from the causeway leading north towards Montivilliers to supplement their materials for maintaining the defences.

Harfleur is likely to have had a militia drawn from the population, and there were also some crossbowmen and men-at-arms. Reinforcements arrived on 18 August, probably entering through the Porte de Rouen, before Clarence could complete the investment of the town. The defence was in the hands of Louis, the Sire d'Estouteville, and Raoul de Gaucourt. Based on accounts relating to the surrender, some 260 knights and men-at-arms were allowed to leave when the town capitulated, and it is prob-able that this was roughly the number of professional soldiers present during the siege. In addition, townsmen would have been engaged in watch-keeping and other tasks in defence of their town.

Harfleur was well known to the English. It was an important com-mercial and naval port and had been used for piratical raids and operations against English shipping and south coast towns. It had been attacked unsuccessfully by the English in April 1360, but in the following month Edward III had embarked from here after the negotiations leading to the Treaty of Brétigny. Furthermore, the area had been raided in 1369 by John of Gaunt and Harfleur itself had been attacked unsuccessfully by the Earls of Arundel and Salisbury in 1378. More recently Henry V's ambas-sadors had passed through the port on their return to England in 1414. No doubt they would have taken the opportunity to assess the defences.

Henry started his investment of Harfleur on 17 August, and by 23 August the siege was sufficiently well established for the inhabitants to send word to Charles d'Albret, the Constable of France, in Rouen that they could no longer make contact by land. They asked for a boat to be provided to help with the provisioning of the town and to enable messages to be passed between the besieged town and the constable. D'Albret arranged for a small galley, which had the advantage of being powered by oars, to be sent downstream on the Seine from Rouen. Although shortly after the start of the siege Charles d'Albret had sent word to the king and the dauphin in Paris of the arrival of Henry, it was not until two weeks after the landings, on 28 August, that the nobility in Normandy and the surrounding areas were called to arms. Rouen was nominated as the point of rendezvous, and as the French army began to gather the dauphin Louis was sent to Normandy as the king's lieutenant and Captain General. The king indicated his intention to follow soon to raise the siege. Orders were also given to ensure that castles were adequately defended.

The first proclamation to communicate these decisions was issued on 30 August in Paris, and over the next ten days it was posted in other places in the Île-de-France, Picardy and Normandy. The arrangements to raise taxes for the war had been put in place in March, but on 31 August the king's council ordered additional taxes to be raised to cover the costs of the gathering army. The taxes envisaged an army of 6,000 men-at-arms and 3,000 archers. On 10 September the king attended mass in the cathedral of St-Denis and the *oriflamme* was entrusted to Guillaume VIII Martel, the Sire de Bacqueville, who was to meet his death fighting at Agincourt at more than sixty years of age.

At some stage early in the siege Henry offered terms to Harfleur. The offer was rejected and a bombardment of the town began, which over the duration of the siege caused considerable damage both to the town's defences and its houses, so much so that the repairs to the fortifications took a number of years and the poor state of buildings within the town proved to be a strong disincentive when Henry was seeking to encourage English people to settle there.

The siege of Harfleur posed the typical problems for the besiegers: the risk of disease, which eventually had a serious impact on Henry's army, and the difficulties of feeding men and horses. Raids into the surrounding countryside were necessary. French troops in the vicinity kept the foraging parties under close surveillance, harrying them when they had the opportunity, and may well also have adopted a scorched earth policy in the surrounding area to hamper English provisioning.

As the siege progressed, Henry moved on to enforce a blockade with ships on the Seine and smaller boats in the area flooded by the Lézarde. By mid-September the cordon around the town by land and water was proving effective, and an attempt was made to break the stranglehold between 14 and 16 September with a small fleet sent from Rouen. The attempt was unsuccessful, and by 18 September the town decided to enter into negotiations for surrender. Meanwhile, although it would not prejudice the success of the siege, Henry was having problems due to insanitary conditions brought on by unseasonably warm weather, polluted water, difficulties in disposing of carcasses and other rubbish, and the generally humid conditions. The result was dysentery which had a serious impact on some parts of the army, leading to the death, among others, of Richard Courtenay, Bishop of Norwich, and the Earl of Suffolk.

At some point during the siege the English managed to cut off the flow of water from the Lézarde somewhere between Harfleur and Montivilliers. As a result the flood water subsided, and the besieging forces were able to move closer to the town on the southern and western sides. The English also constructed trenches to defend the besiegers from fire from the town, and hoardings were made which sheltered guns and gunners and were lifted when the guns were to be fired. Clarence's men were isolated from the bulk of the army and, because of the high ground behind them, positioned close to the walls. Thus they were particularly vulnerable, and their trenches were especially important. Although the French made no serious attempt to relieve the town there were engagements between the besieging army and French troops from the garrison, and possibly from nearby Montivilliers. As early as 18 August Clarence and his men had come under attack while he deployed his men to the east of the town. There was a further sortie by the garrison on 15 September. An attack was made on English defences constructed to the west of the town near the Leure gate. It is possible that this was a diversionary attack timed to coincide with the attempt to break the waterborne blockade. It caused some embarrassment since the French were able to set fire to the English trench works, but the impact was limited. Henry decided on a riposte. During the night preparations were made for an attack next day. In the morning the Earl of Huntingdon drove the French back from the barbican and inside the main walls.

During the siege Henry's attempts to wear down the defences with guns and catapults had some success. However, at night the French carried out repairs using timber and tubs filled with earth, dung, sand and stones, and walls were shored up with faggots, earth and clay. Streets were also covered with sand to prevent stone cannon balls splintering on impact. These efforts, however, could do no more than delay the destruction of the defences. Eventually the outer barbicans were abandoned, with their guns being repositioned inside. There was also an attempt by Clarence's men to undermine the walls on the eastern side of the town. This may have been a reflection of the lack of effect of the artillery fire, or it may have been due to better conditions for mining on this side. In any case, in the face of French countermining and sorties to disrupt the work, the attempt was unsuccessful and the mine was abandoned and subsequently filled in during the English occupation.

Henry made several attempts to negotiate the surrender of Harfleur, but initially the French garrison believed that an army was being mustered to relieve the town. By 17 September it had become clear that the chances of relief were remote. It is not clear whether the garrison then sought to surrender or whether Henry took the initiative and offered terms. Whatever the case, the negotiations collapsed and Henry made preparations for an assault the following day. This was preceded by a call to arms by trumpet and by an all-night bombardment. The defenders decided that enough was enough, and a message was passed asking for terms. The king sent in the Earl of Dorset, Lord Fitzhugh, and Sir Thomas Erpingham to negotiate the capitulation. Henry had wanted the surrender to be made the following day, but he conceded that more time could be given to the inhabitants. The result was that the town would be surrendered if either Charles VI or the dauphin did not come to its relief by 1.00pm on Sunday, 22 September.

In early September news had reached the dauphin that Harfleur was in desperate need of reinforcement. By 13 September he had reached Vernon on the river Seine, and here he received envoys carrying news of the town's plight. The envoys were assured that the king was gathering his army and would come to Harfleur's aid. This was partially true, to the extent that the king was indeed assembling his army, but by the date of the agreement of terms for the surrender of Harfleur there were no more than a few thousand men available. Furthermore, these were dispersed across several locations to enable the French to respond to possible English movements, and the French were not in a position to relieve Harfleur before the due date for its surrender. Once the terms of the surrender had been agreed on 18 September, the Sire de Hacqueville set out to notify the dauphin and ask for assistance. When he arrived at Vernon the dauphin broke the news that the assembly of the army was not complete and assistance would not be forthcoming. However, given that Hacqueville probably took two days to reach the dauphin at Vernon, relief of the town before 22 September would not have been possible even if the French army had assembled.

Although Henry had left the negotiations to others, he took the surrender in person in his pavilion on Mont Lecomte. In a manner in keeping with the customs of the time, Henry took the surrender graciously and entertained members of the garrison, including de Gaucourt. The Earl of Dorset was appointed captain of the town, and the next day Henry entered Harfleur, dismounting on entering the town, to give thanks to God in the church of St Martin. The French captains were free to go, subject to agreeing under oath to submit themselves at Calais on 11 November. De Gaucourt was despatched to carry a challenge from the king to the dauphin. Civilians were separated into two groups: those swearing fealty to Henry and those being retained in custody against payment of ransoms. Women, children, the poor and the helpless, numbering between 1,500 and 2,000, were expelled from the town on 24 September, in part because the town was in no condition to support the population. They took with them their clothing, all that they could carry, and five *sous*. They were escorted by the English to Lillebonne, 32km to the east, where they were handed over to Marshal Boucicaut, who gave them food and water.

Henry wished to establish Harfleur as an English colony on a similar basis to Calais. His first step was to arrange for a garrison of 300 men-at-arms and 900 archers. He also took steps to encourage settlement. Municipal records and title deeds were burned in the market place and henceforth purchase and inheritance of land were restricted to Englishmen, French inhabitants being reduced to the status of lessees. On 5 October the Duke of Bedford, who had remained in England as keeper of the realm, reinforced these provisions, ordering the sheriffs of London to proclaim that all merchants, victuallers and artificers who were willing to reside in Harfleur should go with all speed to the town, where they would be given houses. Orders were also sent out for the repair of the town and for its provisioning from England. The town remained in English hands until it was recaptured by the French in 1435. The English recovered Harfleur in 1440, but finally surrendered it to the French on Christmas Eve 1449.

The capture of Harfleur was a significant accomplishment for Henry V, but it also represented a step change in the English conduct of sieges, with artillery being used extensively for the first time in the siege of a town. Perhaps as many as fifty guns were deployed, and during the siege 7,466 gun-stones were expended, 866 of which were large stones fired from bombards. Throughout the siege this represented an average of 287 stones per day fired into the town.

Caen, 1417

From Harfleur Henry V marched across northern France to Calais to return to England. Near the village of Agincourt he found his way blocked by a French army. His great victory here in October 1415 threw the French into disarray. They had lost many great scions of the nobility and had suffered a huge psychological shock. However, the battle was not decisive and the French still had the capacity to wage war. Henry V had much to do if he were to achieve his objective of being crowned King of France. He was not in a position to exploit his victory immediately and returned to England, but he was now securely established on the English throne and the uncertainty of his position (having inherited the crown through his father's usurpation of Richard II) was now much diminished. He could now count on support at home for the prosecution of the war. Once back in England he raised men and money, and by the summer of 1417 he was ready to return to France. He intended to take possession of the Duchy of Normandy and to pursue his claim to the French crown. Occupation of Normandy would require the taking and holding of towns and fortresses.

Henry's fleet arrived in the mouth of the Seine on 1 August 1417. He might have been expected to disembark in Harfleur, now securely in English hands after a French attempt to retake it by siege in the summer of 1416. Disembarkation at Harfleur would have opened up the Pays de Caux to the east of the river. However, Henry had fought his way across this country two years before, and the combined ravages of the English and French armies would have left little to support his army. Instead he landed at Touques on the river of the same name about 20km to the south-west of Harfleur. This opened up the prospect of rich Norman lands to the west that were untouched by recent events.

The objective for Henry now was conquest. Whereas Edward III had used the wide-ranging *chevauchée* as his principal strategy, Henry was set on taking control of lands which had once been part of the Plantagenet Empire of Henry II and which he saw as his by right. This in turn meant the capture and holding of towns and fortresses. The rich town of Caen, only 40km south-west of his port of disembarkation, was an obvious first target.

Almost two weeks after the landing at Touques, with the intervening time spent on reconnaissance, some probing raids and the capture of some minor fortresses, Henry began to move inland towards Caen on 13 August. The town, which probably had a population of around 6,000, with numbers no doubt inflated by refugees fleeing the English and seeking refuge within the walls, was difficult to defend. It stood at the confluence of the Orne and the Odon rivers, with access to the sea to the north by means of a wide channel. To the north was the old town with its citadel dating back to the time of William the Conqueror. The walls and towers of the old town had been rebuilt following the sacking of the town by Edward III in 1346. Outside the perimeter walls of the old town were two fortified abbeys: to the west the Benedictine house of St-Étienne and to the east the convent of the Trinity, known respectively as the Abbaye aux Hommes and the Abbaye aux Dames. To the south, and separated from the old town by the river Orne, was the newer town on the Ile St Jean. This had been unfortified in 1346 when Edward III had passed this way during his Crécy campaign, but had since been surrounded by walls. It also had the advantage of being surrounded on all sides by the rivers Odon and Orne. Access between the old town and the *bourg* was by means of a fortified bridge.

The captain of Caen had perhaps 200 professional soldiers plus a company of Genoese crossbowmen and some men drawn from the surrounding area. To this could be added support by the inhabitants, but overall Guillaume de Montenay had insufficient resources to defend the two parts of the town and the abbeys. Montenay ordered that the perimeter walls of the two abbeys should be demolished, against the wishes of some of the inhabitants. Preparations were also made to bring down the west towers of the Abbaye aux Hommes which gave an excellent vantage point for the besiegers. Weapons were checked and supplies brought within the walls. Time was not on Montenay's side. The Duke of Clarence arrived on 15 August with the first English troops and was able to occupy the unprotected suburbs to the north and the Abbaye aux Dames before the demolition could be completed. Ladders were used to scale the walls of the Abbaye aux Hommes. Treachery seems to have played a part with a monk, fearing the destruction of his abbey, showing the English troops a way over an unprotected part of the wall. The abbey was captured before the mines prepared to destroy the towers could be fired. While Montenay had been taking military precautions, the wealthier citizens had been moving valuables into the castle for safety.

Three days later Henry arrived with the rest of the English army which was distributed around the town with communications across the rivers being assured by a pontoon bridge constructed by Henry's engineers. Montenay was summoned to surrender the town to Henry as Duke of Normandy and King of England and France. Despite the offer of the

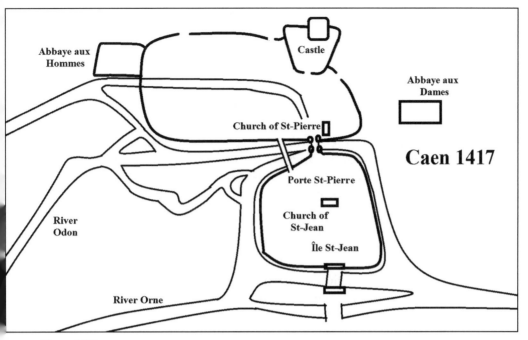

Caen, 1418.

confirmation of existing privileges for Caen, the reply was uncompromising: 'Our town belongs to our natural lord, King Charles. With the help of God we shall faithfully hold it for him, or we shall fall with honour.' With this rejection, Henry set about taking the town. Cannon were brought up on barges. The price paid by the French for failing to destroy the abbeys now became apparent as the cannon were sited on the walls and roofs of the two abbeys, giving them a commanding position to fire onto the walls and buildings of the old town. Round-the-clock artillery fire destroyed much of the town's wooden housing. It was common practice to destroy suburbs outside the walls of a town to remove cover for the besiegers. This had not been done and English troops were able to approach the walls on the north side. Attempts to undermine the walls were also made, with the French countermining and fighting underground to expel the miners. Breaches were made in the wall and on 4 September an assault was launched. Initially the king's division attacked on the western walls from the Abbaye aux Hommes. Montenay sent most of his men to counter the attack, leaving the Duke of Clarence to come over the walls on the eastern side. Caught by attacks from front and rear the French suffered heavy losses and those who could do so fled. The gates were opened and more English troops flooded in. The English forced their way across the fortified bridge into the *bourg*. Henry ordered that the lives of women and priests were to be protected, but the town was given over to plunder and in the ensuing mayhem it is unlikely that the king's orders carried much weight.

Around 1,800 people are believed to have been killed. Surviving civilians and soldiers alike sought refuge in the citadel, with perhaps around 1,000 gaining access before the drawbridge was raised. The citadel was formidable, with its large Norman keep and solid curtain walls, but it had not been built to resist sustained artillery fire. Henry's artillery was brought into the town to fire at point-blank range. Montenay managed to get a messenger away to the constable in Paris with a plea for help. The dauphin set about organizing an army of relief to muster at Étampes on 15 October 1417. However, this was much too late. On the very day that the dauphin summoned his army, 10 September, Montenay agreed terms for the surrender. If a French relief army, led in person by the king, the dauphin or the constable did not arrive to relieve the town by 19 September, the gates of the citadel would be opened the following morning. Messengers were permitted to take the unwelcome news to Paris.

Relief was not forthcoming and at midday on 20 September Guillaume de Montenay surrendered the keys to Henry V. The military personnel were allowed to leave with their horses, equipment, clothing and gold, silver or money up to a value of 2,000 *écus*. They went to join the garrison at Falaise to fight another day. Civilians had the stark choice of swearing allegiance to Henry or being expelled from the town. Those who left took nothing save the clothes they were wearing. At least 700 civilians left even under these harsh terms, bearing safe-conduct passes.

Falaise, 1417–1418

The impact of the fall of Caen, and the only too evident inability of the French leaders to bring relief, was considerable and immediate, particularly throughout the Duchy of Alençon. Alençon and Argentan, both well fortified and strongly garrisoned towns with around 1,100 men in each town, capitulated quickly to Henry V. The captain of Argentan asked for terms as soon as the English arrived outside the gates. At Alençon the captain showed slightly more resolve to the extent that he held out for a day-and-a-half before coming to terms. Sées repulsed an assault but capitulated when the garrison learned that Argentan had surrendered. Strongly garrisoned castles at Exmes and Fresnay surrendered without a fight. The panic spread rapidly to the County of Perche. Verneuil, Mortagne, Bellême and St-Rémy-du-Val were captured easily by English detachments. By the end of October 1417 the Duchy of Alençon was controlled by the English, with only the fortress of Domfront holding out.

Late in November Henry V turned his attention to Falaise: the largest French garrison in Lower Normandy with a strong fortress standing on

arcassonne, showing a defended gate, interval towers, and hoardings. (*Peter Hoskins*)

Arques castle, being constructed on high ground, could not have a water-filled moat, but nevertheless a wide dry moat was dug out of the rock. (*Peter Hoskins*)

La Tour des Archives in Vernon, formerly the keep of the castle, showing machicolations. (*Peter Hoskins*)

The fourteenth-century barbican of Picquigny castle. (*Peter Hoskins*)

Drum towers and the curtain wall of the castle of Angers. The plinth at the base of the walls is clearly visible. The towers were higher when built in the thirteenth century but were cut down in size in the seventeenth century. (*Rebecca Sewell*)

Reconstruction of a mangonel, with fixed counterweight, capable of throwing projectiles out to about 100 metres with a rate of shooting of up to three per hour. (*Nicolas Savy*)

copy of a fourteenth-century springald, able to shoot a 1 metre steel bolt a distance of 300 metres. *icolas Savy*)

trebuchet, with hinged counterweight, capable of throwing a 100kg stone out to 200 metres up to ree times per hour. (*Nicolas Savy*)

A bricole, a man-powered traction machine able to throw a 15kg stone up to a maximum of 80 metres, and generally used for defensive purposes. (*Peter Hoskins*)

A couillard at Tiffauges castle showing the double counterweight for this development of the rebuchet. (*Peter Hoskins*)

A reconstruction of a battering ram at Tiffauges castle. (*Peter Hoskins*)

A reproduction of a bombard at Tiffauges castle showing the wooden protective screen. (*Peter Hoskins*)

reconstruction of a belfry at Tiffauges castle. (*Peter Hoskins*)

The castle of La Réole. Three of the four thirteenth-century corner towers remain. (*Peter Hoskins*)

The thirteenth-century watch tower in Calais. (*Peter Hoskins*)

Rodin's sculpture of the Burghers of Calais. (*Peter Hoskins*)

The remains of the Porte de Rouen, Harfleur. (*Peter Hoskins*)

Henry V stayed at the priory of Graville at the start of the siege of Harfleur in 1415. (*Peter Hoskins*)

(*Above left*) Caen castle.
(*Peter Hoskins*)

(*Above right*) The keep of
Rouen castle, now
known as La Tour
Jeanne d'Arc.
(*Peter Hoskins*)

(*Right*) The Tour St-Vigor
on the ramparts of
Pont-de-l'Arche.
(*Peter Hoskins*)

(*Above left*) The castle, or more properly the Ducal Palace, in Frévent. The first stone castle was built in the tenth century. Construction continued under subsequent Dukes of Normandy, and parts of the remains were built by King Henry II of England at the end of the twelfth century. (*Peter Hoskins*)

(*Above right*) Dieppe castle. (*Peter Hoskins*)

(*Left*) Ramparts in the town of St-Lô. (*Peter Hoskins*)

Bonport abbey. (*Peter Hoskins*)

A surviving gate in Mantes-la-Jolie, named the Port du Prêtre in memory of an attempt by a priest to retake the town from the English in 1421. The gate appears lower than it would have been in the Middle Ages, having lost some height with the construction of quays along the river in the nineteenth century.
(*Peter Hoskins*)

The perimeter tower of
St Martin in Mantes-la-Jolie.
(*Peter Hoskins*)

A stretch of the town walls
in Beauvais adjoining the
Tour Boileau. (*Peter Hoskins*)

Vernon, Château
des Tourelles.
(*Peter Hoskins*)

Vestiges of the
castle motte at
Chizé. (*Peter Hoskins*)

high ground at the western end of the town. Winter was setting in and it looked as though the English were digging in for a long siege if necessary, with lodgings being built from wood and trenches dug to counter the garrison if sallying forth to attack the besiegers. Supplies for the English were brought in regularly from Caen. Henry elected not to assault Falaise but set about an artillery bombardment. He started with the town, battering the walls and towers and destroying housing and churches. The French commanders, Gilbert de La Fayette and Guillaume de Meuillon, had some 600 professional soldiers under their command and could also expect to draw on the population of the town. Some of these were refugees from Caen and it is not surprising in the circumstances that, after about two weeks of bombardment and with no sign of relief in view, the town elected to surrender. On 2 December agreement was reached that if neither the king nor the dauphin relieved the town by 2 January 1418, Falaise would open its gates to Henry. The conditions were that all English prisoners would be released, all stores and arms were to be left in the town, and the garrison would submit to Henry's mercy.

The surrender did not, however, include the castle. This had its own garrison under the command of Olivier de Mauny. Built high up on rock, the castle was impervious to mining and invulnerable to the English guns because of the high ground. Nevertheless, Henry V set about taking the fortress methodically. The dry moat was bridged and shelters constructed against the curtain wall to allow men to work on its demolition. They succeeded in creating a breach almost 40m wide. By 1 February 1418 the garrison had had enough and, with the French still incapable of coming to their relief, made a surrender agreement to open the gates of the castle on 16 February. The garrison was to submit to ransom, and the commander was required to pay for materials and labour to repair the walls. They were also required to assist with the repairs before being allowed to leave.

Louviers, 1418

The rapid collapse of French garrisons continued early in 1418 as the Duke of Gloucester advanced into the Cotentin peninsula in Normandy. Torigny surrendered on the approach of the English, Carentan surrendered without resistance, the castle of Briquebec was abandoned, the fortress of Condé-sur-Noireau was taken by force, and the fortress of St-Sauveur capitulated as an assault was about to start. Other places held out initially but quickly came to terms when siege operations started. Vire resisted a short siege, St-Lô gave up when a siege started, the inhabitants of Valognes were induced to surrender when mining started, and the garrison of Coutances had had enough after a few days. The captain of Cherbourg, however, was made of sterner stuff than others in Normandy and the Duke of Gloucester was destined to lay siege to the town for five months.

Further to the east in Normandy the Duke of Clarence struck to the east of the river Touques towards the end of March. The castle of Harcourt capitulated without a fight. Perhaps surprisingly the abbey of Bec-Hellouin, defended by a rag-bag of refugees led by the prior and a local squire, the abbot having fled, held out for a month. The lands further west on the border with Brittany were not yet under English control, but the only places of any significance still holding out in Lower Normandy were Cherbourg, besieged by Gloucester, Domfront, whose defenders were slowly starving under a siege led by the Earl of Warwick, and Honfleur, which had been isolated by Clarence's operations.

The next major target for Henry V was Rouen. En route to Rouen Henry besieged Louviers on the Eure and Pont-de-l'Arche on the Seine. The siege of Louviers started on 8 June 1418. Louviers had been without walls when Edward III sacked the town in 1346 during the Crécy campaign. Work to remedy this deficiency had started twenty years later, and when Henry's army arrived the town was surrounded by high modern walls and three ditches, manned by a Burgundian garrison. Henry set about bombarding the town with artillery, filling the ditches and undermining the walls. The Burgundians replied with their own artillery, narrowly missing Henry V, and made several sorties to try to silence the English guns. However, after about a week the English guns had made several breaches in the walls and Henry prepared to assault the town. The inhabitants were justifiably fearful of the town being taken by force, and compelled the garrison to negotiate terms. Time was allowed for relief but with the chaotic state of the French government this was a forlorn hope.

Louviers surrendered on 23 June 1418. Henry was not in the humour to be generous. The captain of the town had formerly been captain of Bayeux and had sworn not to bear arms against Henry again. The price for having broken his word was his life. Similarly, Henry hanged eight gunners because of the casualties they had caused. The town was compelled to pay 8,000 *écus* in indemnity.

Pont-de-l'Arche, 1418

Henry V's army now moved north towards Pont-de-l'Arche, with the first elements arriving on 27 June. Pont-de-l'Arche lies on the left bank of the Eure, which is separated from the much wider Seine by a narrow strip of land. The confluence of the two rivers is about 9km to the west. The town was very well protected with walls on all sides, including close up to the river Eure, and a castle within the town which would also have to be taken to gain access to the bridge over the rivers. In 1346 the town had successfully repulsed an assault by Edward III's army, albeit Edward did not have siege equipment.

The French royal lieutenant in Normandy, Robert de Braquemont, had appreciated that holding the English south of the Seine was essential if there were to be any hope of stopping them from broadening their control of Normandy. He had made a conscious decision to leave Louviers to its fate, but had determined that the defence of Pont-de-l'Arche was critical. He had managed to raise a field army from within Normandy and had garrisoned Pont-de-l'Arche with about 1,000 men commanded by Jean Malet de Graville. He had stationed a further 2,000 men north of the river to try to prevent the English from crossing. He had another 800 men in reserve about 15km away. Perhaps unfortunately for the defence of Normandy, de Braquemont was dismissed as the English approached.

His replacement, the Lord of Chastellux, arrived just in time to see the English succeed in crossing the Seine, opening up the approach to Rouen. The English occupied an island in the river about 2.5km to the west of Pont-de-l'Arche near the abbey of Bonport, a Cistercian establishment which, according to legend, was founded by Richard the Lionheart in 1189 in thanks for his safe arrival on the river bank after getting into danger pursuing a deer. About 1km upstream towards the town a noisy diversion was started. While the French moved to counter this supposed crossing, Sir John Cornwall crossed from the island using small wicker-and-skin boats. A small French force on the northern bank tried to counter the landing but could not prevent Cornwall starting to establish a bridgehead. The French sent reinforcements but by the time they arrived about 1,000 men were across and the bridgehead was secure. During the morning the Duke of Clarence followed with a further 4,000 men. The French were beaten back and the town could be sealed off. A pontoon bridge was constructed, prefabricated in England and brought via Harfleur. The fate of the town was sealed, and two days after the English crossing a conditional surrender was agreed with 20 July set as the date for the town to surrender if not relieved by either the king or the dauphin in person.

Things were going from bad to worse for the French. About the time that Pont-de-l'Arche was negotiating surrender Domfront was also in the process of capitulation, agreeing to hand over the castle to the Earl of Warwick on 22 July, just two days after Pont-de-l'Arche was due to surrender. Honfleur, however, continued to hold out and did not enter into an agreement for its surrender until 25 February 1419. Cherbourg had also held on for some time, but with Gloucester having succeeded in undermining the walls and the garrison starving, the town surrendered towards the end of September 1418.

Rouen, 1418–1419

After the surrender of Pont-de-l'Arche and Domfront the English came to Rouen. As with Harfleur, where we have a first-hand account of the siege written by a priest with the army, here we have the story told in some detail in doggerel verse by a soldier, John Page, with Henry's army. Page tells us that the first to arrive was the Duke of Exeter, who came to reconnoitre the defences and summon the town to surrender. He halted outside the town, displayed his banners and sent heralds into the town. They issued the customary call to surrender and set out the usual consequences if the people did not heed the call. The heralds were scorned and sent away and artillery in the town opened fire on the duke's men. There was also a determined sortie by mounted men-at-arms and some of Exeter's men were killed and others captured in the ensuing skirmish. Exeter now returned to Pont-de-l'Arche to report to Henry on the reaction of the town to the call to surrender and to relay his observations on the defences of the town. Late on 29 July Henry V arrived with the main body of the army.

Rouen was the largest city that the English had attempted to take during the war to date with between 20,000 and 25,000 inhabitants. It lay on the north bank of the Seine and was surrounded by a high perimeter wall with a circumference of about 6km. There were five fortified gates and a dry ditch which Page describes as being wide, deep, with steep sides and with deep pitfalls and caltrops at the bottom. These defences dated from the early thirteenth century. Dating from approximately the same period was a citadel in the north, built by King Philip Augustus in 1204 when he took the town from King John of England. In the years since the construction of the walls and the citadel the town had expanded considerably, with sprawling suburbs outside the fortified part of the town. Some of these suburbs, to the north-east, had been enclosed by a more recent wall. Eight parishes, however, remained outside the walls and these had been razed on the approach of the English to prevent their use for shelter or as cover for men approaching the walls. A Benedictine priory to the west and the naval yard, the Clos des Galées, founded in the late fourteenth century to facilitate raids on England, on the south bank of the river had also been destroyed to deny them to Henry's men. The towers and gates were well furnished with guns, some large calibre and some smaller but with a more rapid rate of fire. There were also trebuchets and other stone-throwing machines within the town. The defences were completed by a fortified bridge which linked the town with a fort on the south bank of the river.

The defence of the town was in the hands of Guy Le Bouteillier, with a garrison of up to 1,600 men. This was considerably more than had been available for the defence of Harfleur, but the perimeter was twice as long and without the contribution of the population the defence would have been problematic in the extreme. In the event, Le Bouteillier had men drawn from the population to supplement his professional soldiers. He set up his headquarters in the citadel with part of the garrison, allocated most of the men to sectors corresponding to the gates and formed a mounted reserve to bring speedy help to sectors which needed reinforcement.

On their arrival the English set about sealing off the town. King Henry took up residence in an abandoned monastery to the east of the town and commanded a sector facing the Porte St-Hilaire. The Earl of Salisbury was on the king's left, covering the marshy ground down to the river and the Porte Martinville gate. The Duke of Exeter guarded the northern stretch and Sir Thomas Mowbray, the Earl Marshal, and Sir John Cornwall covered the citadel. The Duke of Clarence was to the west, based in the demolished abbey of St Gervais, and finally the Earl of Huntingdon completed the encirclement with men stationed on the south bank and

Rouen, 1418–1419.

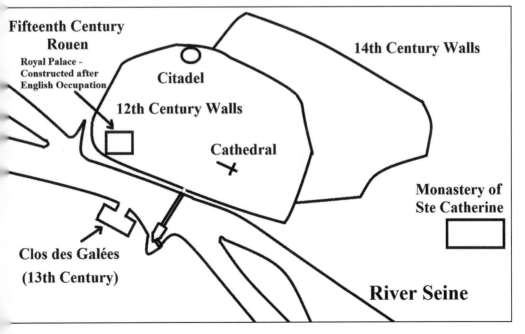

Fifteenth Century Rouen

Royal Palace - Constructed after English Occupation

Citadel

14th Century Walls

12th Century Walls

Cathedral

Monastery of Ste Catherine

Clos des Galées (13th Century)

River Seine

surrounding the fort on the southern end of the bridge. Soldiers in barges patrolled the river, and chains were spread across the Seine both upstream and downstream of Rouen, three chains being placed at different depths in the water. A wooden bridge was built to facilitate communication between the English troops on both sides of the river. At the mouth of the Seine, 130km away, Portuguese galleys blockaded the river on Henry's behalf.

Henry seems to have decided early on not to assault the town. Much as today, street fighting was a hazardous business; to have engaged in hand-to-hand fighting in a heavily populated town with many streets and lanes would inevitably have resulted in heavy casualties. He also appears to have elected to make only limited use of his artillery, although he had brought guns to the siege from the defensive complement of artillery at Harfleur. Guns were certainly placed in front of the gates and possibly on high ground overlooking the walls, but there are no records of the kind of damage inflicted at Harfleur, Falaise and Caen. The likely explanation for this is that Henry wanted to preserve the town as best he could for his capital of the Duchy of Normandy. Also, damaged defences would make the town vulnerable in the event of a French attempt to retake it. So the English settled down to starve the town into submission. The large population made the demand for food difficult to satisfy. An attempt had been made to drive out useless mouths, but with limited success, and extra mouths to feed came in the form of refugees from the suburbs and the countryside. To compound the problem, with the siege starting in July, the harvest had not been gathered in. Inhabitants had been ordered to stock ten months of supplies, but the effect was simply to redistribute to the population supplies held in shops and by market traders.

Having set his siege, Henry now turned his attention to securing his own supplies to ensure that he did not suffer the same fate as his great-grandfather Edward III, who had abandoned the sieges of Tournai in 1340 and Reims in 1359–1360 due to lack of supplies for the besiegers. The plan to supply the army was to create a depot at Harfleur, where supplies were transhipped onto barges to move upstream to Rouen. However, to make this plan work two towns on the north bank of the Seine, Quillebeuf and Caudebec, both of which were garrisoned and had armed ships intended to block the use of the river by the English, had to be neutralized. Quillebeuf fell little more than a fortnight after the start of the siege of Rouen, after the garrison was defeated in a battle beneath the walls on 16 August 1418.

Caudebec was a tougher nut to crack. The Earl of Warwick, shortly after his arrival from Domfront, was despatched to resolve the problem.

The town held, delaying a hundred barges waiting to move upstream to Rouen. Eventually an agreement was reached with the garrison. They would surrender if and when Rouen fell, but in the meantime they would allow safe passage for English barges.

Upstream there was another problem for Henry V. Less than 1km to the east of the town was the monastery of Ste Catherine standing on high ground and with a substantial garrison. This strong point threatened English communications with Pont-de-l'Arche and was a threat in the event of a relief force arriving from the east. An English assault early in the siege was beaten off, but the weak point for the garrison was food and on 1 September 1418 they surrendered for want of supplies.

With the access secure for supplies from England via Harfleur and up the Seine to Rouen, the French strong point at Ste Catherine neutralized, the harvest in and English foragers ranging far and wide to supplement supplies from England, the siege was well established by early autumn. Henry brought in a company of lightly armoured and mounted Irish soldiers to rustle cattle both to supplement English supplies and to deny food to the inhabitants of Rouen. With long lines of communication stretching back to England, Henry V's siege would have been vulnerable to a determined French campaign. However, with the disarray in the French camp, particularly with the feud between the Burgundians and Armagnacs, this was a remote possibility.

Within the walls the situation was much less rosy. Food was running out and with a sense of abandonment striking fear among the inhabitants, appeals for help went out to the Duke of Burgundy, royal councillors and the dauphin. At this stage the government was effectively in the hands of the Duke of Burgundy. He was well aware of the importance of Rouen. If it fell, the chances of recovering Lower Normandy from the English would be much diminished. Undertakings had been given to the citizens of Rouen that they would be relieved, but these were just fine words with little basis in reality. What resources Burgundy could muster were devoted to the feud with the Armagnacs in the Île de France around Paris. The relief of Rouen would have required cooperation between the dauphin and the duke. The dauphin, however, regarded countering the Burgundians as a higher priority than the relief of Rouen and turned his attention to dislodging them from Tours and their other strongholds in the Touraine. Attempts were made to find a modicum of cooperation between the Burgundians and the Armagnacs, but the best that could be cobbled together was an unsatisfactory arrangement with a division of responsibilities and resources between the two camps which would have given

Burgundy the task of relieving Rouen but without being able to call on all of the available resources. In the event, even this proposal came to nothing.

By late October 1418 the situation in Rouen was desperate, and on 28 October a delegation from the town described the plight of the inhabitants to the royal council in Paris: supplies were exhausted and the population was reduced to eating horses, cats, dogs and rats to survive. The case for the town was put by a friar, Eustache de Pavilly. In addition to explaining the military consequences of allowing Rouen to fall, he made it plain that in the eyes of the inhabitants the duke would be held responsible and his house would earn their undying enmity.

The government decided that every effort would be made to come to the relief of Rouen, and orders went out to muster men. The results were poor, and by 24 November the Duke of Burgundy had only some 4,000 men at his disposal at Pontoise, 90km south-east of Rouen. Meanwhile, Henry V had, during November, elected to exploit the divisions between the Burgundians and the Armagnacs to try to reach an agreement with the dauphin. These discussions came to nothing and then the Burgundians came to Henry to negotiate. It was not in Henry's interest to come to an agreement before he had taken Rouen, which now was close to the end of its endurance. In mid-December these talks also broke down.

By Christmas, almost two months after de Pavilly's plea before the royal council, the situation inside Rouen had deteriorated to the extent that about 200 people were reported as dying each day. Bodies were thrown into open pits and piled up in the streets. Unsurprisingly, disease spread and order disintegrated with people fighting for what little food could be found. Guy Le Bouteillier, the captain of the town, organized a sortie to attempt to break through the English lines. The attempt started badly with a drawbridge collapsing under the weight of the mounted men leaving through the gate, and those that did make it to the siege lines were thrown back with heavy casualties. To save food several thousand useless mouths were forced out of the town to be left to the mercy of the English. Any hope that Henry would be merciful and accept moral responsibility for these wretches was misplaced. They were driven back by English archers and took refuge in the ditch surrounding the town, where many died of exposure and starvation.

The Duke of Burgundy had not abandoned hope, despite the difficulties. He moved north from Pontoise to Beauvais, arriving on 29 December 1418 to find more men rallying to his call. Here he was still 80km from Rouen. Once again the number of men who had responded to the call was very disappointing. Nevertheless, a plan was hatched. The duke would approach Rouen from the east. Meanwhile the Burgundian Admiral of France, Charles of Lens, was to seize ships on the Picardy coast, and load them with supplies and men. He would then force a passage up the Seine and break through the siege lines. An appeal was once more sent to the dauphin, but he rejected this and furthermore forbade any men within his allegiance from joining the Burgundian army. Henry V had not been idle while this was going on: he was strengthening his position. Reinforcements were brought in from England, men were withdrawn from garrisons to augment the besieging force, and defences were constructed across the approaches from Paris.

Burgundy was not only short of men, he was short of time, and the prospect of the ship-borne relief reaching the town in time was remote in the extreme. Shortly after the Duke of Burgundy arrived in the Beauvaisis the urgency of the situation was brought into sharp relief by the arrival of a delegation which had succeeded in making its way through the siege lines. They made it clear that if relief did not arrive within a few days, Rouen would have to submit to Henry V. The Duke of Burgundy told the delegation that he expected to have sufficient men to relieve Rouen by 8 January 1419, and they left to take the news to Guy Le Bouteillier. Burgundy had probably been too optimistic even if all had gone in his favour, but in fact events elsewhere were running against him. The dauphin had taken Tours and was threatening areas under Burgundian control and there was simply not the money to pay for the army that he needed. About 3 January Burgundy gave up hope of relieving Rouen and sent a message to the town advising Le Bouteillier to surrender with the best terms he could extract from Henry.

The defenders had not waited for this message and on 31 December 1418 asked to negotiate with the English. These talks started on New Year's Day. The first item on the agenda for the French was to ask for relief for those expelled from the town and who were still alive and trapped between the siege lines and the walls. Henry was unsympathetic, pointing out that it was the garrison which had put them there, not him. The French then asked to negotiate a conditional surrender. Henry's riposte was that Rouen was his by right and that the Duke of Burgundy was well acquainted with the situation and had no need of further messages. However, this apparently uncompromising response was no more than a ritual prelude to talks.

The serious negotiations started on 2 January 1419 in pavilions erected near the Porte St-Hilaire. Despite the desperate plight of the population, these talks dragged on for almost two weeks while townsmen watched from the walls. Divisions were emerging within the city, with the citizens wanting a quick resolution at any price and the professional soldiers wanting to hold out for honourable terms. There were accusations that the soldiers had failed to fulfil their duties and even that Guy Le Bouteillier had deliberately brought about the failure of the sortie intended to break through the siege lines. Among the inhabitants plots were hatched to kill the captains of the garrison, while the soldiery threatened to demolish sections of the wall and set fire to places in the city unless Henry V offered acceptable terms. Despite the unequal positions of the two sides, Henry wanted to take the town intact and gave ground, reaching agreement with the defenders on 13 January 1419.

The terms required the surrender at midday on 19 January 1419 of the town and castle, intact, unless relieved beforehand by an army under the command of either King Charles VI or the Duke of Burgundy. The population and garrison agreed not to intervene in any ensuing battle. Corpses were to be collected and buried outside the walls. The remaining terms reflected Henry V's objective of re-establishing the English Duchy of Normandy: the town's privileges would be preserved, inhabitants could retain their property if they swore allegiance to Henry, non-Norman soldiers could leave with a safe-conduct but Norman members of the garrison had the choice of swearing allegiance to Henry or imprisonment. An enormous indemnity, 365,000 *écus*, was to be paid, with the first instalment falling due after three days and the remainder one month later. To put this sum in context, it was more than one-fifth of the outstanding ransom for King John II. All horses and war materiel were to be surrendered, and the king would take land within the city to build a palace. Eighty hostages were taken as guarantee for the fulfilment of the terms.

The date set for the relief was no more than a formality. By the time the news reached Beauvais the Duke of Burgundy had already given up hope and disbanded his army. On 19 January 1419, two hours after the surrender at midday, Henry V entered Rouen in great pomp, accompanied by the ringing of the church bells. He dismounted on reaching the cathedral of Notre Dame and bare-headed entered the cathedral and gave thanks on his knees for the surrender of the town.

Between Rouen and Montereau

As had been predicted, the fall of Rouen had a wide impact in Normandy. Caudebec surrendered as previously agreed in the event of Rouen's surrender. Elsewhere in Normandy Montivilliers, Fécamp, Dieppe and Eu also capitulated. Honfleur surrendered on 25 February. From the end of

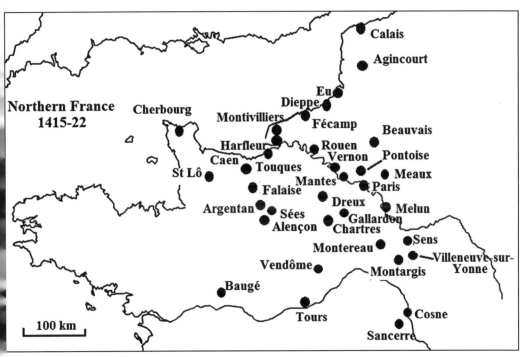

Northern France, 1415–1422.

March only a handful of places held out: the fortresses of La Roche-Guyon and Château-Gaillard and the towns of Gisors and Ivry-la-Bataille. The fall of Lower Normandy also opened up the Île-de-France: Vernon, Mantes-la-Jolie and Meulan were all abandoned on the approach of the English for want of the means to resist a siege. The English were within 30km of Paris, with raiding parties advancing within sight of the walls.

After the fall of Rouen there were diplomatic manoeuvrings between three parties: the English, the dauphin and the Armagnacs, and John the Fearless, Duke of Burgundy, on behalf of King Charles VI. It appeared at one point that the dauphin would reach an agreement with Henry, but news that the Scots were to send an army in support of the dauphin led him to withdraw from the negotiations. The focus now turned to negotiations with the Burgundians. In September 1419 John the Fearless was murdered by the Armagnacs and the new Duke of Burgundy, Philip the Good, concluded an agreement with Henry. In the meantime, following the breakdown of talks with the Armagnacs, Henry renounced a truce which had been agreed with the dauphin and renewed his military operations. The first objective was Ivry-la-Bataille. The town was taken on 1 April 1419. The castle initially held out but surrendered ten days later. Two of the remaining Norman fortresses were the next targets: La Roche-Guyon and Château-Gaillard. The Earl of Warwick set about the castle of La Roche-Guyon. The defence was conducted by Perrette de la Rivière, who had lost her husband and other relatives at Agincourt less than four years before. Guy Le Bouteillier, the former French commander of Rouen but now in Henry's service, used his local knowledge to show Warwick tunnels which could be used to undermine the walls of the fortress. With this information, and despite a spirited defence which inflicted heavy casualties on the English, Warwick was able to take the castle in less than a month. Le Bouteillier was rewarded with the castle. The task of taking Château-Gaillard was given to Exeter. He settled down to a siege which was to last for six months before finally Olivier de Mauny, who had held out with just 120 men-at-arms, surrendered. According to one chronicler, the surrender was necessary simply because the ropes used to raise water from the well broke.

On 21 May 1420 Henry V and Charles VI signed the Treaty of Troyes. The dauphin was declared a bastard and thus disinherited from his claim to the French throne. Henry was to become King of France on the death of Charles. In the meantime Henry would rule as regent. Special provisions were made for Normandy, which would be ruled separately by Henry and only reabsorbed into France on his accession to the throne. Outside of the treaty Charles' daughter Catherine de Valois was to marry Henry. Henry was about twenty years younger than Charles and had every expectation of outliving the French king. In the event, as we shall see, Charles was to outlive Henry by a few months and the infant Henry VI was to accede to the two thrones. Perhaps the most important aspect of the treaty was that Philip the Good, Duke of Burgundy, was now formally allied with the English.

The most urgent task for the Anglo-Burgundians was to relieve the pressure being exerted on Paris by Dauphinist garrisons with their block-ades of the rivers Oise and Marne and the Seine valley. On 4 June 1420 Henry V marched west out of Troyes with the King and Queen of France, King James I of Scotland, Philip the Good and an army of between 8,000 and 10,000 men. The first target was the cathedral town of Sens. Sens had a garrison of only some 300 men and provisions were low. The dauphin's captain managed to hold out for a few days but surrendered on 11 June. Five days later the army arrived at Montereau, the scene of the assassination of John the Fearless.

Montereau, 1420

The town and castle were in the charge of Guillaume de Chaumont, who had been captain when the Duke of Burgundy was murdered. He had about 500 men to defend the town and castle. He tried initially to hold the town, to the south of the river Yonne, but a week after the arrival of the Anglo-Burgundians they stormed the weak walls and the defenders fled into the castle, closely pursued by the attackers. The fleeing garrison suffered heavy casualties, including some who drowned in the river. Pontoon bridges were constructed across the Yonne, and the castle, which was old and vulnerable to artillery fire, could now be surrounded. Eleven prisoners had been taken by the English during the attack on the town and Henry hoped to induce the surrender of the garrison by threatening to execute them if the defenders continued to hold out. The prisoners pleaded with de Chaumont to surrender to save their lives. He refused to do so and Henry duly hanged them all one by one in full view of the defenders. Their deaths were in vain. The English constructed stone-throwers and Philip the Good brought guns from Sens along the river Yonne. De Chaumont started negotiations and on 1 July 1420 opened the gates. The defenders departed under safe conduct, save those who had been involved with the murder of John the Fearless. In view of his role in the assassination Guillaume de Chaumont should not have been allowed to go free but somehow he managed to make his way to safety and rejoined the dauphin with the others. The body of John the Fearless was exhumed, having, as a contemporary described it, been buried dishonourably, and was transferred to the mausoleum of the Dukes of Burgundy near Dijon.

Melun, 1420

After the fall of Montereau two other important towns to the south-east of Paris fell quickly into Anglo-Burgundian hands: Villeneuve-sur-Yonne, taken by surprise by escalade by Burgundian troops, and the river port of Joigny-sur-Yonne 15km upstream which was occupied without resistance. The Anglo-Burgundians now had control of the river route from Burgundy to the Seine valley. This gave them a secure line of communications to support the forthcoming siege of Melun, the next target on the list of towns and fortresses in Dauphinist hands in the Île-de-France, with food, construction material and artillery.

Melun, 65km upstream on the Seine from Paris, had been occupied by the dauphin's men since 1418. The old town was constructed on an island dominated by its castle. The castle had been an important residence for French kings, including Charles V. Thus he had taken an interest in its defences and it had been rebuilt on his orders some fifty to sixty years before the arrival of Henry V. It was a strong fortress with a rectangular keep with eight round towers and high walls typical of the military architecture of the period. The old town was connected to walled suburbs on both sides of the river by fortified bridges with gate towers at both ends. The suburbs were protected by dry ditches which had been maintained by the defenders. Earth taken from the ditches had been used to construct earthworks by the gates to house artillery. The garrison of some 600 to 700 men, mostly Gascons but with a few Scots, was commanded by Arnaud-Guilhem de Barbazan and Pierre de Bourbon. Of great importance for the commanders was the support of the population, who not only guaranteed the pay of the soldiery but also fought alongside the professional garrison.

The Anglo-Burgundians arrived outside the town on 8 July 1420, on the right bank of the river. The Duke of Burgundy occupied the ground to the north of the town with the Earls of Warwick and Huntingdon. Henry V continued a further 15km to the north-west to cross the Seine at Corbeil before returning to take up station on the left bank. The besiegers constructed defences to protect themselves from sorties from the town and from attack from the rear. A pontoon bridge was built to allow the two elements of the army to communicate and the Burgundians installed heavy artillery. The siege began formally on 13 July 1420 with a demand delivered by King Charles VI from below the walls for the town to surrender. King James of Scotland issued a similar demand to the Scots within the town. The response from the town was uncompromising, if familiar: gladly would they open the gates for the King of France but not for the King of England.

Henry V's army in France was thinly spread and it was becoming increasingly difficult to find reinforcements. As a consequence he was keen to avoid unnecessary casualties and did not wish to risk an assault on the town before the defences had been sufficiently weakened by bombardment and mining. However, on the right bank an assault was launched by the Burgundians under the direction of the German Count Palatine. The result was much as Henry had feared. The attackers were repulsed with artillery fire and crossbow bolts and a determined sortie by the defenders caught men still in the ditches waiting their turn to climb the scaling ladders. Chastened by the losses inflicted by the garrison, the besiegers settled down for a long siege. The scene was now set for the besiegers to bombard the walls and start mining. The defenders conducted a resolute and determined defence, launching sorties to attack the besiegers, destroy siege works and take prisoners. They also dug countermines and in one instance broke into an English mine with hand-to-hand fighting with lances ensuing. Artillery damage to walls was repaired at night with earth

and wood. Sharpshooters were deployed on the walls to snipe at prominent figures, and according to one chronicler they managed to kill at least
one Englishman and one Burgundian of senior rank.

Initially the dauphin was too preoccupied by his problems with John,
Duke of Brittany, to give much thought to the relief of Melun, and it was
only in September that an army started to muster at Beaugency-sur-Loire,
130km to the south-west. The army was to be commanded by the Count
of Vertus, Philip of Orléans. The operation suffered an inauspicious start
when Philip died while the army was mustering and the dauphin withdrew
from the army to go to Mehun-sur-Yèvre where he spent the remainder
of 1420. Things went from bad to worse. The army set out in mid-
September under the command of captains of modest rank. They stopped
at Montargis, still 70km south of Melun, and sent forward scouts to reconnoitre the positions of the besiegers. They returned with a pessimistic
report that the besiegers were both numerous and well protected by their
earthworks. That was enough for the commanders and the army dispersed
without attempting to relieve the town. By the end of the month the
conditions in Melun were worsening quickly. Many buildings had been
ruined by cannon balls and stones thrown by siege engines and inhabitants
took refuge where they could in cellars. Supplies of food were now non-
existent, with the garrison having resorted to eating their horses. Inhabitants tried to escape but some were captured by sentries. The state of
affairs in the town was well known to the besiegers.

Hopes among the defenders had been raised at one point by the sight of
a column arriving from the north, but their optimism was quickly dashed
when it became clear that the approaching men were men-at-arms and
archers led by John of Luxembourg and drawn from Picardy and the
Calais garrison as reinforcements for the Anglo-Burgundians. At the first
sighting the inhabitants had rung the church bells and climbed on to the
walls to shout their greetings before descending disconsolately when the
truth became clear. Towards the end the garrison eventually managed to
get a messenger out who took an appeal for help to the dauphin. His reply
was to the point: his forces were too weak and he could offer no hope of
relief. On 17 November 1420 the town surrendered, having held out for
more than nineteen weeks.

Henry's army had suffered heavily through battle casualties and dysentery, that habitual scourge of besiegers. He had lost perhaps as many as
1,700 men, one-third of his army's strength. It is hardly surprising that in
the circumstances he exacted severe terms. The garrison was not permitted to leave with safe-conduct. Englishmen or Scots found within the

walls would lose their lives, as would anyone considered to have been involved in the assassination of John the Fearless. Twenty Scots were hanged for treason to King James and three squires of the Duke of Orléans were beheaded for their involvement in the death of John the Fearless. Among those who lost their heads were two monks, for reasons unknown to us. One of the key men in the murder, Olivier de Léer, was identified but managed to escape. One of Henry's Gascon retainers, Bertrand de Caumont, was judged to have aided his escape in return for a bribe. He was beheaded in front of the army. The town had to pay a fine of 20,000 francs and all armour, weapons and movable goods had to be surrendered and placed in the castle. Eighteen hostages, including six noblemen from the garrison and six prominent burghers, were taken as surety for the fulfilment of the terms of the surrender. The captain of the garrison, Arnaud-Guilhem de Barbazan, was sent to Paris initially and remained a prisoner of war until 1429. Those of lesser rank who escaped execution, some 500 or 600 men, were taken to Paris and imprisoned. Some were subsequently released on ransom under parole not to take up arms again against the kings of France and England, at least two were tried and executed for treason, and many died while they waited in prison to learn their fates.

Between Melun and Meaux

In 1406 Prince James, heir to the Scottish throne, had been sent to France by his father Robert II. The prince's ship had been intercepted by an English privateer and the young prince was taken to England. Robert died shortly after he received the news of his son's capture, and James became king in captivity. He was to remain a prisoner of the English for the next eighteen years. In his absence the Duke of Albany became Governor of Scotland and renewed the alliance with France. Scots fought alongside the French in small numbers for some years but in the late summer of 1419 a substantial army of perhaps 6,000 men, commanded by the Earl of Buchan, arrived in France. For reasons that are not clear they were initially under-employed, but on 22 March 1421 inflicted a serious defeat on an English army led by Henry V's brother, the Duke of Clarence. An impetuous and rash commander, Clarence attacked the Scots at Baugé, against the advice of the Earl of Huntingdon and Sir Gilbert Umfraville, before he had gathered all his army. He attacked a force of between 4,000 and 5,000 Scots and 1,000 French troops with about a third of his force, some 1,500 men. The result was a disaster, with many English killed and most of the survivors captured. Clarence was among a number of great men killed in the mayhem. There was much rejoicing in the French camp and the victorious Earl of Buchan was appointed Constable of France. Buchan urged the dauphin to take advantage of the disarray in the English camp and strike into Normandy. However, too much time was allowed to elapse and it was six weeks before the dauphin marched towards the English at the head of 6,000 men, mainly drawn from the Scots.

The dauphin's first objective was Alençon, held by an English garrison. There had been a number of defections to the dauphin from the Burgundian side after Baugé and the Duke of Brittany, always ready to change with the wind, had allied himself with the dauphin, even if he had little, if any, intention of keeping to this commitment. The Earl of Salisbury had responsibility for restoring the English position. He appreciated that little had really changed in military terms and that the main challenge was to restore belief and morale by showing that English military power remained dominant. He made good use of the time given to him by the delay on the part of the dauphin to follow up after Baugé to consolidate garrisons and appoint new commanders. Salisbury elected to make a direct attempt to relieve the siege of Alençon but was driven off by a superior force and suffered heavy casualties. Undeterred by this setback, he then opted for an indirect strategy and struck south with a classic Edwardian *chevauchée* spreading destruction and cutting the dauphin's supply lines from the Loire. In May the dauphin had no option but to raise the siege.

Henry V was in England when the news of Baugé reached him. He seems to have received the news calmly, but resolved to return to Normandy with reinforcements in June. He also tried to exploit divisions within the Scots to detach the Earl of Buchan from French service. As a consequence of his skilful efforts Earl Douglas did not go to France with a second army, but the French continued to enjoy the support of Buchan and his men. Henry returned to Calais on 11 June 1421 with King James and 4,200 reinforcements. He found a deteriorating military situation, the dauphin, well funded for the first time, and the Duke of Burgundy in serious financial straits. Henry provided funds to bail out the Duke of Burgundy in return for the promise of an army. Meanwhile the dauphin had stormed the town of Gallardon and killed the entire garrison as traitors. Gallardon had been a subsidiary garrison for the much more important town of Chartres about 15km to the west. The garrison was substantially Burgundian, reinforced with some English troops. Gallardon had been taken on 25 June and by the end of the month Dauphinist forces had invested Chartres. The siege was short-lived. The dauphin's force was substantially larger than the potential relief force. However, as soon as news arrived that the English had reached the Seine, some 60km away, the dauphin hastily lifted the siege, ostensibly because of problems with disease and provisioning the army, and headed 80km south to Vendôme. The real reason was almost certainly that the risk of losing all in a battle with Henry V was just too great for the dauphin and his advisers. The Dauphinist army, which withdrew progressively over the next few days, was ordered to reassemble at Vendôme on 15 August 1421.

On 9 July Henry rejoined his army at Mantes-la-Jolie on the Seine. The next day, as promised, Philip of Burgundy arrived. They decided that Henry would pursue the dauphin while Philip returned to Picardy. The English moved south and reached Dreux on 18 July. The town, on the west bank of the Eure, was walled and had a strong castle on a spur of rock. It housed the largest Dauphinist garrison in the region. However, the captain and his deputy were both absent and morale was low. The dauphin and his counsellors agreed that they should attempt to relieve Dreux. Further troops were summoned to muster at Vendôme by 25 August. It was to prove too late. The English had penetrated the outer bailey of the castle, driving the garrison back to take refuge in the keep. On 8 August they sued for terms and surrendered on 20 August. For the most part the garrison was allowed to leave under safe-conduct on condition that they did not take up arms against the Anglo-Burgundians for a year. An exception to the rule was the lord of a local castle who, having previously sworn allegiance to Henry V, had surrendered his castle to the Dauphinists. He paid the price for his disloyalty and was hanged.

Henry V now embarked on a wild goose chase in pursuit of the dauphin. In doing so he exposed his army to considerable risk deep in the heart of hostile territory. It was largely due to the timidity of his opponents that he managed to extricate himself and head north-east towards the Seine and the Yonne once more. The Duke of Burgundy in Picardy fared little better, despite a victory at the end of August over a Dauphinist army close to the Somme: a victory which cost the Burgundians dearly.

On reaching the Yonne Henry retook Villeneuve-sur-Yonne, which had fallen to him in 1420 but had then been retaken by a surprise Dauphinist attack early in 1421. The garrison surrendered to Henry after just five days. Henry now considered that he had freed the Seine and Yonne for river traffic and thus eased the pressure on Paris. However, there remained a further problem for communications with Paris: the town of Meaux on the Marne, 40km east of the capital.

Meaux, 1421–1422

At the end of September 1421 Henry moved initially from Villeneuve-sur-Yonne to Thorigny-sur-Marne, 16km south-west of Meaux. Here he constructed machines for use in the forthcoming siege of Meaux. The Duke of Exeter was sent forward, with an advance guard arriving on 6 October and catching the garrison and population by surprise, to the extent that the northern suburbs were taken before they could be destroyed by the defenders. The remainder of the army arrived three weeks later, bringing the total number of combatants in the besieging force to around 2,000 men, a remarkably small number of men for such a task. Including the many non-combatants who habitually accompanied a medieval army, there were probably around 3,000 in total in the English camp. The size of the besieging force reflected the challenge of holding Paris and the towns in Normandy now in English hands, which tied down the majority of the 8,000 to 10,000 men Henry now had in France.

Meaux was built on both banks of the Marne. To the north, on the right bank, was the *cité*. It was walled, with an old castle in the south-west corner, and at its heart was the cathedral. However, it was weak, with Roman walls which had been reinforced with towers in the fourteenth century. There were extensive suburbs outside the walls. On the opposite bank was the *Marché*. This was an entirely different proposition to the *cité*. The *Marché* was a fortified suburb which sat on a peninsula formed by a tight ox-bow bend in the Marne so that the river flowed beneath the walls on three sides. To complete the circuit a canal had been dug to the south of the *Marché*. Since June 1418 there had been a Dauphinist garrison of several hundred men in the *Marché* commanded by the Gascon captain the Bastard of Vaurus, supported by another Gascon, Peron de Luppé. When it had become apparent that Henry was likely to try to take Meaux, the dauphin's council had sent Guichard de Chissay, a nobleman from the Touraine, to take command. The garrison had been reinforced and the total of defenders was now around 1,000 men.

The besiegers established their siege in a well-practised manner: driving out minor local Dauphinist garrisons, constructing fieldworks to defend the siege lines, building a bridge over the Marne to ensure communications between those on both sides of the river, and setting up markets supplied from Champagne by river. Cannon and stone-throwing machines were installed. The Duke of Exeter had set himself up in the Benedictine abbey of St Farron to the north, the Earl of March occupied the Franciscan convent to the East, and the Earl of Warwick had taken up station near the canal to the south. The encirclement was completed by King Henry at Rutel, 2km to the west.

The garrison conducted a vigorous defence. Breaches caused by artillery fire were repaired and ditches which had been filled by the English by day were cleared again overnight. Sorties were launched to disrupt the siege and artillery fire was used to drive back those trying to approach the walls. The situation for the besiegers was far from ideal as winter set in. Their artillery was taking its time to inflict significant damage and the weather was presenting challenges. The cold and wet turned to sleet and snow and in December the river flooded its banks, forcing the besiegers to move back to higher ground. The flooding was short-lived and after two weeks the English could reoccupy their original positions, but the garrison had taken the opportunity to send out foraging parties in boats to restock their supplies. In these conditions dysentery, the only too common scourge of siege camps, took its toll. There were also casualties, the most notable being the king's cousin, the seventeen-year-old son of Sir John Cornwall. The young Cornwall lost his head to cannon fire, and his father, who was standing beside him, was also wounded. The problem of losses due to casualties and sickness was compounded by desertions, and it has been estimated that Henry had lost one-sixth of his strength by Christmas 1421.

In the circumstances it is surprising perhaps that the dauphin made no serious attempt to relieve Meaux. He was probably poorly placed to raise a sufficiently large force because of financial difficulties. He was also likely to have been deterred by his perennial fear of a set-piece battle with the English. A small force of only forty men led by Guy de Nesle attempted to bring some relief. It is difficult to see what practical help they could have brought but in any case the episode ended in farce. During the night of 9 March 1422 Guy and his men made their way through the English lines and approached the dry ditch below the walls to the north of the *cité*. Ladders had been placed against the walls by the garrison and covered with sheets as camouflage against the stone walls. Some of the relieving force managed to get into the town, but Guy, taking up the rear to drive his men on, trod on an old ladder rung which broke and he fell into the ditch. The clatter of his armour alerted the English sentries. In the subsequent combat he was wounded and captured, along with several of his men.

Morale was already poor among the townspeople. The English were getting close to the walls with a mine, and the inhabitants wanted to surrender before it was too late. Rather than bringing succour, Guy de Nesle's attempt at relief seems to have resolved the garrison to withdraw from the *cité* and consolidate their defence in the *Marché*. The next day the professional soldiers withdrew across the bridge with their possessions. There was panic among the inhabitants who feared that the departing soldiery would burn the *cité* as they went. One citizen called to the English to tell them what was happening. A ladder was placed against the walls for him. He climbed down and was taken before King Henry. Henry ordered an assault but one of his captains had already taken the initiative: he had seized a section of undefended wall and opened the gates. The English poured in, pursuing the garrison towards the *Marché* as the inhabitants took refuge in the churches. Henry's men assaulted the fortified gate defending the bridge, but as the last of the garrison reached the *Marché* the wooden section of the bridge was pulled up. The besiegers now concentrated their efforts on the *Marché*. Artillery was set up on islands in the river, the gap in the bridge was filled and the mills below the bridge, previously used by the inhabitants for grinding their flour, were occupied.

Henry apparently decided that he was not simply going to wait for the garrison to be starved into submission and set about taking the *Marché* by assault, willing it seems to accept the casualties that this entailed. Artillery battered the walls and aggressive operations were carried out on three sides. To the south Warwick crossed the canal and, protected by a wooden shelter, secured a foothold on the strip of land between the canal and the wall. From here his men were able to seize the outworks of the southern rampart. To the west Sir Walter Hungerford threw a bridge across the river, established another foothold and started on a mine. It was impossible to do the same to the east where the walls descended straight into the water. However, Henry was not deterred. A wooden tower was built and set on two barges so that it overlooked the walls. It was provided with a bridge which could be lowered onto the ramparts. The defence had been equally vigorous and heavy casualties were inflicted by crossbow shooting. To add to the loss of the young John Cornwall, there were more senior casualties. The Earl of Worcester was killed by a cannon ball and Thomas Lord Clifford by a crossbow bolt.

Towards the end of April, as the cumulative effect of the attacks of the besiegers and the dwindling supplies took their toll, preparations were in hand for a final assault. The garrison asked for terms. It seems that the initiative was taken by men of lesser rank rather than their commanders. Terms were agreed on 2 May for the surrender of the *Marché* on 10 May 1422. They were harsh. Twelve of the senior men in the garrison were to submit to King Henry's mercy. Four were selected for their prominent role within the garrison during the last three years: the Bastard of Vaurus and his cousin Denis, a lawyer named Jean de Rouvres and Louis Gast the *bailli* of Meaux. The Bastard of Vaurus was accused of having hanged a large number of labourers before the siege. Their bodies were cut down and buried by the English. The Bastard was treated in the same way and hanged from one of the trees where his victims had died. His cousin Denis was also executed, and the corpses of the Vaurus cousins were displayed outside the gates. Rouvres and Gast were sent to Paris for trial and subsequently beheaded. Three others were required to surrender unconditionally, including an unnamed horn player who seems to have aroused Henry's ire; he was also decapitated in Paris. Five other men were singled out for having associations with other Dauphinist garrisons. They included Guichard de Chissay, who had been sent to take command at the start of the siege, and the Gascon captain Peron de Luppé. These five were required to buy their lives by ensuring the surrender of other garrisons.

The main body of the garrison would be allowed their lives, but had to surrender as prisoners of war. These terms, however, did not extend to all. Those who were not guaranteed an amnesty included those associated with the assassination of John the Fearless; Irish, Scots or English soldiers; Frenchmen who had sworn to abide by the Treaty of Troyes; and the professional artillerymen who had inflicted such casualties. Up to 800 men surrendered on these terms when the gates were opened on 10 May and were sent in chains to Paris. Some were able to ransom themselves quickly, others died in prison, and the rest were held for larger ransoms or for political motives. Some were held in castles in Normandy; the remainder were sent to England. Prisoners held by the garrison were to be released.

Finally, everything in the fortress, including personal possessions in addition to the usual stores of food, weapons and horses, was to be collected, inventoried and surrendered. Also included were movable goods in the churches. No stores were to be destroyed or damaged. Those in the Dauphinist cause paid a high price for their seven months of stubborn and determined resistance.

Cosne, 1422

During the siege of Meaux the Dauphinists had been active in the north of France. The fall of the town changed the strategic situation dramatically. The lesson was not lost on numerous towns and garrisons that the loss of Meaux both demonstrated the inability of the dauphin to bring relief and placed the Anglo-Burgundians in a much stronger position. Nevertheless, the Dauphinists remained active further south on the Loire. Towards the end of June the garrison of La Charité-sur-Loire surrendered to the Dauphinists, and shortly thereafter Tanneguy du Chastel, the Dauphinist Provost of Paris, laid siege to Cosne 25km downstream on the Loire. Cosne was garrisoned by the Burgundians, but it was not in a condition to resist a long siege. A messenger was sent to the Duke of Burgundy asking for help. Relief was promised but before many days had passed the captain of Cosne had agreed to surrender the town if a relief force, commanded by the Duke of Burgundy, did not arrive before 12 August 1422.

By now Henry V was sick with the dysentery that was to kill him, but he remained alive to the chance that this presented of bringing the Dauphinists to battle and he agreed with Burgundy that the challenge should be accepted. During the second half of July troops were gathered from across English- and Burgundian-held territories. The army was a good size, perhaps 9,000 provided by the Duke of Burgundy and his allies and 3,000 English, including those of the Earl of Warwick who had been withdrawn from the siege of Le Crotoy on the Somme estuary. The army left Paris in the third week of July with Henry still at its head. By the time the army reached Corbeil, just 30km south of Paris, Henry could go no further. He passed overall command to the Duke of Burgundy as his lieutenant, who proceeded with Henry's brother the Duke of Bedford and his uncle the Duke of Exeter. The army marched on and arrived outside Cosne two days before the appointed day. The dauphin and his army were nowhere to be seen; they had abandoned their siege lines and left just a part of their army under the command of the Earl of Buchan. He was at Sancerre, 15km away on the left bank of the Loire. His mission was to prevent the Anglo-Burgundians crossing the river and passing into Berry.

Henry V lived just three weeks after the relief of Cosne, dying on 31 August 1422. His young son, not yet nine months old, succeeded him as King of England. Less than two months later Charles VI died, and the young Henry became King of France under the terms of the Treaty of Troyes. The Duke of Bedford was appointed to carry on the war as Regent of France until the infant Henry VI reached his majority.

Chapter 7

From the Death of Henry V to the Siege of Orléans, 1422–1429

The Treaty of Troyes had been based on the not unreasonable assumption that Henry V would outlive Charles VI, eighteen years his senior, and that Henry would accede to the French throne. With the birth of his son in December 1421 Henry could reasonably have expected to live long enough to see his son grow to majority before he had to take on the reins of power in the two kingdoms. In the event, as we have seen, this was not to be, with Henry VI coming to the throne of England as an eight-month-old babe in arms and two months later to the French throne. Those among the French who had not accepted the treaty and supported the dauphin continued to oppose the English. The war continued unabated under the leadership of Henry V's brother John, Duke of Bedford, acting as Regent of France.

As might have been expected, the dauphin took encouragement from the sudden turn of events. He proclaimed himself Charles VII of France six days after the death of his father, with his government based in Poitiers, Bourges and Toulouse. Charles also began negotiations with the Castilians and the Scots to raise and transfer 8,000 men to France. Meanwhile Bedford had not been idle and set about besieging Meulan. He had also put arrangements in place to raise taxes in Normandy for the defence of the duchy and to raise reinforcements in England. The first batch, 380 men-at-arms and 1,140 archers, arrived in May.

Meulan, 1423

Meulan, on the Seine 36km north-west of Paris, was key to secure communications between Normandy and Paris. It was an obvious early target for Bedford once he had decided to take the war back to the dauphin. We know little about the conduct of the siege, but its importance lies in the strategic significance of the town. It is also of interest for the rapidity of the surrender and the terms of the composition.

Bedford arrived before Meulan in early January 1423. He brought with him English, Norman and Picard troops and set about besieging the town

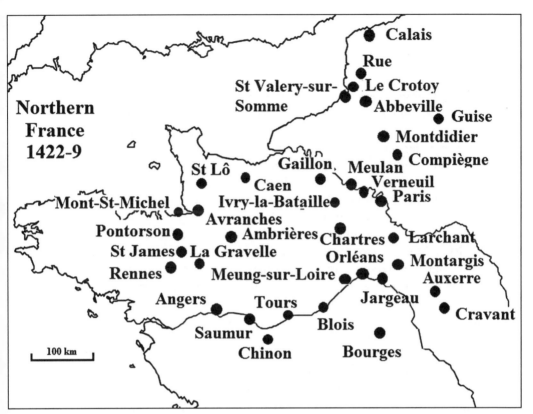

Northern France, 1422–1429.

and the bridge, deploying his men on both sides of the river. The siege continued into February with siege engines battering the walls. Towards the end of February a relief force of some 6,000 men loyal to the dauphin was assembled in Berry and marched to within 20km of Meulan. The force was led by the Count of Aumale, the Earl of Buchan as constable of the dauphin, the Viscount of Narbonne and the Breton Tanneguy du Chastel. If this force was indeed as strong as the chronicler claims then it would almost certainly have outnumbered Bedford's besieging force. It is a mystery, therefore, why the army melted away without approaching Bedford's siege camp. All we are told is that there was dissension between the leaders. It seems that there had been an agreement that the town would surrender if relief did not come by a certain date. The inhabitants were very dispirited when the news reached them that the relief army had left without making any effort to save them. The dauphin's banner was thrown down from a gate in disgust, and some citizens who had been wearing the arms and badges of the dauphin climbed onto the ramparts and tore them up in view of the besieging army. They shouted out that they had had enough of those who had lied to them and raised false hopes for their relief.

Negotiations seem to have progressed rapidly and on 1 March 1423 a treaty was signed to come into force two days hence. The terms were tough. The garrison was to surrender the bridge and the town leaving guns, powder, crossbows, all military equipment, clothing and rations in place and undamaged. The garrison was to surrender to the mercy of Bedford. However, the duke would be merciful, save for certain designated men. The list is a familiar one. Excluded from the duke's mercy were those in breach of oaths sworn after the Treaty of Troyes in 1420, those involved in the murder of John, Duke of Burgundy, and Irish, Scots and Welsh soldiers. Two other men were also excluded for reasons unknown to us, and gunners and those who had taken part in a skirmish near the bridge would be, again for reasons unknown, at the mercy of the regent. The garrison was required to surrender and place in a specified location all personal armour and equipment; similarly all gold, silver, jewellery and plate was to be surrendered and assembled in one place. All horses and their harness were also surrendered. Finally, all those who within the garrison held fortresses or towns for the dauphin were to surrender them to the English. As a consequence several fortresses passed into English hands in the aftermath of the siege. This was not a case of a garrison leaving with safe-conduct and all their possessions, horses and arms.

Having taken Meulan, the Duke of Bedford did not wish to wait for the enemy to come to him but preferred to carry the war to the French. Salisbury was charged with the systematic reduction of Dauphinist strongholds between Chartres and Paris. A further important objective for the English was Mont-St-Michel which stood as an isolated stronghold in English Normandy. In July Sir John de la Pole was given the mission to take Mont-St-Michel. Suffolk and Sir Ralph Bouteiller were set the task of taking the important port of Le Crotoy on the Somme estuary.

Le Crotoy, 1423–1424

Sometime in June 1423, around the feast of St John the Baptist on 24 June, Sir Ralph Bouteiller set siege to Le Crotoy by sea and land. We are told that he set about his task with great diligence and placed his men well. The French had anticipated that the English would see the capture of Le Crotoy as a priority and the captain of the town Jacques d'Harcourt had stocked the town with provisions and artillery. Bedford had commissioned the forging of three new cannon for use at the siege and had drawn 1,500 men from garrisons throughout Normandy to serve with Sir Ralph. We know little of the siege, but after four months a treaty was agreed for the surrender of the town.

Rather unusually, the terms of the treaty required that on 1, 2 and 3 March 1424 the Duke of Bedford as Regent of France, or his representative, would present himself between the towns of Rue and Le Crotoy between daybreak and 3.00pm for personal combat against Jacques d'Harcourt or his representative. If Bedford won the day the town would surrender at 3.00pm on 3 March. The garrison, except, as was now a common term in treaties of surrender, those who had participated in the assassination of John the Fearless, Duke of Burgundy, would be allowed to depart with all their possessions. They could take personal arms and equipment but they were required to leave behind gunpowder, artillery, crossbows and crossbow bolts. The treaty included an inventory of nine small cannon, twenty-three crossbows and nine chests of crossbow bolts. Inhabitants who wished to remain could do so if they swore allegiance to the regent. D'Harcourt was permitted to have a ship to leave the port, but other ships were to be left to the English. There was to be an exchange of prisoners.

During the unusually long period between the signing of the treaty and the surrender of Le Crotoy the English undertook not to attempt to take the town and the garrison would not engage in warlike acts, although d'Harcourt was free to make war elsewhere in France. The inhabitants were also permitted to come and go freely to trade in Rue, Abbeville and St-Valery-sur-Somme. As a reciprocal arrangement the English could go into the town to trade. Any French shipping or men-at-arms who arrived would be turned away and d'Harcourt was prohibited from either improving or demolishing the town fortifications or the castle. Also during this period d'Harcourt, his family and his men could leave the town. D'Harcourt took advantage of this provision, selling his goods in Abbeville and leaving for Mont-St-Michel, sending his family to Montreuil-Bellay near Saumur.

At the end of February Bedford moved to Abbeville in preparation for the surrender of Le Crotoy. When it became apparent that the French were not coming in force, he sent Sir Ralph Bouteiller to fulfil his side of the bargain on 1, 2 and 3 March. The town duly surrendered on 3 March 1424.

Cravant, 1423

If all had gone to plan de la Pole would have been settling down to the planned siege of Mont-St-Michel during August 1423 with men drawn from the garrisons of Caen and towns and fortresses in the Cotentin peninsula, but events were to take a hand and the siege of Mont-St-Michel would have to wait.

At the beginning of July 1423 Dauphinist forces, under the command of the Earl of Buchan, Constable of France, had laid siege to the Burgundian town of Cravant 150km to the south-east of Paris. An Anglo-Burgundian army some 4,000 strong assembled at Auxerre 15km to the north-west and on 31 July relieved the town and defeated the besieging force, inflicting heavy casualties on the largely Scottish besieging force. The Earl of Buchan was wounded in one eye and taken prisoner, along with John Stewart, Constable of the Scottish army in France and some 400 other men in the besieging force.

De la Pole decided that, rather than continue with his mission, there was an opportunity to exploit the French defeat and launch a raid into Anjou. He got as far as Angers but, returning with his booty, he was lured into a trap and heavily defeated at La Bossinière by the Count of Aumale. De la Pole paid the price for his ill-judged venture, being taken prisoner. With many of de la Pole's men killed and captured, the garrisons in Normandy which had provided men for his force were dangerously exposed. Aumale initially tried to press home this advantage by raiding St-Lô and laying siege to Avranches, but he withdrew on the advance of an English relieving force.

Compiègne, Gaillon and Ivry-la-Bataille, 1424

In the spring of 1424 both sides geared up for the coming campaigning season. The dauphin's avowed objective was to open up the way to Reims, the traditional place for the coronation of French kings. Bedford's objective was to consolidate the conquest by eliminating remaining Dauphinist strongholds on the borders of Normandy and pushing the frontier south into the counties of Anjou, Maine and Dreux.

The Duke of Bedford's campaign involved a considerable number of sieges, many of which have left little trace in the records. In late 1423 or early 1424 Compiègne had been taken by escalade by a force of 300 French troops who had been able to approach the town unseen due to the negligence of the night-watch. The town, 70km north-east of Paris in the heart of Anglo-Burgundian France, could not be left in French hands. Sometime towards the beginning of 1424, probably in early February, before the main campaigning season started, Bedford moved to Montdidier, 35km to the north, and assembled an Anglo-Burgundian force to besiege and retake Compiègne. After three weeks, during which there were some skirmishes between the besiegers and the garrison, it became clear to the garrison that there was no prospect of relief. Even though the town had been well provisioned, there seemed little to be gained by continuing to resist. The captain, Guillaume Remon, was absent from the town but had been captured by Sir John Fastolf. Bedford had Remon brought forward in sight of the garrison on a cart with a noose around his neck. This was the final straw and the garrison, loyal to their captain, agreed to surrender if relief did not come within three weeks.

The terms of surrender were generous, perhaps in recognition of the speed of the capitulation. The garrison surrendered the town on 15 March 1424 and left with their arms and equipment. They promptly moved 110km west into Normandy to seize the castle of Gaillon. Lord Scales was despatched to retake the fortress. After two months, the efforts of 800 men and the effects of a sustained bombardment the castle surrendered. This time Bedford was in a less generous frame of mind: no mercy was shown to the garrison and the castle was demolished.

While Scales tackled Gaillon the Earl of Suffolk was sent to retake another castle which had fallen to the French after a surprise attack the previous August. Ivry, now known as Ivry-la-Bataille, is in the valley of the Eure 60km west of Paris. The castle stands on high ground overlooking the valley. The siege was set during June. The captain, Géraud de la Pallière, who had been in command of the successful assault the year before, ran out of victuals and, seeing no sign of help coming, agreed to surrender on Assumption Day, 15 August 1424. There was the usual formula of a cessation of hostilities if no relief came but on this occasion the dauphin felt sufficiently confident to act.

The French assembled a large army at Tours and marched to the relief of Ivry. The army was nominally led by the fifteen-year-old Duke of Alençon, but in reality command was in the hands of the experienced Count of Aumale, accompanied by the Earls of Buchan and Douglas. There were said to be some 14,000 men in the army, including 10,000 Scots and 2,000 heavy Milanese cavalry, thus the French contribution was relatively small. This formidable force did not, however, proceed to Ivry but was arrayed for battle at Verneuil some 40km to the south-west. Bedford arrived at Ivry to take the surrender on the due date. He had perhaps 1,800 men-at-arms and 8,000 archers at his disposal. The two armies met in battle at Verneuil on 17 August. The dauphin's army was waiting for Bedford, having chosen flat ground which favoured their Milanese heavy cavalry intended to destroy the English. Apart from the Milanese both armies were arrayed on foot. The initial Milanese charge drove through the English archers, but the cavalry did not press home their advantage and instead set about pillaging the baggage train. The English rallied, with the archers participating in the general mêlée. The French and Scots were driven back and slaughtered. The result was what has been called a second Agincourt. In total, 7,262 Scottish and French troops are said to have been killed while Bedford claimed to have lost only a handful of men. Among the dead were the Count of Aumale and the Earls of Buchan and Douglas. The young Duke of Alençon was taken prisoner. The Scottish army had been destroyed. It would not be replaced.

Guise, 1424–1425

The defeat at Verneuil was a severe blow to Armagnac hopes and the dauphin abandoned his plans to march to Reims for his coronation. Bedford and his captains took the initiative and seized a number of border strongholds. Étienne de Vignolles, known as La Hire, recognizing the deteriorating military situation for the Armagnacs, abandoned a number of others in the spring of 1424. At the same time 1,600 English reinforcements disembarked at Calais. Some were sent to the Duke of Bedford in Paris while others went to join Sir Thomas Rempston who was with the Burgundian John of Luxembourg in the County of Guise. Guise, 150km north-west of Paris, was the last Armagnac stronghold in the north.

Earlier in the year John of Luxembourg had negotiated with Poton de Xaintrailles to leave Guise with his men under safe-conduct to go beyond the Loire and only to return if they were in the company of the dauphin. Luxembourg and Rempston then set about the siege with a mixed force of English, Burgundian and Picard troops. The remaining garrison had prepared themselves well and had adopted the time-honoured technique of burning the suburbs to deny cover to the besiegers, leaving, we are told, just two of many fine houses standing. Nevertheless, siege engines and artillery were positioned to bring fire to bear on the gates and the walls. The governor of the town sent letters to the Dukes of Bar and Lorraine and the Count of Bar asking for assistance, but in vain. The besiegers and besieged settled in for a siege which was to last five months. By mid-September it was clear to the governor that help was not going to be forthcoming and he decided to treat for the surrender of the town.

As in the case of Le Crotoy the year before, an unusually long period was agreed to enable the dauphin to send relief with the surrender date being set as 1 March 1425. The terms of the treaty, signed on 18 September 1424, provided for a truce until the surrender date, in effect bringing the siege to an immediate end. Luxembourg and Rempston both departed. Rempston took his men to join Bedford in Paris. The treaty was generous, giving the garrison a month from the surrender date to depart with all their possessions and weapons and to go to several named towns in the region to collect possessions and money. There were the usual exemptions from safe-conduct for those who had played a role in the assassination of John the Fearless. Also there were terms frequently found in such treaties: artillery was to be left *in situ* and fortifications were to be neither improved nor demolished. For reasons that are unknown the town surrendered early on 26 February 1425; perhaps the chance of relief was so remote that the governor tired of waiting.

We can only speculate why such long periods were allowed between treaty and surrender at Le Crotoy and Guise. They seem too remote to have acted as realistic bait for the dauphin to be drawn into battle. Perhaps the fact that the towns were remote and had been neutralized by the treaties was sufficient and there was no urgency to take possession of them.

Mont-St-Michel, 1424–1425

Despite these successes there remained a thorn in the side of the English occupation: the island fortress of Mont-St-Michel. Its strength is still evident today with many of the fortifications remaining. The abbey church stood 75m above sea-level on a granite outcrop about 800m wide. Access was only possible over a causeway at low tide and the causeway ran through quicksands. Its natural defensive qualities were enhanced by the granite walls of the abbey, a fourteenth-century barbican, recently constructed ramparts at the foot of the mount and a water cistern cut out of the rock.

Mont-St-Michel was not only a symbol of resistance to the English occupation but also a base for raids by the garrison. In early 1423, presumably to give some control over access to Mont-St-Michel by sea and as a precursor to the planned siege, the English had started to fortify Tombelaine, a priory on a rocky island 3km north of Mont-St-Michel and lying between it and the Norman coast in the estuary of the Cuesnon. Tombelaine had a garrison of thirty men-at-arms and ninety archers. As we have seen, if all had gone to plan Sir John de la Pole would have begun to besiege Mont-St-Michel in July of that year, but his ill-judged and disastrous adventure in Anjou had put paid to all that.

In early 1424 Thomas Burgh, the English captain of Avranches, hatched a plot to take the fortress by subterfuge. With the authority of the Duke of Bedford he paid a considerable sum to a Norman squire in the garrison, Henry Meudrac, to deliver Mont-St-Michel to the English.

Either Meudrac betrayed Burgh or he failed. In either event the attempt came to nothing and on 26 August 1424 Nicholas Burdet was charged to undertake a new siege. Bertrand Entwhistle, Admiral of Normandy, was entrusted with a sea blockade. Burdet began in September by building a wooden fortress at Ardevon, 4km inland from Mont-St-Michel. Burdet had at his disposal 160 men from his own company and a further 360 men drawn from garrisons throughout Normandy. Entwhistle had a number of ships and sailors for the blockade and had been allocated 108 soldiers to serve on board. Entwhistle's naval blockade was discontinued in March 1425, but started again in early April under the command of Laurence Holden, the captain of Tombelaine, with twenty-five ships and 424 men.

The siege on land was conducted from Ardevon with frequent sorties by the garrison of Mont-St-Michel and skirmishes with the besiegers. On 12 May 1425, however, a raid led by Jehan de la Haye, captain of an Armagnac garrison 45km away, seems to have caught the English between the coast and Ardevon. The ensuing combat resulted in the capture of Burdet and the death of a number of the English. On 21 May the Earl of Suffolk took command of the siege, but operations were now scaled down and he had only 240 men conducting the siege. The following month the siege was lifted but 210 and 120 men were left to garrison Ardevon and Tombelaine respectively. The sea blockade was finally abandoned with the siege in June 1425.

Pontorson, 1427

The next two years were marked by dissent within the Anglo-Burgundian camp, largely brought about by rash and ill-judged actions by the Duke of Gloucester. In particular his marriage to Philip of Burgundy's cousin Jacqueline of Bavaria had enraged Burgundy, who had designs on her lands. There were also troubles back in England due to a quarrel between Gloucester and his uncle Henry Beaufort, Bishop of Winchester. Only Bedford could mediate and he returned to England for fifteen months, thus diverting his attention from the conduct of the war. In April 1423 Bedford had achieved a major coup with the Treaty of Amiens securing a triple alliance between England, Burgundy and Brittany. In October 1425, however, the Duke of Brittany, always driven by self-interest, changed sides and with the Treaty of Saumur passed over to the French side.

England formally declared war on Brittany in January 1426, and Sir Thomas Rempston, fresh from his success at Guise, led a raid into Brittany reaching as far as Rennes before withdrawing to the border fortress of St-James-de-Beuvron, now known simply as St-James. The Bretons under

Arthur de Richemont attempted to take St-James-de-Beuvron but withdrew after an unsuccessful siege of two weeks. However, in January 1427 they took the stronghold of Pontorson 14km to the west. This could not be allowed to remain in Breton hands and the Earl of Warwick began a siege of the town on 27 February 1427 with 600 men-at-arms and 1,800 archers, including 300 recruited rapidly from the Channel Islands, to retake it. In due course the garrison sued for terms and agreed to surrender the town on 8 May 1427 if help were not forthcoming. Richemont assembled an army at Angers, which seems to have caused consternation among the English to the extent that a procession was ordered in Paris to pray to God for an English victory. In the event Richemont did not appear and the town duly surrendered on 8 May.

Montargis, 1427

The capture of Pontorson potentially opened the way for an invasion of Brittany. It was time for the Duke of Brittany to change sides again in the face of this threat and in early September he swore allegiance to Henry VI and accepted the terms of the Treaty of Troyes. However, almost coincident with this diplomatic triumph came two serious English setbacks. The first of these was at Montargis, 90km south of Paris, which had been besieged by the Earls of Warwick and Suffolk for more than two months since July with an army said by one contemporary to be 6,000 strong. The inhabitants of Montargis and the garrison were in sore need of resupply, but Warwick and Suffolk had imposed an effective blockade with field fortifications consisting of deep ditches and wooden palisades which surrounded the town.

The besieging army was split into two divisions separated by the river: one under the command of the Earl of Suffolk and the other led by his brother Sir John de la Pole. Warwick had been sent by Bedford to find reinforcements at St-Mathurin-de-Larchant, now known as Larchant, 30km to the north. Attempts to bring the siege to a conclusion were hampered by deficiencies in artillery since many cannon had been broken by use in sieges in the campaigns into Maine and Anjou, and others had been deployed to different places.

The Constable of France, Arthur de Richemont, resolved to relieve the town, gathering a force which was commanded by La Hire and the Bastard of Orléans. In a remarkable surprise attack in full daylight, said by a contemporary to be due to negligence on the part of the guards, the French burst through the English fortifications on horseback and on foot, breaking into the encampment of Sir John de la Pole. Sir John fled across the river on horseback but some 2,000 of the besiegers were said to have been killed or taken prisoner. Among the dead were many who crowded onto a bridge which collapsed under their weight. Seeing the success of the attack, the townspeople and garrison sallied out of the town to join the fight from the rear. On hearing of the attack, Warwick hurried back to rally the English. The French had now withdrawn into the town. Warwick offered battle, but the French were having none of it. With a much rein-forced French presence there was little prospect of bringing the siege to a successful conclusion. The siege was raised and the English departed, leaving all their cannon behind. Montargis held an annual celebration of the relief of the town up until the French Revolution.

La Gravelle, 1427

On the same day as the English defeat at Montargis, some 250km to the west at Ambrières-les-Vallées, a French captain called Ambroise de Loré with between 140 and 160 men ambushed and defeated a stronger English force and captured Henry Blanche, the nephew of Sir John Fastolf, the governor of Anjou and Maine. The result of these two defeats had an impact 45km to the south-west at the castle of La Gravelle. The castle had been besieged for some time by Fastolf's men. The garrison had come to terms to surrender on a set date if relief were not forthcoming. This very routine situation was overturned by a most unusual event: the garrison, hearing of the Armagnac successes at Montargis and Ambrières-les-Vallées, went back on their word and refused to give up the castle. This proved to be a very unfortunate decision for the hostages who had been given up to guarantee the treaty since Bedford ordered their execution. The repercussions of the defeat at Ambrières and the events at La Gravelle led to Sir John Fastolf losing his job.

Orléans, 1428–1429

Despite these setbacks, the English fixed their eyes on a great prize: Orléans. If the English could take the city it would enable them to expand their conquest of Dauphinist France to the south. With a population of 30,000, second only to Paris among French cities, it could not remain in Dauphinist hands if the English were to continue with their siege cam-paign and extend the reach of the conquest.

The Earl of Salisbury arrived before Orléans on 12 October 1428. His army was initially some 4,300 strong, made up of troops drawn from garrisons and some 444 men-at-arms and 2,250 archers who had crossed from England in July. By the time he reached Orléans, however, his army

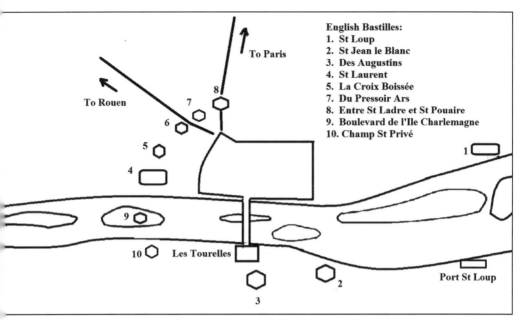

English Bastilles:
1. St Loup
2. St Jean le Blanc
3. Des Augustins
4. St Laurent
5. La Croix Boissée
7. Du Pressoir Ars
8. Entre St Ladre et St Pouaire
9. Boulevard de l'Ile Charlemagne
10. Champ St Privé

To Paris

To Rouen

Les Tourelles

Port St Loup

Orléans, 1428–1429.

would probably have diminished to about 3,500 with men left behind to garrison places taken on the way south. Salisbury brought with him seven large bombards firing stones of 46, 41 and 36cm in diameter for attacking the town and sixty-four much smaller cannon which fired balls of about 1kg and were for anti-personnel use. Among the army were what one chronicler described as 'false French' in allegiance to Henry VI. To defend the city there was a trained garrison initially of only around 200 men, but many among the population would have borne arms. It was the most populous town to be besieged by the English during the war. The town stood on the right bank of the river. It had thirty towers and five gates, and a bridge over the Loire strongly fortified by a fortress known as Les Tourelles on the left bank. The Dauphinists had had plenty of time to prepare for Salisbury's arrival. Suburbs had been razed to deny both shelter for the besieging army and cover for assaults on the walls, and some gates had been walled up. Among the buildings destroyed were the suburbs on the left bank near Les Tourelles, including the Augustinian church and monastery.

Stocks of food and munitions would also have been increased. The timing for the siege was far from ideal; winter was approaching and the harvest had been taken in. In sum, this was a huge challenge for the besieging army.

With the force available it would have been impossible completely to seal off the town. The English set about constructing a series of bastilles, in effect forts, around the north-west and to the east. To the south great efforts were devoted to taking Les Tourelles. With a large population to feed, however, a complete encirclement would not be essential. A blockade that reduced the flow of supplies could be effective given time. However, the porous nature of the blockade meant that men, including senior officers, came and went throughout the siege and the strength of the garrison may have varied quite considerably from time to time. The siege was also distinguished by frequent skirmishes between defenders, who could easily sally forth from the town, and besiegers.

We are fortunate to have an anonymous contemporary journal, written almost certainly by an inhabitant of the town. This gives us an exceptionally detailed account of the siege. Some of the figures undoubtedly need to be treated with considerable scepticism, but the journal does give a vivid picture of the conduct of this important siege, a pivotal moment in the latter years of the war, the vigorous defence and the ebb and flow of fortunes. On 17 October our witness tells us that besiegers fired 124 gunstones weighing 55kg causing a great deal of damage but killing just one woman. The same week English gunfire destroyed a dozen mills on boats on the river. Fortunately for the town's inhabitants a horse-powered mill remained in use. Around this period there were several skirmishes close to Les Tourelles. On Thursday, 21 October the English began to concentrate on Les Tourelles with an attack on outer fieldworks made of earth and faggots of wood. The professional troops and the men of the town fought hard and the attack was repulsed after four hours of combat. The chronicler reports that there were many fine acts of arms on both sides. The women of Orléans also contributed to the defence, bringing supplies and weapons to the men. Both sides suffered casualties. Our chronicler tells us that 240 English troops were killed, which seems an improbably high figure in comparison to the overall strength of the besieging force.

The next day the English returned to the attack with a mine tunnelled under the fortifications surrounding Les Tourelles. The bridge from the fortress crossed an island in the middle of the river. The French could see the way things were going and as a precaution destroyed one of the spans of the bridge between the island and Les Tourelles and constructed field fortifications on the island. On Saturday, 23 October the effect of the mining led the professional soldiers in the garrison to conclude that Les Tourelles could not be held for much longer. On the Sunday the besiegers, having inflicted serious damage with guns, took Les Tourelles. However, their joy at the success was quickly extinguished. The Earl of Salisbury, along with other senior commanders, climbed up Les Tourelles to get a good view of Orléans. Their vantage point was a room with a barred window which looked directly along the bridge and into the town. Unbeknown to the English, the French had set up a cannon trained directly on the window, with a master-gunner biding his time for the right moment. A gun-stone shot from the cannon broke through the bars of the window and a piece of wood detached from a wooden ledge struck Salisbury, taking away half his jaw and an eye. He died of his wounds eight days later at Meung-sur-Loire. It was claimed among the Dauphinists that Salisbury's death was a result of divine intervention. Two reasons were given for God having intervened: Salisbury's broken promise to the Duke of Orléans, held in England since the battle of Agincourt thirteen years before, that he would not attack his lands while he remained a prisoner, and the destruction of churches and monasteries by the English under his command. Sir Thomas Margrave was struck by a splinter from the same shot and died of his wounds two days later.

The English seemed to be every bit as concerned as the French that the bridge should not be used and destroyed two arches and constructed a rampart of earth and faggots. The same day the Bastard of Orléans and other prominent men in the service of the dauphin arrived with 800 men, including men-at-arms, archers, crossbowmen and Italian infantry. Whether these men remained to reinforce the garrison or were the personal retinue for the Bastard of Orléans is not known.

On 8 November part of the besieging force was withdrawn to Meung-sur-Loire and Jargeau about 20km downstream and upstream respectively. This could have been to relieve some of the pressure on bringing supplies to the siege camps or to enforce the blockade on river traffic. A garrison of some 500 men remained at Les Tourelles and presumably men remained to hold the various bastilles. On their way to Meung-sur-Loire and Jargeau the English burned buildings in the Loire valley. Later in the month the garrison and inhabitants destroyed further religious buildings in the suburbs which so far had been left untouched.

At the beginning of December John Talbot came to Les Tourelles with 300 men and supplies. He set up batteries of guns which fired on the walls and within the town. The chronicler tells us with some surprise that there were, however, no casualties – all the more surprising given that a gun-stone is reported as having fallen on the table of a diner in his house on 5 December. Two days later the English seem to have been gathering for an assault across the bridge in the early hours of the morning under the cover of darkness, but the garrison got wind of the plan and church bells were rung at 3.00am to summon the defenders. If an assault was intended the besiegers thought better of it and withdrew. Later in the month the

French installed three large bombards, capable of firing stones of 55kg, to fire on Les Tourelles.

On Christmas Day there was a mutually agreed truce, but once the day was past the mutual bombardment resumed, with the chronicler claiming that many of the besiegers were either wounded or killed. Before the end of the month yet more buildings in the suburbs were destroyed. On New Year's Eve two Dauphinist knights issued a challenge for two English knights for two jousts with lances. The challenge was accepted and the jousts took place in front of an audience drawn from both sides. One of the Dauphinist knights unhorsed his opponent with the first pass, but neither of the other pair was able to achieve a victory.

On New Year's Day there was a skirmish in the middle of the afternoon. There were casualties and prisoners taken on both sides and the English captured an artillery piece. The French were driven off and, with remarkable objectivity, the author of the journal tells us that the French came off worse. Among the Dauphinist wounded was the fighting Abbot of Cercanceaux.

The next day the English tried to take the ramparts by escalade near the Porte Renard on the western side of the city. However, despite trying to achieve surprise by attacking at two in the morning and in heavy rain, the night watch saw the attack developing and the church bells were sounded. The defenders rushed to the point of attack and the attackers were driven off. The English launched attacks again in the early hours of the following day, 4 January, with the men encouraged by great shouts and the sounding of trumpets near the Porte Renard once more and Les Tourelles to the south. Again, the night watchmen sounded the alarm and the attacks were driven off by a resolute defence which included cannon fire.

The porosity of the blockade and the importance to the inhabitants of resupply are shown in many entries in the journal recording the arrival of livestock and other supplies. The first recorded occasion was on 3 January 1429 when during the morning 950 good fat pigs and 400 sheep arrived via the Port St Loup on the Loire south-east of the town. It seems that they arrived at a time of growing need and were received with great joy as a consequence. The incomplete encirclement also allowed considerable bodies of men to come and go. Two days after the arrival of the livestock Louis de Culant, Admiral of France, passed to the south of Les Tourelles with 200 men and followed the same route as the animals, crossing the Loire near the Port St Loup. The defenders seemed to take encouragement from this visit and the following day sallied forth for an inconclusive skirmish with the besiegers. On 10 January supplies of gunpowder and food sent from Bourges made their way into the city. However, this time it appears that the English attempted to intercept the supplies. In what seems to have been a fierce combat, which included the use of cannon, the English were driven off with men killed and captured and the supplies were delivered successfully to the city.

Throughout the weeks that followed attacks on the defences and sorties by the defenders were almost daily occurrences. On 11 January artillery fire from the town took off the roof of Les Tourelles, killing six of the English garrison. The following day the besiegers launched a further unsuccessful attack near the Porte Renard. On Saturday, 15 January a sortie from the town led by the Bastard of Orléans in person threatened to take by surprise an English detachment from the bastille St Laurent on the right bank to the west of the Porte Renard. However, the approach was detected and the English rallied sufficiently quickly and in enough strength to drive off the French who withdrew into the town through the Porte Renard.

On 16 January Sir John Fastolf arrived with 1,200 men and supplies of food, cannon, gunpowder, bows and other equipment. The chronicler reports that the following day the besiegers fired on the town and that one gun-stone fell into a crowd of a hundred people. We are told that there were no casualties but that one man had a shoe knocked off! As if there were not enough to keep both sides occupied, a challenge was issued on the same day by six French knights to fight six of their opposite numbers. The chronicler claims the French went to the appointed place but that the English failed to respond to the challenge. An English cannon shot from Les Tourelles the next day, however, made its mark, killing a native of Orléans serving as a crossbowman.

On 24 January the Dauphinist captain La Hire arrived in the town with thirty men-at-arms, running the gauntlet of English cannon fire as they entered via the Porte Renard close to the English bastilles. On 26 January the English tried to take advantage of the sun in the eyes of a French skirmishing party. They drove them back towards the walls but in doing so came under fire from guns on the wall, suffering twenty men killed while the French are said to have suffered the death of just one archer. The Porte Renard was the target for a further English attack the next day. Perhaps between 400 and 500 men from the English bastilles launched the attack. The defenders rushed to meet the threat, with some men even descending directly from the ramparts. The result was disarray, with the French initially withdrawing back inside the town. However, the Marshal

St-Sevère brought them into good order and they came out once again to drive the English back.

At some date ambassadors had been sent from the town to ask the dauphin for help. They returned to Orléans on Friday, 28 January and on the Saturday a number of prominent knights, including Poton de Xaintrailles, arrived, having spoken recently with the dauphin. What reassurances, if any, these bodies of men brought we do not know. However, on the same day safe-conducts were issued by both sides to allow Lancelot Delisle, a captain in the besieging force, and La Hire from the town, to hold talks. It seems that the talks outlasted the agreed period of safe-conduct and the French garrison, playing strictly by the rules, opened fire as Delisle returned to the siege lines. His head was taken off by a cannon shot fired from within the town.

The pattern of assaults and skirmishes continued with yet another attempt on the walls on 29 January near the Porte Renard. The fighting seems to have been intense, with men killed, including an English knight, wounded and taken prisoner on both sides. The following day the French came out of the town to try to prevent the English tearing up vines and their support posts for firewood. In the skirmish that followed the English are said to have lost seven men killed and fourteen captured. Among the French losses was a bourgeois, Simon de Beaugener, shot through the throat by an arrow. That same night the Bastard of Orléans left the town with several knights and squires to go to Blois. His exit from the town caused some consternation among the English, who feared that this was the start of an attack on their bastilles.

February brought a continuation of a high level of activity, with the dauphin's supporters seeming to take more of the initiative in the first few days. A sortie by the garrison on 3 February tried to draw out the garrison of the St Laurent bastille. However, the English drew up their men in defensive order and stayed firmly in place, leaving the French to withdraw into the town. Three days later a sortie from the town led by Marshal St-Sevère and La Hire with 200 men surprised thirty men with Lord Scales near the monastery of the Madeleine and killed and captured fourteen of them.

The next week brought more arrivals from elsewhere in France. Messengers from the dauphin arrived on 7 February and the next day saw the arrival of 1,000 men accompanied, among others, by William Stewart, brother of John Stewart and cousin of the Earl of Buchan. During the night a further two detachments joined the garrison: 200 and 120 in the service respectively of Guillaume d'Albret and La Hire. However, moving in and out of the besieged town was not without risk, and on 9 February a party of twenty-five men was intercepted by the English and one of the knights with the party, Bourg de Bar, was captured. However, on the same day Gilbert de la Fayette arrived with 300 men. On 10 February the Bastard of Orléans left the town to go to Blois to meet with the Count of Clermont and John Stewart. He was accompanied by 200 men, perhaps a reflection of his status or possibly of the dangers of running the gauntlet of the siege lines. There are said to have been some 4,000 men gathered at Blois with the objective of intercepting reinforcements and supplies heading for the English army at Orléans. The following day, 11 February, others left Orléans to go to Blois: Guillaume d'Albret, William Stewart, Marshal St-Sévère, Xaintrailles and La Hire, reportedly accompanied by 1,500 men.

On Sunday, 12 February Sir John Fastolf approached Orléans accompanied by the provost of Paris and 1,500 men: English, Picard and Norman. They brought with them around 300 carts loaded with food, military equipment, cannon, bows and sheaves of arrows. However, scouts brought news that the garrison was aware of the convoy and was intent on intercepting it. John Fastolf drew up the carts in a ring, tied carts and horses together, planted sharpened stakes before each archer to disrupt charging cavalry and then arrayed his men in defensive formation, ready for what became known as the Battle of the Herrings. The initial force for the attack was said to be about 1,500 strong, very much the same strength as Fastolf's force. The word went out from the Count of Clermont to the various captains not to assault the English encampment, but to await his arrival with 3,000 or 4,000 men. There was some frustration among the other commanders, in particular La Hire, who felt that by waiting they were simply giving the English time to dig in and reinforce their position. The frustration was increased by the fact that La Hire's company was in sight of the English and could see them going about reinforcing their position. The Constable of the Scottish army, John Stewart, arrived with 400 men and was not inclined to wait to see the English position grow stronger.

In mid-afternoon Stewart sent forward archers and crossbowmen to shoot at the English working outside the park to drive them back inside the ring of carts. Other companies were now arriving to take part in the assault on the English, among them those of the Bastard of Orléans and William Stewart. They brought with them around 400 men. The English noticed that the main body of men was still some way off and advancing slowly. They took the opportunity to come out from their enclosure and fall upon the archers and crossbowmen, who were on foot, killing, we are told, some 400 of the French.

The English pursued the fleeing men. La Hire saw an opportunity to take advantage of the scattered English troops, but with only sixty to eighty men to accompany him he had little chance of defeating the English, although his men are reported to have killed some in Fastolf's force. The French losses included many senior leaders, John and William Stewart and Guillaume d'Albret being among the most notable. The Bastard of Orléans was wounded in the foot by an arrow. He was saved by two of his archers who pulled him from the fight and put him on a horse. The English made no attempt to continue the pursuit and the survivors among the Dauphinists withdrew to Orléans, arriving late in the evening, with La Hire bringing up the rear to protect stragglers from attacks from the men in the English bastilles.

Around this time Joan of Arc comes on to the scene. At Chinon in 1429 she advised that the dauphin should withdraw to the Dauphiné from where he could protect the Lyonnais, the Languedoc and the Auvergne. It was decided that she should meet with the dauphin. She explained to Charles that she had been sent by God to help him and that with the grace of God and by force of arms she would raise the siege of Orléans and take him to Reims to be crowned. She withdrew and Charles consulted his council. Doctors of theology were instructed to interrogate her. They were favourably impressed, but she was taken to Poitiers to be interrogated further. While she was at Poitiers money was raised to pay for men, rations and artillery to try to come to the relief of Orléans. The conclusion of the interrogation was that the dauphin should have confidence in her, and she was armed, given good horses and a standard. A squire and a page were appointed to accompany her.

On 18 February the Count of Clermont left Orléans to go to Chinon to see the dauphin. With him went a number of senior leaders including Louis de Culant, the Archbishop of Reims and the Bishop of Orléans. Some 2,000 combatants are said to have gone with them, much to the consternation of the inhabitants. Attempts were made to pacify them with promises of Clermont returning with men and supplies, and the Bastard of Orléans and Marshal St-Sévère remained. Nevertheless, the inhabitants remained concerned about the much reduced strength of the garrison in the face of their perception that the English strength was growing day by day. The citizens tried another tack: sending Poton de Xaintrailles and a number of representatives of the population to plead with the Duke of Burgundy, who was allied with the English, to ask him to set aside his alliance and raise the siege for the sake of the Duke of Orléans, still a prisoner in England, and for the good of the realm. If this account is true it seems an extraordinary move given the long-standing feud between the houses of Orléans and Burgundy.

On 20 February there was a further inconclusive skirmish, and two days later a curious incident. The Earl of Suffolk, Lord Scales and Sir John Talbot sent a herald with a tray of figs, raisins and dates as a gift for the Bastard of Orléans. Suffolk had asked for some black fur to add to a gown. The request was honoured and a herald was sent to the English lines with the return gift.

On 27 February the Loire was in flood to such an extent that the inhabitants thought the ramparts surrounding the St Laurent bastille and Les Tourelles would be washed away. To their evident disappointment, even with the water up to the cannon emplacements on the ramparts, the English worked day and night and succeeded in keeping the waters back. Despite this distraction the English managed to fire a number of cannon shots causing considerable damage to houses within the walls. In return, the garrison fired on Les Tourelles bringing down a large section of wall.

The new month brought no change to the pattern of frequent skirmishes, either as the English probed the defences of the city or as the French tried to disrupt the besiegers' activities. On 3 March a sortie from the garrison set out on just such a mission with the target a trench that the English had dug to allow them to approach the walls unseen and in cover from gun fire. The French seemed to have had the better of the day, taking nine prisoners and killing five men, including the nephew of the late Earl of Salisbury. A further sortie on the same day attacked one of the English bastilles and captured a cannon and quantities of booty and military equipment. However, the English rallied and the French were driven back to the ditches and walls. This last skirmish of the day left a number of the French dead, wounded or captured.

On 4 March the journal writer laments an English raid by 300 men on two villages to the west of Orléans with the English seizing food stocks and taking workers in the vineyards prisoner. The tit-for-tat artillery exchange also continued, with an unnamed English lord killed by a cannon shot on 5 March and a report of widespread damage within the city due to English cannon fire.

Reinforcements arrived for the English: 40 from England, 200 from Jargeau and others from garrisons in the area. The French were aware of these new men arriving. They remained on the alert and took precautionary measures in case an assault should be forthcoming. We saw earlier the courtesy of the exchange of gifts between the Earl of Suffolk and the Bastard of Orléans, but an incident reported on 10 March shows another side of medieval life: the Bastard of Orléans hanged two French men-at-arms from trees in the suburbs for having broken the terms of a safe-conduct.

The English now started to construct a further bastille, St Loup, about 2km to the east of the city on the right bank and opposite the Port St Loup on the other bank which had been used as a route into the city by resupply parties. On 11 March St Loup was the centre of attention with the English falling on workers in the vineyards outside the walls and taking several prisoners. The tit-for-tat nature of operations can be seen the following day when a sortie from the garrison took six English prisoners; three days later English soldiers from the bastille St Loup, dressed as women collecting wood, again surprised workers outside the walls and took nine or ten more prisoners. It is interesting to note that even with the English bastilles at no great distance from the walls the occupants generally felt safe enough, and the task sufficiently important, to work outside. Since labourers were prepared to work outside the walls it seems reasonable to assume that generally there was an effective system of lookouts and alarms which failed on these occasions.

On 16 March Marshal St-Sevère left the city to deal with family matters, promising the inhabitants that he would return as soon as possible. That such a senior personage could pass so easily in and out of Orléans shows once again the porosity of the siege lines. The same day the English took a cart from St Loup to their bastille at St Laurent on the other side of the city, passing the gates to the north and causing much consternation among the population who feared that this was the prelude to an assault. Our diarist also shows us something of the daily life of the city in reporting the death from natural causes of the Provost of Orléans on 17 March.

It is possible that about this time the English brought larger cannon to Orléans, because on Saturday, 19 March, the eve of Palm Sunday, fire from bombards was reported as surpassing any previous fire, with a great deal of damage done. One gun-stone killed seven people including a pewter worker called Jehan Tonneau. A further five inhabitants were killed outside the town-house of a recently deceased inhabitant, Berthault Mignon.

More than six months had passed since the start of the siege, but even now the English continued to tighten their grip on the city by building more fortifications. On 21 March a substantial force drawn from the garrison and the inhabitants sallied forth to try to disrupt the construction of a new bastille to the north-west called the Boulevard des Douze Pierres.

It seems that the new fortification was not yet complete since the English retired rapidly to the bastille St Laurent, taking everything with them. There was then an ebb and flow of fortunes. The English came out in force and drove the French back towards the walls, but they in turn were driven back by artillery fire from Orléans. There were said to be casualties on both sides, including an English man-at-arms called Robin Heron.

There was a further skirmish the following day when the French once more sallied forth, this time to the north of the city. They were met by an English force which initially drove them back until once again the tide of fortune turned and the French gained the upper hand. One unfortunate Englishman fell into a well and was killed by the pursuing French. About this date Joan of Arc was at Blois and dictated a letter to the King of England which she had delivered to the captains of the English force at Orléans. The letter called upon Henry VI to surrender the keys of all the towns held by the English in France. She claimed to be acting in the name of the King of France and God. If the English did not withdraw peacefully she would come and drive them out by war. The English captains do not seem to have been impressed and mocked all that she had written.

Several days of relative peace followed, although on Maundy Thursday a shot from an English bombard killed three inhabitants. There was a truce on Easter Sunday and it was not until the Friday after Easter, 1 April 1429, that fighting resumed when the French came out to try once again to counter the construction of the Boulevard de Douze Pierres. The two sides seem to be have been well balanced, since nothing ensued other than a stand-off with an exchange of artillery fire resulting in several men wounded on both sides. The French returned the next day with the same objective. This time the English were ready and 400 men emerged from the bastille of St Laurent to counter them, charging into the arrayed French troops led by senior French commanders including La Hire and the Bastard of Orléans. The result was once again inconclusive with casualties on both sides, many inflicted by artillery fire.

On 4 April there was a combat between pages of both sides, with the boys throwing stones and pebbles at one another, an event which seems to have attracted spectators from both sides. The fight resumed the following day, with one of the English page boys killed by a stone and several hurt on both sides. The English, however, seem to have had the better of the day, capturing the banner of the French boys.

There are frequent references throughout the journal to the arrival of supplies for the inhabitants and the garrison of Orléans. There were three successful deliveries of livestock in January, with a further large consignment of 250 head of cattle intercepted by the English. There was one reported delivery in February, but in March the pace was picking up, with five successful deliveries, including one of gunpowder, and a successful interception of supplies destined for the besiegers. In early April the flow of supplies into the city was impressive with six convoys breaking through the lines, and a barge destined for the English at St Loup intercepted, in the first nine days of the month. These brought a variety of supplies, including butter and cheese, but also 64 head of cattle and 135 pigs. On 13 April money was also brought into the city to pay the garrison. The English were clearly both aware of and concerned by these deliveries, and in a bid to cut off supplies built a further bastille to the north of the city, between St Ladre and St Pouair, astride the road running south into the city from Paris. This does not seem, however, to have stemmed the flow, with further supplies breaking through the cordon on 16 April. Meanwhile, skirmishing continued, with three English troops killed and fifteen taken prisoner near Les Tourelles on the same day.

On 17 April Poton de Xaintrailles returned to the city after treating with the Duke of Burgundy. The proposition to Burgundy was aimed at dividing the Burgundians and the English. If the siege were raised Orléans would surrender to the Duke of Burgundy and he could appoint the town's governors. The city revenues would be divided between King Henry VI and Charles of Orléans, still a prisoner in England, but the Duke of Burgundy would have effective control of the town. We do not know Burgundy's reaction but he clearly consulted the Duke of Bedford. The regent would have none of it, ruling that the agreement would be in breach of the Treaty of Troyes which provided for conquests to pass to the king. Denied his prize, Burgundy withdrew his men, thus weakening the besieging force.

The next day an attack by the French on the English in the early hours of the morning initially brought reward for the attackers with the capture of a banner and much booty taken in the form of silver, furs, bows, arrows and other military equipment. However, the English rallied and, despite a banner-bearer being killed by a cannon shot, drove the attackers back with numerous men among the French killed and wounded.

Despite the new bastille intended to tighten the besiegers' grip on the town, supplies and men continued to arrive in Orléans throughout the remainder of April, with gunpowder being brought in on horseback on 21 and 23 April and reinforcements arriving on 24, 25 and 28 April. On this latter day there was a major skirmish, with the English launching an attack and the garrison and citizens coming out to try to drive them back from the walls. The oft-repeated pattern was seen: the English were initially driven back with men killed and wounded, some falling into the ditches surrounding their bastilles, and then the French withdrew with losses inflicted by cannon fire and archers.

The next day news arrived that the dauphin had sent Joan of Arc with food supplies, gunpowder, cannon and other equipment with the intention of raising the siege. To divert the attention of the English from the arrival of the convoy the garrison sallied out in large numbers towards St Loup, which stood on the line of march of the reinforcements. Both sides suffered casualties, but on this occasion the French seem to have got the better of things, entering the bastille and capturing an English banner. Joan stopped initially at the village of Chécy, about 9km east of Orléans and 7km beyond the bastille of St Loup. She was met with great joy by the Bastard of Orléans and other leaders. It was decided that, to avoid too much disturbance among the population when the maid arrived, Joan should enter the city at night. She did so at eight in the evening, mounted on a white horse, wearing armour with her banner carried before her.

How much the subsequent events can be directly attributed to Joan is arguable, but there can be little doubt that her arrival gave the morale of the garrison a great boost. Nor can there be any doubt that from now on the tide was running with the French.

On 30 April there was another of the many indecisive skirmishes between the garrison and the besiegers, but from now on the combats had more purpose and inexorably went in favour of the French. That night Joan sent two heralds to the English camp demanding that they return a herald held ever since she had sent letters to the English from Blois. She threatened that if all the heralds were not returned, English prisoners held in Orléans and elsewhere would be put to death. They sent back the heralds but with a contemptuous message that they would burn her when they caught her and that she would do better to return to tending cows. She went forward the same night onto the bridge that led to Les Tourelles to speak to Sir William Glasdale, who commanded the garrison. She told Glasdale that if he surrendered he and his men would be granted their lives. The response was again contemptuous and to the same effect: she was nothing but a milkmaid and they would burn her if they caught her. The same scene was repeated when she approached the English at another point.

On 2 May Joan rode out of the city to reconnoitre the English fortifications, accompanied, it is said, by a great crowd of citizens. The lifting of the siege began in earnest on 4 May. Joan and the Bastard of Orléans led an attack with around 1,500 men on the bastille of St Loup. The bastille was well fortified and defended valiantly, but in the end it fell to the French with 114 of the English said to have been killed and the remaining forty of the garrison taken prisoner. The bastille was demolished and burned to the ground. The English tried to bring support to the bastille of St Loup, with men coming out from the bastille of St Pouair to the north of the city. The alarm was sounded and 600 men came out of the city to counter the attempted relief. Not only were the English driven back, but after a stubborn resistance the St Loup bastille also fell to the French.

Ascension Day, 5 May, was ostensibly a day of truce. A council of war among the French concluded that their next objective should be Les Tourelles. This would be a tough nut to crack. The fortifications were strong and the garrison composed of seasoned troops. However, the fall of the bastille of St Loup had opened the way for an attack and it was a logical next step for the French to take it. The French, led by Joan, the Bastard of Orléans, Marshal St-Sevère and La Hire, with, it is said, 4,000 men, left the town and crossed the river near St Loup. From there they turned west along the river and took the bastille of St Jean le Blanc which stood between them and Les Tourelles. The English sallied forth from Les Tourelles in great numbers but were driven back. Next to fall to the French was the bastille of the Augustinians, the last of the fortified places between the French and Les Tourelles, resulting in the death of men in the English garrison and the liberation of French prisoners. That night the French turned besiegers and settled down in front of Les Tourelles and the associated ramparts. Throughout the night inhabitants of Orléans brought bread, other food and wine to the French soldiers.

The next day the French assaulted the ramparts before Les Tourelles. As was to be expected, the fighting was fierce. The French tried to capture the place by escalade in several places, but were driven back with men falling from ladders as they faced cannon fire, the shooting of archers and hand-to-hand combat with axes, lances, lead mallets and bare hands. The French suffered numerous casualties with men killed and wounded. Joan was also wounded, with an arrow passing cleanly between her shoulder and throat without the arrowhead lodging in her body. The Bastard of Orléans and other senior commanders were of the opinion that it would be better to call off the attack and return the next morning.

Joan persuaded them to continue with the attack and they drove the English back from the ramparts towards Les Tourelles. The drawbridge broke under the press of men, with many Englishmen drowning under the weight of their armour. Among them was the captain of the garrison, Sir William Glasdale. Les Tourelles fell to the French, and with it and its control of the bridge over the Loire went any English hope of continuing the siege. The next day, 8 May 1429, the English lifted the siege and departed from Orléans.

It would perhaps be too much to claim that the English withdrawal from the siege of Orléans marked a turning point in French fortunes. There were still defeats and disappointments to come, but with the benefit of hindsight it certainly seems a pivotal point when high morale and belief started to return to those French loyal to the dauphin. Of course, Joan of Arc played her part and the contemporary writer Christine de Pisan recognized the turning point in French fortunes with the coming of Joan: 'Who has yet seen something occur, So far beyond what they expected? The whole of France should now ensure, the story be well recollected, that France (which as I said above) was near destroyed might rise again.' Writing to King Henry VI after the failure to take Orléans, the Duke of Bedford also seems to have recognized the significance: 'And alle thing there prospered for you til the time of the Siege of Orléans, taken in hand God knoweth by what Advis.' Unfortunately the letter is undated so we do not know if this reflected his judgement in the immediate aftermath or later.

Chapter 8

From Orléans to the
Truce of Tours, 1429–1444

Jargeau, 1429

At the end of the siege of Orléans Joan of Arc tried to persuade the dauphin to march to Reims to be crowned king. Charles was not convinced. A march 240km north-east into the heart of Anglo-Burgundian territory would be a risky enterprise despite the success at Orléans. It made more sense to exploit the success along the valley of the Loire. The English held Meung-sur-Loire and Beaugency-sur-Loire, respectively 15km and 20km downstream from Orléans, and Jargeau 20km upstream. Taking these places would relieve Orléans of further pressure. The first objective was Jargeau. It took around a month to gather and supply the necessary men, but on 11 June the twenty-year-old Duke of Alençon, accompanied by La Hire and Joan of Arc, set the siege of the town and castle. The town was held by the Earl of Suffolk with a garrison variously estimated as being between 300 and 700 men.

The French quickly took the suburbs and set up their artillery which, the following day, brought down the largest tower. Suffolk offered to surrender in fifteen days if relief did not arrive. It is likely he was aware that Fastolf was on his way from Paris with an army, and in this case he could hope for relief. Most unusually, and contrary to the code of chivalry, the offer was refused, perhaps at the instigation of Joan of Arc rather than the professional captains who would have been only too aware how the precedent set could turn to their disadvantage at another time. The French launched an assault and Suffolk once more offered to surrender. This time the request was simply ignored. The result was the death of several hundred of the English garrison. Among the dead was one of Suffolk's brothers. Suffolk himself and another of his brothers, Sir John de la Pole, were captured.

Beaugency-sur-Loire, 1429

The Armagnacs now moved downstream to Beaugency, leaving the fortress of Meung-sur-Loire alone where Sir John Talbot and Lord Scales

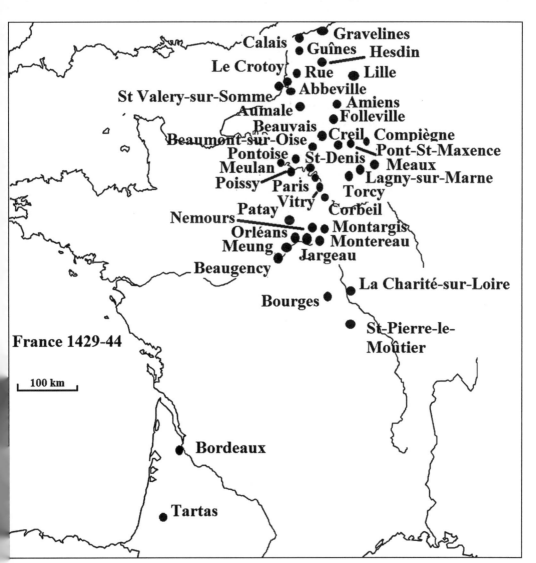

France, 1429–1444.

were headquartered. They besieged Beaugency on 15 June. On 16 June Arthur de Richemont arrived with 1,200 men. He was still subject to a banishment order issued by the dauphin two years before. His arrival was welcome because of the men he brought but also represented a potential problem since he was in breach of his banishment. Pragmatism won the day, possibly since scouts had brought the news that there was an English army of 4,000 men nearby at Meung-sur-Loire, and Richemont's reinforcements joined the besiegers. This information does not seem to have been available to the captain of Beaugency, Matthew Gough, who decided that the arrival of Richemont's men meant that resistance would be hopeless. He offered to surrender on 18 June, only three days after the start of the siege, providing that he could evacuate his men under safe-conduct. In return for this guarantee his men would not engage in combat for ten days.

Thus Gough's men could not join the gathering English army. The force which had been seen by scouts near Meung-sur-Loire started to withdraw towards Paris. The army comprised the men from Meung-sur-Loire under Talbot's command, the remnants of the Orléans siege army, and men under the command of Fastolf sent from Paris by the Duke of Bedford. Fastolf, a cautious commander, was in nominal command and rejected Talbot's plea to go to the relief of Beaugency. Once news arrived that Beaugency had already surrendered, Talbot reluctantly accepted Fastolf's plan for a managed retreat. On the day of the surrender the French moved quickly following Gough's evacuation and caught the English at Patay 30km north of Beaugency. Fastolf had had news of their approach and had started to take up a defensive position. However, the English were caught by surprise before their defensive preparations were complete and they were cut to pieces, with the archers unable to bring their usual devastating shooting to bear. More than 2,000 men were killed in the English army, and most seriously all of the senior English commanders except Fastolf were captured. The fall of Orléans had been a setback, but the defeat at Patay was a disaster. With the destruction of a good-sized English army and the capture of many senior captains, the possibility of the dauphin heading for Reims for his coronation was now on the cards. Within a month he had entered Reims and been crowned Charles VII.

Charles VII's Coronation Campaign

The coronation of Charles VII was used to try to detach the Duke of Burgundy from the English. The Duke of Bedford was well aware both of the impact of Joan of Arc on Armagnac fortunes and of the risk of Burgundy changing sides, and he went to some lengths to court Burgundy with a ceremony in Paris and a large payment from the revenues of Normandy to raise more troops in his territories. He also took practical measures to strengthen his position, including consolidation of some garrisons and raising troops in Normandy. The walls of Paris were strengthened, ditches cleared of rubbish, and artillery positioned.

Several important towns opened their gates to Charles VII, forming a semi-circle around the east of Paris. Bedford recognized the threat to Paris and returned to the city accompanied by Cardinal Beaufort bringing 500 men-at-arms and 2,500 archers. He then took his men out of the city and manoeuvred to keep himself between Paris and the Armagnac forces. Charles VII was initially reluctant to attack Paris, preferring to continue to work on bringing Burgundy across to his allegiance. The result was a four-month truce between the Burgundians and the Armagnacs which took effect at the end of July and covered much of the territory in Burgundian hands but excluded towns on the Seine including Paris. Meanwhile the Armagnacs had invested the Norman town of Évreux 90km northwest of Paris. The town had agreed to surrender on 27 August if not relieved. Bedford left Paris and arrived to save the town on the day due for surrender.

At the end of August the Duke of Alençon with Joan of Arc took St Denis, now part of Paris but in the fifteenth century about 10km north of the capital, and raided up to the walls. Bedford launched an appeal to raise an army to counter this new threat. Before the army could be mustered, however, Joan and Alençon attacked Paris on 8 September, although without the support of the king. The hope was that the population would rise in support of the Armagnacs. This hope proved forlorn, and the attack was driven back. Joan was wounded in the leg by a crossbow bolt and her standard bearer was also shot and killed by a crossbowman. The attackers, who had lost perhaps 500 dead or mortally wounded, withdrew. More

Normandy, 1429–1444.

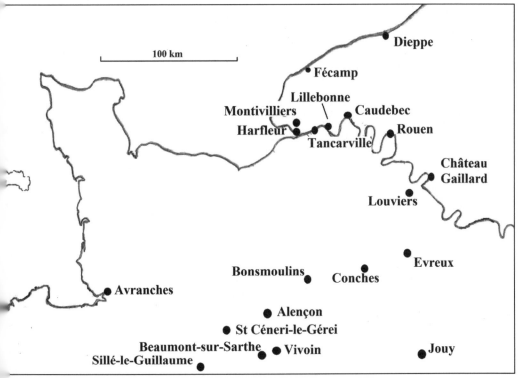

importantly, the first crack had appeared in the myth of Joan's invincibility. The withdrawal from Paris marked the end of Charles VII's post-Orléans campaign and on 21 September he disbanded his army. That was not the end of campaigning for the year, however, and in late November 1429 the Armagnacs laid siege to La Charité-sur-Loire.

La Charité-sur-Loire, 1429

La Charité-sur-Loire lies 50km east of Charles' provisional capital of Bourges. It was the principal stronghold of Perrinet Gressart, a mercenary captain in the pay of both Bedford and Burgundy, who had held the town for almost six years. Gressart was uncomfortably close to Bourges and had been a source of many problems for the Armagnacs throughout his occupation of the town. Furthermore, La Charité controlled an important bridge over the Loire. If it could be taken it would remove a significant problem and give the Armagnacs control of this major river crossing.

The task of taking La Charité was given to Charles d'Albret and Joan. They initially took by assault another Gressart town, St-Pierre-le-Moûtier, 45km to the south. The timing was far from ideal, with all the problems of a siege in mid-winter of bad weather and shortage of provisions. In addition, they were short of gunpowder, crossbows and other military equipment which had to be provided by neighbouring Armagnac towns. La Charité had a large abbey and was surrounded by strong walls. It had proved impregnable in the past but nevertheless, with the evident lack of resources for a long siege, it is not surprising that an attempt was made to take the town by assault. The assault failed and d'Albret and Joan settled down for a siege using what munitions they had to bombard the town. However, with a lack of money and food as well as military supplies, the siege could only be maintained for less than a month and before Christmas the siege was raised. As they departed they left behind their heavy cannon, almost certainly because of the difficulty of moving them. As evidence of this, one of the bombards, named 'the Shepherdess' after Joan and used at Orléans and the siege of Jargeau, had to be dismantled and split into two loads, one requiring seven horses and the other twenty-nine, for transport as a gift to the Duke of Burgundy. Once again Joan had failed.

Compiègne, 1430

The gravity of the situation in France had now become apparent in England and subsidies, the first granted for seven years, had been authorized by parliament to be levied in January and December 1430. In January 3,199 men crossed the channel commanded by the Bastard of

Clarence. In February a further 4,792 soldiers were raised to go to France with Henry VI.

Under the terms of the truce between Burgundy and Charles VII Compiègne should have passed into Burgundian hands. The inhabitants, however, had refused to surrender to Burgundy, and thus the town was an early and obvious objective for the Burgundians and the newly rejuvenated English cause after the end of the truce. On 20 May 1430 a combined Anglo-Burgundian force started to besiege the town, which stood on the north bank of the river. It was surrounded by walls and towers, which in turn were protected by a moat filled with water drawn from the Oise. There was a single bridge, lined with houses, which spanned the river. The town, whose captain was Guillaume de Flavy, had anticipated such an eventuality: the defences had been strengthened and supplies of food and military stores stocked.

The besiegers – the Burgundians led by the Duke and John of Luxembourg and the English by the Earls of Huntingdon and Arundel – started to construct bastilles and to bombard the town as they had done at Orléans. In the early hours of 23 May Joan managed to slip through the siege lines with 200 Piedmontese mercenaries. She came without the blessing of the king, acting on her own initiative out of frustration at having been side-lined. Towards evening on the same day she sallied forth with her men, crossing the bridge to take on the besiegers. They succeeded in clearing the bridge and the access on the far bank and attacked Luxembourg's men. The fighting ebbed and flowed, and twice they drove the Burgundians back but were themselves repulsed each time. On the third attempt they were intercepted by English troops and in the ensuing fighting Joan was captured by Luxembourg's men. Accounts of her capture vary: perhaps the gates had been closed when Joan's men tried to withdraw or perhaps it was simply the press of men on the bridge which prevented them gaining the safety of the town. In any event it was the beginning of the end for Joan. She would eventually be sold to the English and taken to Rouen where, after interrogation and trial, she would be burned at the stake.

The siege was to continue for five months, with the two contingents now under the command of Huntingdon and Luxembourg. It was marked by frequent skirmishes and a deteriorating situation for the garrison and the inhabitants. However, the size of the besieging army had diminished with Burgundy drawing off troops to deal with problems elsewhere in his domains. The Armagnacs decided to attempt to relieve the town and late in October an army under the command of the Count of Vendôme and Marshal de Boussac launched attacks on the Anglo-Burgundian bastilles, taking a number of them by assault and driving the besiegers into an ever-reducing number of fortifications. Huntingdon and Luxembourg considered that their position was untenable and decided to withdraw. As they did so they left behind much of their artillery, including three large bombards, and copious other stores including wine.

Louviers, 1431

Joan's capture was good news for Bedford, but it was not sufficient in itself to turn the tide and re-establish English military fortunes. Henry VI was scheduled to arrive at Calais on St George's Day 1430 and the military situation needed to be such as to allow his safe passage to Paris. The estates-general of Normandy raised money for the payment for sieges of frontier fortresses, including Torcy, Aumale and Conches-en-Ouche, which were a threat to the duchy. A siege was also under way to recover the strong fortress of Château-Gaillard which had fallen to La Hire the year before. The Armagnac revival had not only galvanized the Norman estates-general to raise taxes but also encouraged towns to raise local taxes to put their defences in order.

One of the first tasks was to retake Louviers. The town stands on the Eure, but is only 4km from the Seine. It had been captured by the Armagnacs in December 1429 when La Hire with 500 or 600 men took the town by surprise and by escalade. It had since been a serious strategic embarrassment for the English. The garrison had preyed upon English shipping attempting to take supplies to Paris. It also stood on the route between Rouen, the seat of English government in Normandy, and Paris and so long as it remained in Armagnac hands it would be too dangerous for the young Henry VI to travel to Paris for his coronation. The English tried to take the town initially by ruse, exploiting the penchant of the garrison to attack English ships on the Seine. Two ships carrying grain were despatched from Rouen without either escort or safe-conduct. The objective was to lure the garrison out from the safety of Louviers to be ambushed by the waiting English. Perhaps the trap was too obvious. In any case the garrison did not fall for the trick and at the end of May a full siege began.

The importance that the administration of Normandy attached to the retaking of Louviers is demonstrated by the commitment by the Norman estates-general of a tax grant made in June for this purpose. In addition, they raised money to pay for 400 men-at-arms and 1,200 archers to serve at the siege. Men were drawn from garrisons throughout the Duchy of

Normandy. In June twenty cartloads of assorted artillery pieces were brought to join the besieging army. The siege demonstrates the problems of maintaining a large siege force for a protracted period. Food for horses became such a serious problem that valets escorted by archers took horses further afield to graze. This created another problem in that the treasurers would not pay the wages of those employed taking horses to graze because they were not engaged at the siege. At some stage during the siege the Armagnac captain of the town, La Hire, was captured, possibly by Jean de Messier, captain of the castle at Dourdan, when he left Louviers to seek help or relief for the town. Despite the loss of its captain the garrison continued to hold out. However, by October the end seemed in sight when 100 stone balls were ordered from quarries at Vernon 25km away. On 25 October 1431 the town surrendered, the garrison leaving honourably with their possessions. The captain of the siege army, Thomas Beaufort, had been even less fortunate than La Hire, dying three weeks before the town surrendered. In contrast, the townspeople were less fortunate than the garrison, with the English soldiery looting the town and the authorities razing the walls to prevent the town becoming an Armagnac fortress again in the future.

St-Céneri-le-Gérei, 1432

The fall of Louviers opened up the route to Paris. On 30 November 1431 Henry VI arrived in Paris, a date carefully orchestrated to coincide with St Andrew's Day, the Burgundian patron saint, and on 16 December he was crowned King of France. The coronation of Henry VI, despite the venue being the third-best option of the Parisian cathedral of Notre-Dame rather than at either Reims or St-Denis, might have been expected to herald a period of English recovery. However, the coronation seems to have been insensitively handled, creating widespread discontent. Worst of all, a few days before the coronation the Duke of Burgundy had agreed a six-year truce with Charles VII, blaming the lack of English material and financial support for the necessity to come to terms with the Armagnacs. Henry VI returned to England in early February 1432, never to return to France.

While the king was being received back in London the English administration in Normandy received a great shock when Marshal de Boussac achieved a remarkable, albeit short-lived, coup. He assembled 600 men-at-arms at Beauvais and advanced to within 5km of Rouen, 70km to the west; still undetected, he hid his men in woods. Guillaume de Ricarville was sent forward with 120 men on foot and a handful of men on horseback to be admitted to the castle by a traitor in the garrison: a Swiss called Pierre Audebeuf. The garrison were taken by surprise in their sleep and those that could, including the captain, the Earl of Arundel, fled. Most of the castle was quickly in Ricarville's hands without the attackers suffering any casualties. He went back to where he had left the bulk of his men to bring reinforcements into the castle, only to find that they refused to come because of a dispute over the shares of booty. Ricarville was left to do the best he could with the men at his disposal. He gave up much of the castle, withdrawing into the great tower with all the supplies his men could gather. In view of the fate of those who succeeded in the initial coup, those who refused to join Ricarville could be considered to have made a sound if disloyal decision. The English brought in reinforcements and artillery. After thirteen days of bombardment the tower became indefensible and Ricarville surrendered. He and his men received no quarter, with 150 men being executed. Audebeuf was decapitated and quartered as a traitor. The extent of the discontent among the French within the English-held territory is perhaps shown by the fact that the failed attempt on Rouen was only the first of around a dozen attempts to betray towns to the Armagnacs during 1432.

Bedford recognized the importance of giving reassurance to the king's Norman subjects, and had devoted considerable effort to trying to prevent Armagnac raids into the duchy. This required him to destroy their bases and take frontier fortresses. After the success at Louviers he kept, at the request of the estates-general of Normandy, 300 men-at-arms and 900 archers in the field under the command of Lord Willoughby. Willoughby's task was to retake several fortresses on the frontier of the Duchy of Normandy. One of these, St-Céneri-le-Gérei, was a particular target since Ambroise de Loré had led a daring raid to Caen, 90km to the north, in September 1431 disrupting and causing panic during the Michaelmas fair.

Willoughby with Matthew Gough set siege to St-Céneri with a large artillery train. They deployed a range of artillery, including some large bombards, and dug ditches around the fortress. There were the usual sorties and skirmishes. When de Loré, marshal of the Duke of Alençon, received news of the siege he was authorized to launch a relief operation with the Lord of Beuil. He deployed his force of approximately 700 to 800 men to two adjacent villages, Beaumont-sur-Sarthe and Vivoin, 25km to the south-east of St-Céneri. Local lords were summoned to join de Loré and he waited three days in the villages for reinforcements to arrive. A further 300 to 400 men turned up, bringing the overall strength up to perhaps 1,100 men. The two villages were separated by the river Sarthe, with a single bridge allowing communications between the two. Aware of this weakness in the French disposition Matthew Gough led a detachment of the besieging army riding through the night to fall upon the French at Vivoin. He achieved complete surprise and initially overwhelmed the Armagnacs. However, the noise of combat drew the attention of de Loré to the battle under way. Although outnumbered, de Loré took 80 men-at-arms and 160 archers across the bridge. Other captains led their men across also and the French numbers grew as the combat continued.

The French eventually carried the day, but not without losing men killed and captured, including de Loré. The Armagnacs believed he had been killed after his capture, although he was actually rescued later in the day, and in revenge killed English prisoners. The English captain Matthew Gough was also captured, and the surviving English withdrew and returned to St-Céneri.

The following day the Armagnacs advanced towards St-Céneri. Willoughby decided to lift the siege and withdraw to Alençon with what remained of the siege army. The withdrawal was made in haste, hampered by members of the garrison coming out of the castle and attacking the English as they broke camp. They left behind their cannon, two siege engines, probably trebuchets, and copious quantities of food and wine.

Lagny-sur-Marne, 1432

Lagny-sur-Marne, 27km to the east of Paris, was a threat to resupply for the capital, and in May 1432 Bedford set siege to the town for the second time in two years in an attempt to relieve the pressure on Paris. He built a temporary pontoon bridge across the Marne upstream of the town and constructed a fortified camp, protected by ditches, that was larger than the town. The siege conditions were difficult, with floods and heat so intense that men were dying of heatstroke within their armour, and even Bedford is said to have collapsed suffering from exhaustion. The English artillery bombarded the town walls and gates, causing breaches in several places. Nevertheless the garrison continued to hold out until, in August 1432, Charles VII sent a relief army commanded by a number of senior captains, including the Bastard of Orléans and Raoul de Gaucourt.

The Armagnac relief army advanced close to Lagny, taking up positions arrayed for battle about 2km from the town with a small river between them and the English. There were skirmishes between the Armagnacs and the English, but under cover of these activities Raoul de Gaucourt fought his way into the town with eighty men as reinforcements and supplies, including twenty to thirty beef cattle and a quantity of flour. Having brought this relief the Armagnacs withdrew in battle order, moving towards Paris. Bedford offered battle, which was declined. Reinforcements from England had been promised for some time but they had not yet arrived. This left Bedford with a dilemma: either he continued the siege or he went to ensure the security of Paris. He could not do both. Paris was clearly more important and the siege was hastily raised on 20 August 1432, with once again artillery and supplies abandoned. Lagny would remain a source of disruption of resupply of food and firewood to the capital.

St-Valery-sur-Somme, 1433

A bad year for the English cause drew to a close with fruitless tripartite truce negotiations in November 1432 between the English, the Burgundians and the Armagnacs. As the campaigning season of 1433 approached, the picture was far from rosy for the Duke of Bedford and the English hold over its territories in France. With Burgundy effectively out of the fighting due to his truce with Charles VII, the burden of the war now fell entirely on the English. Negotiations for a truce continued through the early months of 1433, again without success. Bedford had around 9,700 men at his disposal: 1,600 occupied in the siege of St-Valery-sur-Somme on the Somme estuary, 1,200 in the field with the Earl of Huntingdon to safeguard the frontier of Normandy, 900 men in the field with the Earl of Arundel in Alençon and Maine, and 6,000 tied down in garrison service throughout English-held territories. However, it became clear that Charles was incapable of holding the Armagnacs to the terms of the truce with Burgundy, and great inroads had been made by the Armagnacs in taking Burgundian towns and fortresses. In June Montargis, 90km south of Paris on the Loing, fell to a ruse carried out by men in the pay of the Duke of Burgundy. This opened up the opportunity for the Burgundians to retake places lost to the Armagnacs over the last two years, and the Duke of Burgundy was soon campaigning again in alliance with the English.

Both Burgundy and Bedford had a reason to want St-Valery taken from the Armagnacs. For the English it was dangerously situated in their rear and only 85km south of Calais. For the Burgundians its capture by the Armagnacs earlier in 1433 had been a flagrant breach of the truce between the Armagnacs and Burgundians. On 25 June 1433 the Duke of Burgundy ordered the Count of St-Pol to lay siege to St-Valery. To his force were added 1,600 English troops under the command of Lord Willoughby. The Armagnacs had some 300 men to garrison the town. St-Pol and

Willoughby set about bombarding St-Valery, but it seems the garrison had little stomach for a prolonged siege and preferred to negotiate for favourable terms before positions hardened too much.

In return for a sum of money the garrison agreed to leave the town, but they asked to be allowed to depart with all their possessions and prisoners if relief did not arrive by a given date. The terms were granted, even the most unusual provision concerning prisoners, and the garrison marched out under safe-conduct on 20 August 1433.

St-Céneri-le-Gérei, 1433

While the siege of St-Valery was under way, the Duke of Burgundy, who now had the bit between his teeth, had been campaigning in person. He would remain in the field until November. Lord Talbot, who had now been released following his four years in French hands since the battle of Patay, fought alongside Burgundy with 1,600 English troops. They recovered many Burgundian towns on the Yonne.

The pendulum had swung back in favour of the Anglo-Burgundians, and the Earl of Arundel was also having success in Maine. Among his targets were those fortresses occupied by de Loré's men which Willoughby had been unable to take just a year before. Bonsmoulins surrendered without the expenditure of much effort and the defences were razed. Next on the list was, once again, St-Céneri-le-Gérei.

This was a much tougher proposition. The presence of de Loré's wife and children possibly hardened the garrison's resolve. They would not have wanted de Loré's family to fall into English hands, but they may also have reasoned that with his family trapped in the town he would be sure to come to their relief.

Arundel set about the siege with artillery bombardment and mining. The besieged conducted a vigorous defence with sorties to disrupt the siege. Relief was being planned, with de Loré indeed intending to lead an army, but the marshalling of the force was slow and before they arrived the fortress had fallen. The siege lasted three months, but at long last the bombardment created a wide breach in the walls. In the fighting to try to defend the breach the captain of the castle and some forty or fifty of the garrison were killed. The remaining men had little option but to surrender. However, since this was not a negotiated capitulation but a surrender forced by the success of an assault, generous terms could not be expected. The remaining members of the garrison, presumably including the family of de Loré, were permitted to leave under safe-conduct but on foot and without possessions. The fortifications were demolished.

Sillé-le-Guillaume, 1433

Having taken St-Céneri, Arundel moved off quickly to besiege Sillé-le-Guillaume, 23km to the south-west. He does not seem to have set a siege, but rather to have encamped in a village close by and relied on a demonstration of the strength of his army to bring the garrison to terms. The captain, Aimery d'Anthenaise, agreed to surrender in six weeks if relief was not forthcoming.

The Duke of Alençon, Charles d'Anjou and the constable Arthur de Richemont, took command of the army which had been raised for St-Céneri and came to Sillé just before the deadline. They lodged their men close to those of Arundel, the two armies being within earshot of each other, and there was some skirmishing. During the night the English crossed the small river separating the two armies, and Arundel drew up his men in battle order. The French also took up battle order, but Alençon's scouts reported that the English were in a very strong position. The French would not attack such a strong position and the English were not going be drawn out of their defensive positions. Thus, the two armies stood facing each other throughout the day.

Alençon took the view that, although there had not been a battle, his arrival with a relief force had fulfilled the terms of the agreement between Arundel and the garrison. He therefore sent a herald to demand the release of the hostages given up by the garrison to guarantee the terms of the surrender treaty. Arundel accepted the argument and released the hostages and prepared to move off. However, once the Armagnac relief force had dispersed he returned to Sillé and, catching the garrison by surprise, stormed and captured the fortress. There were further successes for Arundel, and as 1433 drew to a close it was clear that the Anglo-Burgundians had bounced back from the disastrous preceding year. However, despite the resurgence in the fortunes of the Dukes of Bedford and Burgundy, there was still a sense of insecurity within Anglo-Burgundian territory with La Hire, based in Laon, raiding far and wide, including up to the walls of Paris. The recapture of St-Valery by the Armagnacs in January 1434 also took a little icing off the cake.

Creil, 1434

In early 1434 La Hire continued his raiding, in one ambush intercepting a convoy of 2,000 pigs and sundry cattle and sheep. The Armagnacs followed this up with an attack on Vitry, now within Paris but then about 8km from the capital. La Hire's brother, Amado de Vignolles, then took the town of Beaumont-sur-Oise, giving the Armagnacs a base only 40km from Paris. Lord Talbot had brought 1,000 men from England in March as reinforcements. He initially went to Rouen but then set out for Paris, capturing Jouy en route and hanging the entire garrison. In Paris it was decided that Talbot should besiege Beaumont. However, on hearing of his approach Vignolles abandoned the town to occupy the stronger fortress at Creil, 20km upstream but still within striking distance of Paris. Talbot destroyed the fortifications at Beaumont and pressed on to besiege Creil. The garrison conducted a determined defence. Vignolles, who seems to have been well respected by his men, was killed by an arrow in one of numerous skirmishes between the defenders and besiegers. His death sapped the morale of the defenders and they came to terms, surrendering the town after six weeks on 20 June. They departed under safe-conduct with their possessions.

St-Denis, 1435

Following the fall of Creil Talbot continued to build on his success, driving the Armagnacs out of towns and castles north of Paris. The Earl of Arundel also continued to have success while Lord Willoughby carried on with his joint operations with the Burgundians, with St-Valery-sur-Somme changing hands yet again.

However, in 1435 the English began to see their gains slip away again. Bedford faced the usual military challenge of keeping troops in the field and maintaining a large number of garrisons. Furthermore there was the perennial problem of raising taxes in England and Normandy to finance the war. In early 1435 Bedford faced the first popular revolt in the region of Caen, and there was also developing discontent in Paris. All of this was set against the background of a particularly severe winter from late November 1434 well into 1435.

On the military front La Hire retook fortresses that Talbot had captured only the year before. St-Valery-sur-Somme was once again back in French hands. Rue on the opposite bank of the Somme to St-Valery had also fallen into French hands and opened up the prospect of Armagnac raids to the north. The Earl of Arundel was sent to recover Rue but was killed in a clash with the Armagnacs, depriving the English of a capable commander. The Armagnacs were tightening the blockade of Paris; first Pont-Ste-Maxence on the Oise 50km north of Paris fell, and then St-Denis, barely 8km from the centre of the capital. Elsewhere, Alençon and Loré had broken the siege of Mont-St-Michel, which had been restarted in 1434.

The military successes of the Armagnacs were a prelude to tripartite negotiations ostensibly aimed at achieving a peace settlement, or more accurately for the English a prolonged truce since they would not agree to a peace treaty until Henry VI came of age. In the event, the negotiations were a charade aimed from the Armagnac side at separating the Burgundians from their alliance with the English and from the Burgundian side at allowing the duke to reconcile himself honourably with Charles VII. The result was the Treaty of Arras signed on 21 September 1435. Burgundy was now allied to the Armagnacs. The English were now alone, having seen their other allies, the Duke of Brittany and the Holy Roman Emperor, make peace with Charles VII the year before. A week before, on 14 September 1435, the Duke of Bedford had died in Rouen. The English were not only now devoid of allies but had lost the services of an astute and determined political and military leader.

Earlier in the year, however, in response to the military situation Bedford had secured a grant by the estates-general in Normandy to raise 800 men-at-arms and 2,300 archers. In England loans had been raised to pay for a further 2,500 men. Military operations continued while the peace negotiations were under way, and a key objective was to retake St-Denis and relieve some of the pressure on Paris. It had been easily taken by surprise by the Armagnacs on 1 June by 1,200 men. The garrison had been slaughtered, along with all inhabitants of English nationality. Its recovery was to take almost five weeks, at a considerable cost in English lives. Its fall, just three days after the Treaty of Arras, was the last time that the Burgundians fought alongside the English.

Among the Anglo-Burgundian captains were the marshal, the Sire de l'Isle-Adam, Lords Talbot and Scales, the Bastard of St-Pol and Louis of Luxembourg. They set the siege with some 6,000 men in mid-August. Chief among the captains in the garrison was the Marshal of Rieu. There were around 1,600 men to defend the town. Siege engines were brought up to the walls and gates to attempt to destroy the fortifications.

Fearful of an assault the garrison maintained a strong guard on the walls day and night. With the walls and gates badly damaged, the besiegers decided to try to take the town. The attack was made against several places on the walls. Men crossed the water-filled ditches up to their necks carrying ladders to climb the walls. The defenders feared for their lives if the town were taken and fought ferociously. After two hours the assault was called off. The Anglo-Burgundians suffered more than eighty killed, their bodies lying in the moat and at the foot of the walls. The defenders, however, had also suffered heavily and were in fear of a new assault. They hoped that the Armagnac constable, then at the talks in Arras, would come to their relief but in the meantime set about repairing the breaches in the walls. It became clear, however, that help would not be forthcoming and the Marshal of Rieu negotiated a treaty for his men to depart under safe-conduct with their possessions. They could perhaps be considered fortunate in view of the indiscriminate slaughter when they took the place.

Paris, 1436

The English success at St-Denis was, however, isolated. On the day of the surrender Meulan, 20km to the west, was taken by surprise by the French closing the net again around Paris. Attacks on Normandy by mercenary captains and Ambroise de Loré resulted in the fall of the very strong town of Dieppe to the French after a surprise attack. Revolt in Normandy followed with Normans rallying to the side of the new masters of Dieppe. The objective of the French was to take the coastal towns held by the English and so important for resupply and reinforcement of English France.

Fécamp, Montivilliers and Harfleur fell into French hands, as did Tancarville and Lillebonne, extending the reconquest up the Seine towards Rouen. There was great concern in Normandy at this turn of events with the estates-general at Rouen imploring Henry VI in December 1435 to send help. He promised to send a great army of 2,100 men-at-arms and 9,000 archers. The army would be commanded by the young and inexperienced Duke of York. Gathering and despatching this army was slow, and numbers fell short of those promised. Although some men arrived in January 1436 the final detachment of 4,500 men did not arrive until late May.

Fortunately for the English cause, Talbot stepped in to stem the Armagnac tide, taking control of the defence of Rouen and reinforcing Caudebec, gathering cattle from the surrounding countryside and driving them into the two towns to deny them to the enemy. As the reinforcements arrived from England some were allocated to the Rouen garrison. However, the situation in the Paris region was deteriorating rapidly. Towns surrounding Paris, including Corbeil, St-Germain-en-Laye, Bois-de-Vincennes and Pontoise were in Armagnac hands. In face of this crisis 800 men were sent to Paris under the command of Sir Thomas Beaumont. Paris, although nominally held by the English, owed its allegiance to the Duke of Burgundy. The loyalty of the population was in doubt, and the arrival of Beaumont, an experienced commander and veteran of Orléans, was timely. However, the tide was running against him: after the Treaty of

Arras the Duke of Burgundy was at peace with Charles VII but not yet at war with England. By early April this had changed and the English in Paris faced the combined Armagnac and Burgundian army gathering at Pontoise.

The English made preparations for a siege: destroying crops and burning villages on the Seine between Pontoise and Paris to deny them to the French, seizing food supplies and marshalling supplies within the city. Beaumont took the initiative and set out to intercept the enemy. A disaster followed with 400 of his men killed and Beaumont himself captured. St-Denis fell into enemy hands once again. In the event there was no need to besiege Paris. L'Isle Adam, who had taken St-Denis the previous year for the Anglo-Burgundians, was now in the French camp. Entry was made into the city on the strength of presentation to the guards of a general pardon from Charles VII which resulted in the gates being opened. There was some resistance from English and loyal inhabitants, but they were driven to take refuge in the Bastille. They were so numerous and crowded that they could not have held out for long with the available supplies. However, the French had no appetite for a siege and the English and their French supporters were allowed to leave the city on 17 April 1436. Paris's days under English occupation were over. The fall of Paris was not strictly speaking the result of a siege, but all the ingredients were there, with a beleaguered population and a powerful army at the gates. The collapse of morale and the lack of any prospect of relief were sufficient to bring about the fall of Paris without the need for either assault or a prolonged siege.

Calais, 1436

After Bedford's death there would no longer be a Regent of France acting for Henry VI. The Duke of York was appointed with restricted powers as lieutenant-general, and the Lords Scales and Talbot bore the brunt of the military responsibilities. By the end of 1436 these capable commanders had recovered many of the losses of previous months, although Harfleur, Fécamp and Dieppe remained in enemy hands. Despite these successes, and although the English were to remain in Normandy for another fourteen years, with the fall of Paris the English hold on France was doomed.

Meanwhile, the Duke of Burgundy cast greedy eyes towards Calais. The English got wind of what was afoot and Cardinal Beaufort, who had been destined to go to Anjou and Maine, was diverted to Calais with 2,000 men. Beaufort took the offensive, raiding into Burgundian territory in Flanders. The Duke of Burgundy brought together a powerful army with a formidable artillery train. There were more than 125 cannon, including ten great bombards, one of which, the Burgundy, needed forty-eight horses to pull the cart carrying the barrel and a further thirty-six for the chamber. He also had some 450 hand-guns, and 450,000 crossbow bolts. Burgundy arrived in the Calais Pale in mid-June and took and demolished the out-lying fortresses of Oye and Marck. By 9 July he was encamped outside Calais and awaiting the arrival of a fleet of thirty-five ships to complete the blockade.

Early in the siege there was a fruitless assault on the town, resulting in casualties on both sides, including La Hire who was wounded in the leg by an arrow. The Duke of Burgundy also had a close shave. Going out on reconnaissance with some of his captains a near-miss by a gun-stone killed a trumpeter at his side, unhorsed one of his companions and killed three horses. There were frequent sorties from the garrison resulting in skir-mishes which were generally in favour of the English. While the siege was under way, Burgundian detachments were sent out to reduce the fortresses at Balinghem, Sangatte and Guînes. The first two fell but Guînes held out despite an artillery bombardment.

The Burgundian shipping was holed up in Sluys, unable to make the voyage to Calais due to adverse winds. To the great frustration of the besiegers they could see English shipping coming and going at will delivering reinforcements, supplies and weapons. To add to the frustra-tion of the Burgundian army the garrison also put their cattle to pasture outside the walls each day. This provoked a number of attempts to cap-ture the livestock. On one occasion English sentinels spotted a force of some 200 Flemish trying to approach the cattle covertly. In the ensuing fighting twenty-two Flemish were killed and thirty-one taken prisoner. Humphrey, Duke of Gloucester, a long-time adversary of the Duke of Burgundy, sent a herald to the Burgundian camp to deliver a challenge to battle. This could be either in the Calais Pale or wherever Gloucester could find Burgundy if he withdrew from the siege before his arrival. The herald regretted that he could not set a date for battle since Gloucester's arrival was at the mercy of favourable winds and tides.

The Burgundians began to construct a wooden bastille close to the town to improve surveillance of activities within the walls. The English saw this as a threat to their sorties and over several days raiding parties attempted without success to prevent its construction.

On 25 July the Burgundian fleet finally arrived off Calais. In the evening of their arrival four ships filled with stones were scuttled in the harbour to try to prevent its use by the English. The garrison bombarded the shipping involved and sank one ship. The next morning two further ships were scuttled. Unfortunately the enterprise had been ill-conceived. The ships had been sunk in shallow water, and as the tide went out they were seen to be stranded on the sand with a clear channel remaining for access by English ships. To add insult to injury, townspeople came out, undeterred by artillery fire, to break up the ships for firewood. The Burgundian fleet then sailed away, its commander considering the waters off Calais too hazardous to remain on station.

The Burgundian army included a number of Flemish companies. They were dispirited by the failure of the fleet to enforce the maritime blockade which they considered had been promised to them to ensure a successful and rapid conclusion to the siege. A drawn-out siege was not part of the deal. The Flemish were also concerned about news that the Duke of Gloucester's army was ready to sail for France. On 27 July Burgundy called together his senior captains to try to hold his fragile army together. The same day the English launched a strong attack against the bastille and this time they prevailed. The bastille was destroyed and 160 Flemish killed, with many others taken prisoner. Some of these prisoners were killed outside the town gates as revenge for an English knight killed after having been taken prisoner. The Burgundian army now disintegrated as first the men of Ghent and then those from Bruges deserted, the latter leaving behind provisions and artillery. By the end of July the siege was over and the Duke of Burgundy withdrew first to Gravelines and then to Lille.

Le Crotoy, 1437

In 1437, thanks to the enterprise of Lords Talbot, Scales and Fauconberg, the English conducted a spirited defence of the lands and places that remained under their control. A host of towns and castles fell to them, and small castles, which could have an impact out of all proportion to their size, were demolished. There was a vacuum at the top after the end of the Duke of York's tenure as Lieutenant-General before his successor the Earl of Warwick arrived in the autumn. Shortly after Warwick's arrival, during October 1437, the Burgundians laid siege to the strategically important fortress of Le Crotoy on the Somme estuary.

The siege started on the initiative of the Lord of Auxi, captain-general of Abbeville and of the frontiers of the County of Ponthieu, and the Seneschal of Ponthieu. Once they had invested the town they sent news to the Duke of Burgundy, reporting their action and requesting his assistance. Burgundy sent representatives to see what help was the most practicable. Intelligence indicated that the garrison had only sufficient stores to last a month, and an effective maritime blockade could be expected to bring a swift capitulation. Burgundy, still smarting after his failure at Calais, was only too willing to assist, and called for ships to be sent from Dieppe and St-Valery. Burgundy took control himself, albeit from the safety of Abbeville 20km to the south-east, and gave orders for the construction of a large bastille surrounded by deep ditches, garrisoned by 1,000 men and provided with artillery. There were the usual skirmishes between the besiegers and the garrison, and on one occasion the lieutenant of the castle of Le Crotoy was captured by the Lord of Auxi.

The strategic value of Le Crotoy as an entry port for the English in Picardy was such that measures were quickly taken to relieve the garrison. The Lords Talbot and Fauconberg, with Sir Thomas Kyriell, were despatched with an army claimed by one chronicler to be 4,000 strong. This is almost certainly an exaggeration, but whatever its strength it was clearly effective. Burgundy, on hearing of the approach of the English, summoned men to join him at Abbeville and some 5,000 to 6,000 men are said to have been mustered. However, rather than descending directly to tackle the besieging army, the English bypassed Le Crotoy, burning towns and crops and spreading panic in the surrounding area in a raid which lasted ten days. This approach, whether by design or accident, was very effective. Men were withdrawn from the siege and Burgundy's newly assembled field army to reinforce town garrisons, thus leaving the besieging army more vulnerable to an English counterattack.

Concerned about developments Burgundy sent the Lord Croy and the *bailli* of Amiens to confirm that the men in the bastille were well prepared and confident of holding their own. They reported that all was well, but in the event, as the English turned their attention to Le Crotoy, the besiegers panicked and retreated in disorder, abandoning the siege and leaving behind copious quantities of equipment, arms and artillery. The Duke of Burgundy withdrew to Hesdin and dispersed his army. The siege had lasted six to seven weeks. Its failure was another humiliating setback for Burgundy.

Meaux, 1439

The summer and autumn of 1437 were very wet and crops failed throughout northern Europe and England. The crisis led to severe shortages and soaring prices for grain during 1438. In northern France the war, with supplies required for garrisons and field armies, raiding parties destroying crops and scorched earth tactics only served to aggravate an already severe situation. Military operations continued during the winter of 1437/8 and throughout 1438, but on a reduced scale with neither side launching major campaigns. For the French the main focus was on improving access to Paris for supplies by taking places held by the English and those loyal to their cause. Montereau, Montargis and Nemours were among towns that fell to the French. The English lacked the strength to take such towns as Dieppe and Harfleur held in their rear by the French and had to content themselves with reducing smaller towns and fortresses within the Duchy of Normandy. Unable to sustain a significant field army in the north, Charles VII turned his attention to Aquitaine. A number of towns and fortresses fell to the Armagnacs and they even reached the suburbs of Bordeaux. However, they lacked the artillery and sufficient troops to launch an attempt to take the city.

There was war weariness in both France and England, but with the ebb and flow of fortunes both sides were reluctant to negotiate peace when the tide of fortune seemed to be turning in their favour. Nevertheless, by early 1439 both sides came together near Calais to try to negotiate at least a long truce to last between fifteen and thirty years. These talks were to come to nothing, and in the meantime the war continued.

English-held Meaux, on the Marne 40km east of Paris, was chosen as a target by the French for the summer of 1439. This was the last remaining English stronghold east of Paris and its fate could be expected to have an important impact on the talks under way in Calais.

Richemont was charged with taking Meaux. He began a siege on 20 July 1439, with an army said to be 4,000 strong. Meaux consisted of the walled town and a fortified market which served as a stronghold within the town's perimeter. The besieging army was lodged in buildings in the suburbs, including the abbey and a monastery. The town had a bastille protecting one of the gates. This was quickly taken by the French, who set about constructing seven further bastilles, five of which were on two islands in the river and directly facing the market stronghold. Siege engines and artillery also began their work. A little more than three weeks after the start of the siege Richemont and his advisers concluded that the defences had been sufficiently degraded to permit an assault. On 12 August the French stormed the town. Around sixty of the garrison were killed and forty to fifty captured. The remainder of the garrison withdrew to the safety of the market.

Messengers managed to get through the siege lines to carry a message to Rouen seeking help. Talbot, Scales and Fauconberg gathered their forces and set out to relieve Meaux, again we are told with around 4,000 men. Richemont refused an English challenge to battle, and only a number of skirmishes and minor engagements ensued. The English had the better of these exchanges, with two bastilles being taken with a loss of between 100 and 120 French killed and numerous others captured, along with twenty boats laden with supplies. Talbot decided that he would require a larger force to complete his task and set off to Rouen with most of his army to gather more men. Before leaving he reinforced the market with 500 men and stocked it with plentiful supplies. His intention had been to return quickly to finish the job. Unfortunately he was delayed and returned on 16 September 1439 to discover that the captain, Sir William Chamberlain, had surrendered the day before in the face of Richemont's artillery. The garrison was allowed to depart under safe-conduct to go to Pontoise or Normandy, taking their possessions with them. The unfortunate Chamberlain was arrested by Talbot and subsequently charged with treason for surrendering the town while it was still supplied. He was acquitted, having pleaded the case that, although still well provisioned, he could not be expected to hold out against the artillery ranged against him without sign of the promised relief.

Avranches, 1439

The Earl of Huntingdon had landed in Gascony in July 1439, and had retaken a number of places occupied by the French the year before. He had then threatened to strike towards the Languedoc. Although the war in the south-west was something of a sideshow compared with the struggle in the north, Huntingdon could not be allowed a free hand and troops were mobilized to serve under the Count of Foix, the Lord d'Albret and the Viscount of Lomagne. These measures served to dissipate the threat to the Languedoc. Despite this distraction Charles VII did not lose sight of the situation in Normandy. He despatched the Constable of France, Arthur de Richemont, the Duke of Alençon, and the Lords of Laval and Lohéac to besiege Avranches.

Men were withdrawn from the siege army which had recently taken Meaux, and despatched to Avranches with a large artillery train including heavy bombards. The castle, standing on a cliff, was a difficult nut to crack. Several weeks of bombardment had made little impact and had given the garrison time to get a message to Rouen. Edmund Beaufort and the familiar trio of the Lords Talbot, Scales and Fauconberg set out with a large army to relieve the town. The English encamped at the village of St-Leonard, 6km west of the town, on the estuary of the Sées. The besieging army was on the far bank of the river and beyond them lay the town. There was a bridge at Pont-Gilbert, about 1km from the town, but its use was impracticable with the French present in strength. At low tide the river could be crossed at fords, and the French took advantage of these to cross the river to skirmish with the English. Despite probing attacks by day and night, the English army was unable to overcome Richemont's men and cross the river near the town. On 22 December the English broke camp and crossed the Sée towards the river estuary, crossing the sands at low tide and entering Avranches from the rear and out of sight of the French. The French must have been extraordinarily lax with their reconnaissance, since this manoeuvre seems to have been conducted in secret and the ensuing sortie by the relieving army and the garrison caught Richemont and his men entirely by surprise. The result was a rout, with the fleeing French leaving artillery, supplies and personal equipment behind.

Harfleur, 1440

Much of Richemont's army at both Meaux and Avranches had included large numbers of *écorcheurs*, little more than companies of bandits as content to rob those loyal to Charles VII as his enemies. They posed an increasing threat to the king and his efforts to restore order to his country. Their abject retreat from Avranches did nothing for their cause. In late 1439 Charles introduced a range of sweeping reforms which, *inter alia*, outlawed freelance companies and created a single royal army. As well as ridding France of the *écorcheurs* these reforms were to improve significantly the effectiveness of France's armies and shift the balance of power increasingly in favour of Charles' armies as the war progressed. However, ridding the country of these bands was easier said than done. In the spring of 1440 a revolt erupted, known as the Praguerie, when the Bastard of Bourbon and the Duke of Alençon refused to expel the *écorcheurs* from their armies. The revolt was to last throughout the summer and once again resources and efforts were diverted from the war against the English as the French fought among themselves.

The diversion of French forces to suppress the Praguerie provided an ideal opportunity for the English to take the initiative. In February 1440, before the start of the revolt, the Earl of Somerset had launched a raid into Picardy, taking three fortresses and putting a garrison into Folleville, midway between Beauvais and Amiens. However, there was a more important objective: Harfleur. The town had been taken by the Armagnacs five years before. It served as a base to disrupt English shipping, particularly resupply up the Seine to Rouen. The possession of the port by the Armagnacs also denied the English an important and useful port of entry into Normandy.

Somerset, acting lieutenant for the Duchy of Normandy, delegated command of the siege to his brother Edmund Beaufort. With him went Talbot and Fauconberg, and Somerset occupied himself with ensuring the flow of supplies and raising men to counter the anticipated arrival of a relief army. By June the siege was under way, with the port blockaded. The besiegers were 6,000 strong. In the town were 400 trained soldiers together with the town militia and a number of mariners. The captain of the town was Jean d'Estouteville, son of the captain when the town surrendered to Henry V twenty-five years earlier.

The garrison made numerous sorties to try to disrupt the siege, killing and capturing men of the besieging army, but the English dug ditches and erected palisades to defend their positions. The English were sufficiently confident of their defences for the Earl of Somerset's wife and other ladies to join the siege camp. The English began a bombardment of the town gates and walls, using bombards, other gunpowder artillery and stone-throwing machines. The hard-pressed garrison was short of supplies, and several messages were sent to Charles VII asking for relief. He promised to help, but with the distractions elsewhere with the Praguerie the siege had been under way for four months before a relief army, 4,000 strong, was assembled by the Count of Eu, the Bastards of Bourbon and Orléans, and La Hire. With the rear-guard was Raoul, Lord of Gaucourt, who had brought reinforcements into the town during Henry V's siege, and had now been appointed to overall command of Harfleur.

When the relieving army arrived a determined attempt was made to break the siege. The Bastard of Orléans launched an attack on foot. La Hire held a cavalry reserve and the Count of Eu attempted to break the maritime blockade. On land an ill-judged sortie by around 500 English troops led to the deaths of forty or fifty men when they were intercepted by La Hire's cavalry, and a further thirty were killed during a sortie by the garrison. However, despite these successes the overall attack on land failed to break the English defence. The Count of Eu fared no better, with his force driven off with the loss of several ships. The French withdrew to Montivilliers, 4km to the north, to lick their wounds. They remained there for eight days, facing increasing problems of supplies for both men and horses. In a desperate last throw the Count of Eu issued a challenge to Somerset either for single combat or a battle between 100 chosen men from each side. The offer was rejected and the French had no choice but to withdraw. Both Harfleur and Montivilliers, which after the demands of feeding the relief army was in no position to continue to resist, surrendered towards the end of October. The garrisons were permitted to leave under safe-conduct, unarmed, to return to their homes. The Duke of Burgundy, fearful of pillaging in his lands, stopped men passing into his territory.

Creil, 1441

The French wasted little time in responding to their failure at Harfleur. They retook Louviers, which had been left defenceless after the demolition of its fortifications by the English ten years before, and captured Conches-en-Ouche, 34km to the south-west of Louviers. Charles VII now decided to attempt to clear the remaining English strongholds around Paris. The most important of these were Creil, 48km north of the capital, and Pontoise, 28km north-west of Paris.

On 8 May 1441 the king arrived before Creil. He brought with him an impressive array of great captains, including the Constable de Richemont, Xaintrailles and La Hire, and a formidable artillery train under the command of his master of artillery, Jean Bureau. The effectiveness of the artillery was such that within twelve days the damage was so significant that the garrison was in fear of an assault and indeed, once the artillery had breached the walls, an assault was made on 24 May 1441. Ladders were placed against the walls to enter by way of the breach. The captain of Creil, Sir William Peyto, led a desperate attempt to defend the breach. The Armagnacs were driven back in fierce hand-to-hand fighting, but it was clear that further resistance was futile. The next day the garrison agreed terms and left for Normandy. They were granted safe-conduct but compelled to leave on foot taking only the clothes that they were wearing and the money that they could carry.

Pontoise, 1441

The French king now turned his attention to Pontoise, setting siege to the town on 6 June 1441. There was a garrison of around 1,000 to 1,200 men. The English had been anticipating a siege and since May had been re-supplying the town. The French king lodged in the abbey of Maubuisson just across the Oise from the town. The English were not going to allow the besiegers to establish their defences and sallied forth to attack the French, eventually being driven off with prisoners taken and men killed on both sides. The king ranged his men to the south of the river and prepared solid field fortifications with ditches and palisades, both to protect the men from artillery fire from within the town and to provide a strong place in the event of the arrival of a relieving army. A pontoon bridge was constructed across the river to enable the French to take the abbey of St Martin and install a garrison. A bastille was constructed housing 3,000 to 4,000 men under the command of Charles d'Anjou and Prégent de Coëtivy, Admiral of France. From here the French were able to bring artillery fire to bear on the fortifications around the bridge, and take them on or around 20 June.

However, before further progress could be made by the besiegers, Talbot arrived with a relieving army, said to be between 5,000 and 6,000 strong, and installed Lord Scales as captain to stiffen resolve among the garrison. Talbot did not attempt to draw the king into battle, but secured a route into the town via a gate upstream, which, for reasons that remain obscure, the French had failed to besiege. He returned four further times with supplies over the next three months. On each visit he left more men for the defence and took away the wounded and the sick. While Talbot was making his first visit to Pontoise the Duke of York arrived in Rouen to take up his commission as lieutenant-general of Normandy. He brought with him 900 men-at-arms and 2,700 archers.

York set out to raise the siege, crossing the Oise at Beaumont-sur-Oise, 16km north-west of Pontoise, using boats taken overland by cart and bridges made from small leather boats, wood and rope. The French tried to prevent the construction of the bridge but they were not in sufficient strength and were driven off with men killed. After York's arrival the king withdrew from the abbey of Maubuisson to Poissy 14km to the south. He left the siege under the command of the Admiral of France and La Hire with the army concentrated in the bastille at the abbey of St Martin. The besieging army could not be drawn out from behind their formidable defences, secure as they were with artillery, palisades and deep ditches. Talbot tried to lure them out with a diversionary attack on Poissy, pillaging the abbey, but to no avail. York could not hope to take their positions and withdrew, leaving new men in the garrison to bolster the defence. He withdrew downriver and constructed a further bridge, both to secure his return to Normandy and to prevent supplies from Paris reaching the besiegers. However, the blockade was by no means complete, with ships laden with supplies reaching the besiegers and their cargo hastily transferred to carts and packhorses and taken within the bastille. There was a good deal of skirmishing, including around the bridge constructed by York, with losses on both sides, but no progress was made towards raising the siege. York went back to Normandy having promised to return to Pontoise.

Following York's departure Charles VII resumed the siege with a vengeance, returning to lodge in the abbey of Maubuisson. There were numerous skirmishes between the besiegers and the garrison, with an Armagnac lord being killed by a cannon shot. The garrison repaired the damage overnight with barrels filled with earth and wood. However, sustained bombardment created several breaches in the walls and on 16 September an assault was launched which captured the church of Notre Dame, which stood outside the walls, and resulted in the death of twenty-four of the thirty or forty English soldiers defending it, the remainder being captured. The church tower served as a vantage point to coordinate artillery fire, and on 19 September sufficient damage had been done to the walls, towers and gates to permit a general assault on the town. Simultaneous assaults were made in four places with both Charles VII and the dauphin participating. The assault was bloody and, as was so often the case with medieval warfare, the defeated suffered disproportionate losses, with forty of the attackers losing their lives against between 400 and 500 of the garrison. Sir Nicholas Burdet, who had been installed by the Duke of York, was killed and Lord Clinton, also installed by York, captured. The victors searched throughout the rest of the day and night for those who had hidden themselves, including fifty-three people found sheltering in the Cock and Peacock Inn. Some were put to the sword and others joined the ranks of the prisoners.

The siege had lasted fifteen weeks, and the town having been taken by assault there was no obligation for the king to be lenient. The prisoners were led away to Paris roped together and in rags. Those who could not pay ransoms were executed by drowning, thrown into the Seine bound hand and foot. An unusual feature of this siege was an exchange of ballads in verse, initiated by the English, towards the end of July, trading insults and threats.

Tartas, 1441–1442

The fall of Pontoise marked the end of the English presence in the Île-de-France. However, behind the increasing French ascendancy lay not the time-honoured ebb and flow of fortunes but Charles VII's military reforms, more personal commitment by the king and the increasing efficacy of his artillery led by his talented master of artillery, Jean Bureau. There were isolated English successes, but the failure of York and Talbot to save Pontoise despite considerable resources and effort was a serious setback. The swing of fortunes had the usual effect on attempts to negotiate peace, with the French not wanting to agree to peace while they were making good progress militarily. Proposed dates for talks were repeatedly put back by Charles VII. The English sent ambassadors to Calais in February 1442. They departed in June without their counterparts having arrived.

The focus remained mainly in the north during 1442, but the French could not afford to ignore events in the south-west. In July 1441 the seneschal of Bordeaux, Sir Thomas Rempston, with the Earl of Hunting-don, laid siege to the town of Tartas, in the domains of the Lord d'Albret, 110km to the south of Bordeaux. Eventually, with little sign of relief and after a long and stubborn resistance, the defenders of Tartas entered into an agreement to surrender the town. On a given day the strongest force before Tartas would determine its fate. If the English prevailed the town would pass into English allegiance; if not, it would remain loyal to Charles VII. This was about much more than the fate of one town well away from the main theatre of operations. If Tartas went across to the English, with it would go all the other towns and lordships in the hands of d'Albret. This would have a serious impact on the balance of power in the south-west and Charles VII was determined not to allow this to happen.

Initially the day set for the challenge was 1 May 1442 but at the request of the English the date was put back to 24 June. The king pulled together an army with many of the great nobles of France, including the dauphin, Prégent de Coëtivy, the Counts of Maine, Eu, Foix and de la Marche, and the constable, Arthur de Richemont. Charles drew up his army between 10.00 and 11.00 in the morning as agreed and stayed arrayed for battle throughout the day. The English did not arrive. The Lord of Cognac and Augerot de St-Per, who had been charged by the English with responsi-bility for seeing the agreement enacted, came before Charles VII and handed over the keys to the town along with Charles d'Albret, the son of the Lord d'Albret, who had been held as a hostage.

Dieppe, 1442–1443

The great French effort in the south-west to relieve Tartas had not, however, left the English with a free hand in Normandy. The Bastard of Orléans had been left to keep the English at bay. There were tit-for-tat exchanges of towns and fortresses, but the main focus of attention was Dieppe, the only stronghold remaining in French hands on the Norman coast. Talbot took the matter in hand but the six-month contracts of many of men had ended and he was hard-pressed to find resources for the siege. By the end of October 1442 he had gathered sufficient men and materials to set a limited siege. He could not hope to enforce a total blockade either by land or by sea. To the east of the town he built a large bastille on high ground overlooking the town and port. The bastille was constructed of wood and surrounded by ditches. It was garrisoned by 500 men under the command of Sir William Peyto. Some 200 pieces of assorted artillery and stone-throwing machines were installed in the bastille and a bombardment of the town of Dieppe and its fortifications began.

Without a complete blockade of the town it was relatively easy for the French both to supply and reinforce the garrison. Several columns entered the town during the siege. The first, of between 800 and 1,000 men, was led into the town on 30 November 1442 by the Bastard of Orléans to join the 300 men already present. A few days later a further column arrived with 700 to 800 men. In March around another 100 men arrived. On 12 August 1443 the largest column yet arrived in the town. The dauphin, the Bastard of Orléans, Raoul de Gaucourt and the Count of St-Pol brought with them 1,600 men to add to the men already present. The arrival of such a significant force led by the dauphin was a clear prelude to an attempt to take the bastille. Between 500 and 600 men were initially deployed before the bastille. During a night of heavy rain the English made two sorties to disrupt the French preparations but were driven back.

At 8.00am two days later the anticipated assault began. The French deployed five or six wheeled wooden bridges to span the ditches surrounding the bastille and two or three cranes to lift them into position. The Armagnacs were then able to rush the walls but the resistance was fierce and around a hundred of the attackers were killed and several hundred more wounded. The citizens of Dieppe brought out up to eighty ballistae to shoot at the defenders. The assault was renewed and after fierce hand-to-hand fighting the French carried the day. More than 300 of the defenders lost their lives, and surviving native French speakers fighting for the English were executed for treason. Eight men-at-arms, four archers and two artillerymen were hanged. Among the captured was the captain Sir William Peyto. The dauphin went barefoot to the church of St James in Dieppe to give thanks for his victory, and gave orders for the bastille to be demolished and the captured artillery taken into Dieppe to enhance its defences.

The Truce of Tours

While Talbot had been struggling to bring the siege of Dieppe to a successful conclusion, the Earl of Somerset had been campaigning independently of the Duke of York with virtually non-existent communications between them. Somerset had the strength to have had a potentially critical bearing on events in Dieppe, but instead continued to operate in Maine and then disbanded his army and returned to England in January 1444. The limited successes of Somerset and the fall of Dieppe were significant setbacks to English hopes. The pressure for peace was growing and in the early months of 1444 talks for a truce began. The result was a truce to run from 1 June 1444 until 24 May 1446.

Chapter 9

The Expulsion of the English from France, 1449–1453

The Truce of Tours, originally negotiated to last until 24 May 1446, lasted almost five years, but by the early months of 1449 breaches of the truce became more became and more numerous and by July there was an irretrievable breakdown. At the end of the month war had formally broken out once again. This final phase of the war is striking in many ways: the speed of the collapse of English power in Normandy and the north of France in 1449–1450, with all but Calais having succumbed in little more than a year after the breakdown of the truce, the high incidence of towns and strongholds surrendering to the French without even token resistance, and the short duration of the sieges in contrast to the long and stubborn resistance in so many places during the English conquest.

Verneuil-sur-Avre, 1449

Before the final breakdown of the truce the town of Verneuil-sur-Avre was taken by Pierre de Brézé. A disgruntled miller who had been beaten by an Englishman for sleeping on guard-duty travelled 40km to Évreux to offer his services to the French. On 19 July de Brézé arrived at Verneuil at the break of day. The miller persuaded his fellow night-watchmen to leave their posts early so that they could go to church. He then showed the French where to place scaling ladders beside his mill to enter the town. The French seem to have achieved total surprise and caught the garrison of 120 English soldiers unprepared. Some were captured, others were killed and the rest took refuge in the castle. However, with the aid of the miller the French drained the moat and took the castle by assault. There remained one last strongpoint: the Grey Tower. It was strongly fortified and also surrounded by a moat. It was considered impregnable if well provisioned. On this occasion it was inadequately supplied to sustain a long siege. Nevertheless the remaining English withdrew to the tower with a small number of townspeople.

On the same day that the survivors withdrew into the Grey Tower, the Count of Dunois, also known as the Bastard of Orléans and recently

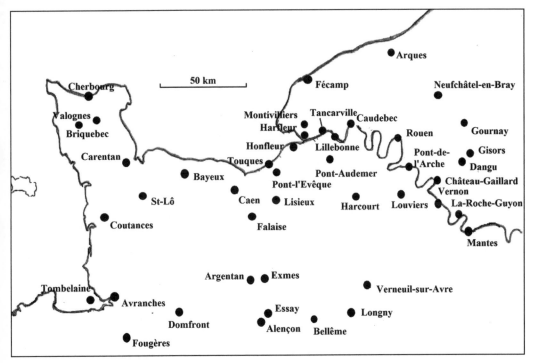

Normandy, 1449–1450.

appointed the king's lieutenant for war, arrived with an army and settled down to besiege the stronghold. At Rouen Sir John Talbot had meanwhile received a plea for relief from the surviving garrison at Verneuil. He assembled a force to bring help, expecting to find simply those French who had taken the town by surprise. However, Dunois had got wind of Talbot's relief plan and, leaving 800 men under the command of Florant d'Illiers to continue with the siege, he set out to intercept the English column. When Talbot neared Verneuil on 31 July he found himself confronted by this much larger French army. He initially drew up his wagons in a defensive array but then prudently decided that the relief of Verneuil was beyond his resources and instead elected to withdraw to the safety of Harcourt castle.

We know little of events following Talbot's withdrawal until the surrender of the Grey Tower. It seems that the besiegers, no doubt in view of the reputedly impregnable fortifications, simply sat and waited for the garrison to run out of food. The garrison continued to hold out until around 23 August when the tower was finally surrendered. Only some thirty men were found within, most of them Normans in English service. Others had escaped at night before the surrender, taking with them anything of value. Their escape was attributed to the negligence of the night watch and Florant d'Illiers was accused of incompetence. The captured Normans were named as renegades but pardoned by Charles VII as a gesture to encourage other Normans in the service of the English to return to the fold.

Vernon, 1449

Even before the fall of Verneuil the French reconquest of Normandy had started to gather pace. An army under the command of the Counts of Eu and St-Pol joined that of the Bastard of Orléans. Pont-Audemer was taken by assault by the combined army and Pont-l'Évêque surrendered without a fight after the garrison fled on the approach of the French. Within days of the surrender of Verneuil, Lisieux and Mantes-la-Jolie had also surrendered without resistance.

On 27 August the *bailli* of Évreux came before Vernon on the river Seine and called for the surrender of the town and castle. This time there was resistance. The commander of the garrison, John, son of the Irish Earl of Ormond, responded with derision to the call for his surrender, gathering together from locksmiths all the old keys they could muster and delivering them to the *bailli*. His arrogance was, however, misplaced and premature since the Counts of Eu and St-Pol arrived the next day and laid siege to the town. There were skirmishes between the besiegers and the English garrison of 120 men. In one such skirmish, when the French took an island with an artillery emplacement and the bridge over the Seine, a lieutenant of the garrison commander was wounded by an arrow which passed through both cheeks. The town inhabitants decided that they wished to surrender. The English garrison would have preferred to resist, but Ormond recognized the difficulties of sustaining a defence against the wishes of the population. An agreement was reached for surrender on Saturday, 30 August if no relief was forthcoming. Such relief would have had to come from the English garrison at Rouen. This was only 64km away, but the timescale was totally unrealistic even if the forces could be gathered. On the ordained day the gates were opened and the garrison marched away under safe-conduct.

Harcourt, 1449

Towns and strongholds were being offered generous terms to come back into the French fold and abandon the English cause. In view of the rapid progress of the reconquest, even in the first few weeks after the end of the truce, and the weakness of the English position it is hardly surprising that submission without resistance became the norm with only scattered examples of determined resistance. By early September Louviers, Longny and Gournay had opened their gates to the French. The castles of Dangu and La Roche-Guyon had also surrendered without a fight. In the latter case the Welsh captain could obviously see the way the wind was blowing and self-interest dictated that, since he was married to a rich French-woman, going over to the enemy was by far the better option.

The fortress of Harcourt was the first to show any substantial resis-tance, holding out for fifteen days, but even this place had fallen by early September. The captain was Richard Frogenhalle, who had at his disposal around 700 or 800 men. The French were not content simply to sit and wait and the siege was marked with skirmishes between the opposing forces, with chroniclers remarking on the losses on both sides due to cannon fire. The Count of Dunois was incensed that Frogenhalle had broken an oath not to take up arms against the French again. In the tradi-tional way of indicating that someone had broken the code of chivalry a painting of Frogenhalle, suspended by the feet, was hung upside-down outside one of the gates. To break the resistance of the defenders Dunois brought up heavy artillery which immediately caused significant damage to the walls of the lower bailey. The garrison decided that unless relief came they could not hold out against such firepower. A date was set for relief and when it was not forthcoming the garrison marched out on 15 September 1449 under safe-conduct, with all their possessions, even, it seems, the disgraced captain.

Rouen, 1449

During September towns and strongholds in English hands fell with great rapidity. The Duke of Somerset, Edmund Beaufort, and John Talbot in Rouen were helpless. The English troops in Normandy were scattered across the duchy on garrison duties. There were simply not enough men to create a field army to counter the French armies, and despite his repu-tation as an aggressive and resourceful commander there was nothing that Talbot could do to relieve places under threat. Clearly captains of garri-sons could not expect help and it is hardly surprising that the mere pres-ence of substantial French forces was sufficient to encourage surrender. Among places to fall to the French in September were Fécamp, St-Lô, Alençon, Argentan, Gisors, Coutances, Carentan, Touques, Essay, Exmes and Valognes.

At the beginning of October the French turned their attention to Rouen, the centre of the English administration in Normandy. It had taken the English almost six months to bring the town to its knees in 1418–1419. It was to be a very different story this time. On 6 October Charles VII arrived at Pont-de-l'Arche, 20km south of Rouen. He despatched heralds to summon the town to surrender, but they were intercepted by Talbot before they could deliver their summons. It is said that Talbot tore up the summons and threw it at the feet of the heralds, who fled in fear of their lives. Understandably irritated, Charles VII advanced on Rouen on 9 October with a substantial force. At this stage he hoped that his presence with a display of force would suffice to encourage the inhabitants to rise up against the English garrison. Charles only remained for one day. Dunois stayed with the force for three days, in appalling conditions of heavy rain, during which the garrison launched numerous sorties to disrupt the French operations. At the end of the three days the heralds were once more despatched with their summons. Again they were intercepted and sent packing.

On 12 October Dunois withdrew to Pont-de-l'Arche but returned on 16 October to attempt to exploit a plot by some of the inhabitants to assist the French to enter the town by seizing two interval towers and the section of ramparts between them. Dunois urged his men up scaling ladders and onto the ramparts and the attack seemed to be on the point of success. At this moment Talbot, who had clearly lost nothing of his aggressive spirit in such circumstances, arrived at the head of 300 men and drove the French back. Some were killed in the hand-to-hand combat and others by archers as they withdrew from the walls. The French lost fifty to sixty men killed or captured.

However, although the assault had failed it had had a serious impact on the inhabitants, who were frightened by the prospect of a major assault and incensed by the killing of some of their number by Talbot's men during the fighting. Leading citizens met in the town hall on 17 October and resolved to sue for terms with the king who had now returned to Rouen. King Charles had anticipated such a move and gave an undertaking not to attack the town before 18 October. He also issued safe-conducts for notables from the city to come to the French camp. The citizens took advantage of these safe-conducts immediately and negotiations were arranged for the following day. Somerset, alarmed by the prospect of the populace rising against the garrison, decided to send two representatives of the English administration to participate in the talks.

Charles offered the Rouennais generous terms: a general amnesty, the preservation of privileges and the restoration of those suppressed during the English occupation. The delegates returned late on 18 October. It was only early the following day that a deputation of citizens came before Somerset and relayed to him the terms offered by King Charles to the garrison. If Somerset allowed the town to surrender he would be permitted to leave and go where he wished. If the English continued to resist they must expect to pay the price when the town was taken by assault. Somerset rejected the offer, saying that he would rather die than surrender, and exhorted the citizens to continue to resist since the walls remained intact. Meanwhile a mob descended on the town hall to hear the report from those who had attended the talks. There was general acclamation of support for the terms on offer. The willingness of the citizens to surrender is understandable in view of the apparent general collapse of English power. However, recollections of the suffering thirty years before during Henry V's siege and the parlous state of food reserves, given that no supplies had been able to enter Rouen for six weeks, must have weighed heavily in their deliberations. Somerset, seeing the way events were going, decided to evacuate the town and concentrate the garrison in the palace, the castle and the barbican controlling the gate at the bridge. As they withdrew into these strong places they were pursued by the mob and seven or eight of them were killed. The gates were opened and the French entered the town. The fortified monastery of Ste Catherine, 1km to the east on high ground, was garrisoned by about 120 English troops. With the arrival of the main French army and the positioning of heavy artillery before the monastery the captain of the garrison decided that discretion was the better part of valour and surrendered. The garrison were allowed to depart with their possessions and left to join the English holding Honfleur. They were allowed to go on condition that they took nothing from the land without payment. They said that they had never taken food without payment but now had no money. King Charles gave them money to pay for food during their 75km march. The king took up residence in the monastery.

By the evening of 19 October the English had withdrawn from the barbican and the bridge, concentrating on the palace and the castle. Some 1,200 men remained with Somerset and Talbot. There was initially no attempt by the French to storm the palace and the castle, or even to set a siege. However, with a shortage of supplies, the loss of the support of the population and a formidable French army present Somerset did not face a rosy prospect and he asked for talks with the French. These were conducted with Charles at the monastery of Ste Catherine. Somerset then returned to the palace to consider the terms.

On 22 October the French set about the siege of the palace and castle in earnest. Trenches were dug around the palace and bombards and cannon sited before the gates. The following day Somerset asked to see Charles once again. The king rebuked the English for not having accepted the generous terms on offer earlier and now demanded more stringent conditions. Somerset's delegation returned to the palace and saw the cordon tightening as the French continued with their preparations. Finally, on 29 October Somerset set his seal to a surrender document. He was to surrender not only Rouen but the castles at Arques, Tancarville and Lillebonne and the towns of Caudebec, Montivilliers and Honfleur. An indemnity of 50,000 *écus* was to be paid within one year and all debts to local traders and inn-keepers were to be settled. A number of prominent hostages were to be handed over to the French as surety, including John Talbot. The departing English were allowed to take their possessions and arms, save heavy artillery which was to be left behind. Somerset marched out of the palace on 4 November. The terms of surrender were received with shock and outrage when the news reached England. The siege had lasted little more than three weeks, and there had been neither assault nor bombardment. The surrender of so important a place in such circumstances could be seen as treasonable. Perhaps Somerset got wind of the attitude at home for, having set off from Honfleur, he elected to go to Caen rather than return to England.

Harfleur, 1449

While attention was focused on Rouen, Gisors and Neufchâtel-en-Bray surrendered. By the end of November Fougères, Bellême and the great fortress of Château-Gaillard had also surrendered, the latter after a siege of five weeks about which we know little. However, in view of its reputation for impregnability it is probably indicative of the poor state of provisioning in English-held towns and fortresses. The shock of Rouen galvanized parliament into action, but it was too little too late. In late November 1,000 longbows, 2,000 sheaves of arrows, 2,880 bowstrings, 1,800 pounds of gunpowder and other armaments were sent to Caen and Cherbourg and authorization was given for reinforcements to be raised. Sir Thomas Kyriell was indentured on 4 December 1449 to raise 425 men-at-arms and 2,080 archers but it was not until March 1450 that these much-needed men arrived in France.

Harfleur was the next major place to receive the attention of the Bastard of Orléans. He arrived on 8 December with sixteen great cannon, some 10,000 combatants, and a host of others to support the army. Twenty-five ships were positioned in the mouth of the Seine and the headquarters for the siege was established in the priory of Graville which had been used by Henry V for his lodgings on his first night ashore in France in 1415.

The conditions for the besiegers were severe. There were no houses to lodge the men and precious little in the way of natural protection from trees or woods. The men were reduced to sleeping on straw in brushwood shelters. Initially they had to suffer severe frosts, but this gave way to heavy rains and flooding from the sea during high tides.

The king was lodged at Montivilliers, 5km to the north, but came forward to watch the preparations to take the town. Great trenches had been dug to protect men approaching the walls, the cannon had started to bombard the walls and mines were being dug. The king, armed and wearing his helmet and carrying a shield, is reported to have gone into the mines himself to approach the walls of Harfleur. Despite the poor conditions for the besiegers and the strength of the garrison – 1,600 men and a further 400 who had come from abandoned towns and fortresses – it was clear that, faced with a shortage of supplies, they could not for long resist the formidable French force encircling the town. On Christmas Eve the captain of the town entered into negotiations. On Christmas Day the surrender document was signed by the captain of Harfleur, Thomas Aurigan, providing for the surrender of the town on New Year's Day and permitting the garrison to depart peacefully with their possessions. Eight hostages were surrendered to the French to guarantee the terms of surrender. They were taken to Montivilliers and duly returned to Harfleur on New Year's Day when the English started their evacuation. Many were evacuated by sea and in view of the numbers involved and the tides two extra days' grace were granted to allow an orderly departure. Apart from five years between 1435 and 1440 the town had been in English hands for almost thirty-five years. It was now lost for ever.

Honfleur, 1450

Early in January 1450 a force sent to Honfleur camped outside the castle and engaged in skirmishes with the English garrison, 300 or 400 strong. On 17 January the Bastard of Orléans arrived and set about besieging the town. Trenches, ditches and mines were dug, and cannon and stone-throwing artillery positioned. The English seemed determined to resist and returned fire with artillery, with the notable effect of killing among others the prominent squire Renaud Guillaume de Bourguignon. However, as with so many places, resistance was not to be long-lasting. At some point an agreement was reached which provided for surrender of the town on 18 February if relief was not forthcoming. There were substantial numbers of English troops with Somerset in Caen, fewer than 60km away, but the English did not attempt to relieve the garrison of Honfleur. The

French had entrenched their positions and prepared for battle, but on the due date the gates were opened and the English departed under safe-conduct.

The Beginning of the End

Thomas Kyriell had duly arrived in Cherbourg in March with the long overdue reinforcements from England. With the help of 1,800 men assembled from other garrisons to add to the 2,500 he had brought with him, he laid siege to Valognes 20km to the south. After three weeks the town fell. It was the last English success in Normandy but it was to prove short-lived, with the town returning to French hands by the summer. Kyriell set out to take his army to Caen. Why he had landed at the isolated port of Cherbourg at the end of the long Carentan peninsula and not sailed directly to Caen is a mystery. In any event he was intercepted by the French near Formigny and heavily defeated. If the numbers reported as killed (around 3,700) and taken prisoner (around 1,200) are accurate, the army was to all intents and purposes eliminated, with few men escaping. There would be no way back now, and it was simply a matter of time before the last strongholds fell.

Bayeux, 1450

Vire had fallen to the French in late April and now the French, led again by Dunois, the Bastard of Orléans, turned their attention to Bayeux. The siege began at the beginning of May. The French began digging trenches and mines, but of greatest importance was the use of artillery. Throughout the reign of Charles VII two brothers, Jean and Gaspard Bureau, had made great advances with ballistics and brought about a revolution in the use of artillery. Jean was Charles' Master of Artillery and was present at the siege of Bayeux, where the devastating effect of well-directed modern guns against traditional medieval fortifications was starkly demonstrated.

Within sixteen days the artillery fire had reduced the walls to rubble, and all that was left was to take the town by assault. Nevertheless, the commanders were hesitant to do so. There were around 900 men in the garrison and the commanders wanted to avoid the potential heavy loss of life. Their worst fears were realized when two unauthorized assaults were made in the same day. Both were repulsed with heavy casualties, partic-ularly due to artillery fire and shooting by archers. The assaults, although unsuccessful, gave the English captain of Bayeux, Matthew Gough, food for thought. He had beaten off two assaults, but he had also suffered losses and in due course he would be defeated or must surrender. The longer he held out, the less favourable the terms were likely to be.

Negotiations were opened and quickly concluded and the town surrendered on 16 May 1450. The terms of the surrender document survive in detail, and show something of the human side of a siege and not simply the military aspects. We see remarkable chivalry and humanity on the part of the French towards the remaining English, who, in addition to the combatants in the garrison, included 300 to 400 women and an unquantified number of children. Nevertheless, the terms were in some respects more stringent than those granted at earlier sieges since the return to war to the extent that with the end in sight for the English occupation the French had no desire to see the English depart to fight another day. The garrison was not allowed to leave with their possessions, armour or weapons. Exceptions were made for specified clothing that they were allowed to take, and they were also allowed a defined sum of money, ten *écus* for men-at-arms and five for the others. The garrison was required to return all jewellery and items of value taken from churches in the town and suburbs. However, married women were allowed to keep their clothing and jewellery. The combatants were each to carry a stick, a sign of safe-conduct. They were to return to England and not rejoin other garrisons. They were specifically excluded from going to Caen, the next target on the French list, but they could leave through the port of Cherbourg. Provision was made for the wounded to stay for a month to recover from their wounds, and those Englishmen who had established their lives in Normandy could remain if they swore allegiance to Charles VII. Finally, in recognition of the many women and children who would need to make the journey of more than 90km to Cherbourg, the English were allowed to keep horses for the women. The French also provided carts to transport those women for whom there were insufficient horses.

Caen, 1450

Avranches, Tombelaine, Briquebec and Valognes had all fallen during May. On 5 June 1450 it was the turn of Caen to receive the attention of the massed French armies. The constable, Arthur de Richemont, took up position to the west towards Bayeux. He brought with him 1,200 lances, 4,000 to 5,000 assorted archers and infantry and 2,000 franc-archers. Dunois took up position to the south with a further 500 lances, 2,500 archers and infantry and 2,000 franc-archers. The franc-archers, along with improvements in artillery, were another important military innovation during Charles VII's reign. They were professional infantrymen raised in return for exemption from the *taille* tax. A bridge was thrown across the Orne to allow communication between the two encampments, and on 9 June further men-at-arms and archers arrived and crossed by the bridge to take up station to the north of the town. Over the next few days further troops arrived to join the already very considerable force surrounding Caen.

The French assaulted the ramparts adjacent to the Bayeux gate and after a ferocious combat established a foothold on the walls. However, they were exposed to flanking fire and withdrew. The English walled up the gate. There was a further assault on the walls near the suburb of Vaucelles on the banks of the Orne to the south. After savage combat, with a number of the garrison killed or taken prisoner, the French held on to this section of the walls. In the sector commanded by Richemont mining brought down a section of wall and a tower. There was hand-to-hand combat as the French fought to exploit the breach and the English struggled to prevent a major incursion. However, both sides were conscious of the bloodshed in 1417 when Henry V took Caen, and neither side wanted a repetition. One chronicler tells us that the king wanted to preserve the town and avoid the violation of churches, the rape of women and the deflowering of virgins. However, the same chronicler gives more practical reasons for the French accepting the English request for talks.

The practical reasons were that the English garrison was recognized as tough and competent and the castle was very strong. The chronicler goes on at some length to explain that the castle was one of the strongest in Normandy, with high walls built of strong stone, deep ditches and sitting on rock. There was a large square keep with four towers. If the English withdrew into the castle considerable effort and losses would be entailed in taking it. It would be much better to secure the surrender of the town and castle through negotiations. Somerset, who was in the castle with his family, negotiated the surrender and signed the agreement on 25 June 1450. The agreement provided for the surrender of the town on 1 July. The garrison and the English inhabitants were allowed to depart with their belongings, personal arms and horses, but they were to go directly to England and would be escorted to the port of Ouistreham for their departure. All artillery and crossbows were to be left behind. Provision was made to hire carts and carriages to help with the transport of possessions. The English were to settle all debts before departing. There was also an enormous indemnity of 300,000 *écus* to pay. Twelve Englishmen, six Norman knights in English service and four prominent citizens were required as hostages for delivery of the town and castle as agreed.

Somerset must have been well aware of the enormity of his surrender of Caen. Indeed, it seems that he offered 4,000 *écus* to a Scotsman, Robin Campbell, lieutenant of Charles VII's Scots bodyguard, to kidnap Dunois or other French leaders and lead 1,500 Englishmen out of Caen. Some of the men would seize Charles and take him to Cherbourg while others would neutralize the French artillery by firing the powder kegs and spiking the guns. The plot failed. It only came to the notice of the French court some years later, but the delay did not save Campbell, who was executed for treason.

Falaise, 1450

St-Sauveur-le-Vicomte had also fallen to the French during June and by the beginning of July only Falaise, Domfront and Cherbourg remained in English hands. On 6 July Poton de Xaintrailles and Jean Bureau came to set the siege of Falaise, garrisoned by 1,500 men. Part of the garrison, on seeing the approach of the French, came out and attacked Bureau and his artillery train. Xaintrailles came to his aid and drove the English back into the town. The French began digging trenches and positioning their heavy artillery. Despite the initial aggressive defence the commanders of the garrison recognized that they had no prospect of relief and that surrender was the only option left to them. On 10 July they signed an agreement for the surrender of the town and castle.

The terms were straightforward, perhaps more honourable than those for other recent surrenders since eleven days' grace were accorded for the arrival of relief. Failing that relief the town and castle would be surrendered on 21 July 1450 and the garrison would leave under safe-conduct with their possessions. As at Caen they were to return directly to England. The two commanders of the garrison were lieutenants of John Talbot, who had been held by the French as a hostage for the fulfilment of the surrender terms for Rouen. Since Honfleur had not been surrendered as agreed, Talbot was still in French hands. His loyal lieutenants secured his release as a condition of the surrender of Falaise. The twist in the tail was that Talbot must go on pilgrimage to Rome. Twelve hostages were given up pending the surrender of Falaise. Of course, there was no hope whatsoever of relief and the garrison duly marched away on 21 July.

Cherbourg, 1450

Domfront was invested by the French two days later and surrendered on 6 August. Now only Cherbourg remained in English hands in Normandy. Troops detached from Falaise under the constable, Arthur de Richemont, and with Jean Bureau in charge of the artillery had set the siege of Cherbourg on 6 July, the same day that Falaise had been besieged.

Cherbourg was renowned for its strength. It had never fallen by assault since the construction of the walls in the mid-fourteenth century. The town stood on a rocky peninsula and had three concentric walls. The sea also turned the town into a virtual island at high tide. Because of its easy access to the sea Cherbourg could readily be reinforced and resupplied from England. It had taken Gloucester five months to take it in 1418, and he had only succeeded then due to treachery within the French garrison.

Despite the difficult conditions with the sea and the heavy defences the French set about digging trenches and mines to approach the walls. Bureau, as ever innovative and imaginative, placed guns on the sands even though they were subject to flooding at high tide. He covered them with waxed hides held down by stones during high water. Thus, along with guns more conventionally positioned around the town he was able to bombard the town from all sides. The garrison returned fire on the French and inflicted two notable casualties: Prégent de Coëtivy, Admiral of France, and the Breton squire Tugdual le Kermoysan, *bailli* of Troyes. On the French side four guns exploded in use, a not-unusual occurrence in the period. In June the town had been resupplied with the ingredients for making gunpowder, bowstrings, bows, arrows, malt, wheat and hops. Two gunners had been sent at the same time.

Thus, on the face of it the town should have been able to resist for a considerable time. Nevertheless, the captain of the town, Thomas Gower, surrendered on 12 August. The public surrender document was a conventional agreement, and since Cherbourg had held out for five weeks it seemed that the captain and its garrison had behaved creditably. However, hidden from public view was bribery. Thomas Gower's son Richard, like Talbot, had been held as a hostage since Rouen. He was released unconditionally. Money was also involved: 2,000 *écus* were paid to members of the garrison, 2,000 *écus* for the ransom of Dickon Chatterton, the captain of Pont-Douve, and other unknown sums for the ransoms of other prisoners held by the French. The French also agreed to pay the expenses of the garrison to return to England and spent money on gifts for undisclosed, but presumably influential, members of the garrison.

The last English-held place in Normandy had fallen, not principally through military action but effectively by being sold for the personal interests of the captain and his garrison. The reconquest of Normandy had taken little over a year. The rapidity of the collapse of English power may seem surprising but when the truce ended the English military situation was already precarious. The administration of Normandy was in a parlous state, and, despite pleas to parliament in England, there was little understanding at home of the need for support for the duchy which the English at home thought should finance its own defence. Once the French started to take strongholds and towns the collapse of English Normandy gathered pace. There was little point in holding out in the face of strong forces when there was virtually no prospect of relief. There were comparatively large numbers of Anglo-Norman men in the duchy. However, they were scattered in garrisons and although Kyriell had, for a short period after his arrival with reinforcements in early 1450, had more than 4,000 men at his disposal there was never a substantial English army in the field to counter the large French forces. The initiative rested entirely with the French and they could pick off towns and strongholds at their leisure. Add to that the improved quality in French armies and the increasingly numerous and effective artillery, and the cards were stacked against the English. As captains saw other places fall without relief, they could only reasonably conclude that they would also need to surrender. It was simply a question of terms.

The Recovery of Aquitaine: the First Campaign, 1450–1451

There had been some activity in the south-west in 1449 and the early part of 1450. The French had taken Cognac and St-Maigrin in May 1449. In September 1449 Mauléon fell to the Count of Foix and in February 1450 he took the fortress of Guiche. Fifteen other strongholds rapidly fell to Foix. However, it was only after the final fall of Normandy that Charles VII turned to the south-west to take Aquitaine.

With the arrival of substantial French forces in the autumn of 1450 many of the characteristics of the situation in Normandy were present in Aquitaine: scattered garrisons, the absence of an Anglo-Gascon field army of any consequence, capable French forces which held the initiative, effective French artillery and a lack of timely and sufficient support from England. A further similarity between Normandy and Aquitaine was the short duration, with the occasional exception, of sieges. An important difference was that whereas the English occupation of Normandy only went back thirty years, the English had been present in Bordeaux for more than three centuries. The English had acquired lands in Normandy through grant or purchase, but in Aquitaine land had remained in the hands of the

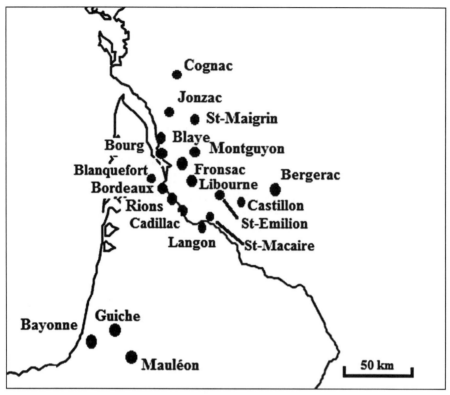

Aquitaine, 1450–1453.

Gascons. The English kings, in their capacity of Dukes of Aquitaine, had generally ruled with a light touch. There had been English officers appointed to the duchy, but much of the administration had been left in local hands. The privileges granted to Gascon merchants and towns in Aquitaine were generous and taxation was not imposed to raise money for the English crown in its own right. Thus there was a high degree of preference for the English over the French throughout much of the duchy. In the end, as we shall see, these circumstances led to a late resurgence in English fortunes when reinforcements eventually arrived in the autumn of 1452, but the overwhelming French strength eventually prevailed.

Mauléon, 1449

Towards the end of September 1449 the Count of Foix, in the company of the Counts of Comminges and Estrac, with men drawn from Foix, Bigorre and Bearn, arrived before the town and castle of Mauléon. The town took little time to decide to come to terms and the garrison withdrew into the castle. The castle was reputed to be one of the strongest in Aquitaine and was perched high on a stone promontory above the town. Nevertheless, the Count of Foix, knowing that the garrison was small and ill-provisioned, decided to lay siege.

The King of Navarre got wind of events and quickly raised a force of Navarrese, Aragonese, English and Gascons with the aim of relieving the siege. However, on his arrival he appreciated that the size of the besieging force was too strong. He attempted to negotiate the raising of the siege with the Count of Foix. Navarre emphasized his responsibility to the King of England to hold safe his possessions and demanded that the Count of Foix, who was also his son-in-law, raise the siege. The count replied that he was the lieutenant of the King of France and had no intention of doing as his father-in-law demanded. The King of Navarre withdrew. The implications for the garrison were clear and they came to an arrangement with the Count of Foix, marching out under the cross of St George before the end of September.

Montguyon, 1451

The French campaign for the recovery of Aquitaine started in October 1450 with the king sending forces south and taking Jonzac and Bergerac. Sometime in the autumn 300 men-at-arms and 2,700 archers arrived from England under the command of Richard Woodville. However, although there was an inconclusive skirmish between French and Anglo-Gascon forces near Bordeaux on 1 November, it was only the following spring that operations began in earnest. The Count of Dunois, Charles VII's lieutenant-general, had arrived from Normandy by the spring. Montguyon fell to him on 6 May after a short siege of which we know little other than the terms of surrender which allowed the garrison to depart with their possessions and personal arms.

Blaye, 1451

After taking Montguyon Dunois started to close the net on Bordeaux. The first target was Blaye. The town lies on the banks of the Gironde 40km downstream from the city. Taking it would make access to Bordeaux extremely problematic for the English.

Dunois arrived before the gates of Blaye on 14 May 1450. The size of the French force is unknown but Dunois was joined by other companies at the start of the siege together with a number of ships sent to blockade the town from the river. The ships also brought supplies for the besieging army. On arriving, the French ships found that five ships had been sent from Bordeaux to bring supplies and help to the besieged town. The French ships were manned by men-at-arms and archers or crossbowmen and immediately attacked the Anglo-Gascon ships. These were also manned by soldiers, but caught at anchor they were at a disadvantage. After fighting which resulted in a number of men killed and wounded the Anglo-Gascons weighed anchor and were driven off by the French and pursued as far as the port of Bordeaux. The French returned to Blaye and sealed off access from the Gironde.

The size of the besieging army continued to grow with the arrival of more men. Trenches, ditches and mines were prepared and an artillery bombardment started. Within a short period breaches were opened up in several places in the walls of the town. Just before sunset on 20 May, as the defenders were changing the guard, the French launched an assault on the town at several points. The defenders were quickly overwhelmed with 200 of the garrison killed or taken prisoner. The survivors, some 200 men, withdrew into the castle. Among those trapped were the mayor of Bordeaux and his deputy and the Lord of Lesparre. It was clear that there could be no escape, either by river or by land, and the garrison entered into negotiations for the surrender of the town.

There was no pretence at time being allowed for relief. The surrender document was signed on 24 May and required the town to be given up that same day. The terms were far from generous. All possessions, gold, silver, arms and artillery were to be forfeited, inventoried and left undamaged. The garrison put themselves at the mercy of the king and Dunois. If they were released they were not to take up arms against the French for four months.

Bordeaux, 1451

Before the end of May Bourg, 15km upstream on the Gironde from Blaye, St-Émilion and Castillon on the Dordogne and Rions on the Garonne all fell to the French. During the first three weeks of June Libourne and Fronsac on the Dordogne capitulated. The position of Bordeaux was becoming increasingly desperate. Sometime in early June the French arrived before the walls of Bordeaux. It was clear to all that there was little point in resisting and the leading citizens and commanders asked for talks. On 12 June 1451 a treaty was agreed for the surrender of the town on 23 June if no help was forthcoming from the King of England by that date. Clearly that was impossible. As the Anglo-Gascon signatories acknowledged, this was for the sake of form and to respect their oaths to the

English king. Charles VII appreciated the special situation in Bordeaux and Aquitaine and his conditions were generous. In return for the surrender of Bordeaux and the remaining places held by the English in Aquitaine the king granted to the inhabitants of Bordeaux freedom from taxes, the preservation of existing privileges granted by the English kings, and a period of six months to decide if individuals wished to remain or leave. Those who chose to leave could take their possessions with them and go with safe-conduct. At sunset on 23 June 1451 the French drew up their army to await the English relief and a herald mounted the ramparts to cry: 'Help from those of England for those of Bordeaux.' No help came, and under the terms of the treaty Bordeaux was required to surrender. In the event, Bordeaux asked for more time and it was only on 30 June 1451 that the keys were handed to Dunois and he entered ceremonially into the town.

Bayonne, 1451

The only place of any consequence to continue to resist was Bayonne, far to the south and close to the Pyrenees. Dunois marched south and arrived outside the town on 7 August 1451. He was in the company of the Count of Foix and numerous other great lords. They came with large numbers of men-at-arms, archers and spearmen, together with the now usual formidable artillery train.

The inhabitants abandoned the suburbs of St Léon, although they were well protected by ditches and palisades. They had rightly concluded that they offered little protection against the artillery being deployed. As they withdrew into the town the garrison set fire to churches and houses in the suburbs. They were closely pursued by the French and it was said by one chronicler that if the French could have entered the town then with a hundred good men they could have taken Bayonne that day. However, the ditches surrounding the town were deep and the walls high. The French involved in this early fighting were not equipped with scaling ladders and had to abandon the attempt to enter the town.

In the succeeding days fresh reinforcements arrived but the garrison conducted a vigorous defence. At one point the defenders came out of the town on the seaward side to attack the besiegers. In the fighting that followed the Frenchman Bernard de Bearn was wounded by a shot from a culverin which pierced his shield and penetrated his leg. There was further fighting when the French took a fortified church surrounded by a palisade. In the circumstances of the determined defence Dunois was reluctant to order an assault before he had reduced the fortifications with his artillery.

A bombardment had started but as yet the large bombards had not yet arrived.

When the bombards arrived their appearance was enough to convince the garrison that further resistance was futile. On 18 August negotiations for the surrender of the town started. As the talks began a dozen armed French ships with 600 soldiers arrived close to the town. There could be no escape by sea. It is said that on 20 August, against a clear blue sky, clouds were seen in the form of a white cross surmounted by a crown which changed into the *fleur de lys*, representing the arms of France. Seeing this sign Bayonne's inhabitants are reputed to have said that as it was the will of God, they would become French. Banners bearing the cross of St George were lowered and the gates of the town opened. The Counts of Foix and Dunois took possession of the town the following day, 21 August 1451. It seemed that it was all over for the English in Aquitaine.

The Recovery of Aquitaine: the Second Campaign, 1452–1453

However, it was not quite all over. The officials appointed by Charles VII to administer Bordeaux and Aquitaine reneged on the king's promises concerning exemptions from taxation and the maintenance of privileges. In July 1452 the Bordelais sent representatives to plead their case with Charles. They failed to obtain his support, and the following month emissaries were sent to England. In September 1452 John Talbot, appointed Henry VI's lieutenant in Aquitaine, set off with between 4,000 and 5,000 men in a last attempt to save Aquitaine. With the French controlling Bordeaux, Blaye and Bourg the English could not penetrate up the Gironde. The landing was made on the Gironde estuary about 100km north-west of Bordeaux on 17 October 1452. After so many years in the English camp the leading citizens required little encouragement to return to the fold, and there was popular support for the return of the English with Talbot. Within less than a week Bordeaux was back in English hands with Talbot entering the city on 23 October 1452. The seneschal had been trying to negotiate with the inhabitants to allow him and his garrison to depart with safe-conduct. However, the gates were opened to the English before the agreement was concluded and the seneschal and his men were captured. A number of towns, including Blanquefort, Libourne, Castillon, Rions, Cadillac, St-Macaire and Langon, quickly came back to the English fold. The only major places to remain in French hands were Fronsac, Bourg and Blaye.

The French had not anticipated a major English expedition coming to Aquitaine and it was only in June 1453 that they arrived in force ready to deal with the renewed Anglo-Gascon activity. Meanwhile in the spring Talbot had laid siege to and taken Fronsac. Around 9 July 1453 the French laid siege to Castillon, now known as Castillon-la-Bataille. Talbot rode to its relief, also seeing an opportunity to confront the main French army in battle. On 17 July the anticipated clash took place, resulting in a decisive defeat for the Anglo-Gascon army. Talbot, in accordance with an oath given when liberated after his release from French imprisonment in 1450 not to take up arms again against Charles VII, rode into battle unarmed and without armour and was killed. The Battle of Castillon was the last throw of the dice for the English, and the death of Talbot and the defeat constituted a fatal blow to morale in the duchy. It was now only a matter of time before the rest of Aquitaine fell once again to the French.

Cadillac, 1453

The day following the Battle of Castillon the French laid siege to Cadillac. We know little of the siege, but it was only on 17 September that an assault was made. The town fell rapidly and the garrison withdrew into the castle. They tried to purchase their freedom but in the end were compelled to surrender. The garrison commander, a Gascon called Gaillardet, was executed.

Bordeaux, 1453

From early July operations by the Counts of Foix and Clermont in the Medoc had the aim of reducing the flow of supplies to Bordeaux. By the middle of the month the French were ready to lay siege to the city. The siege of Bordeaux was a difficult enterprise. It was surrounded by three concentric walls some 6km in length. There were twenty towers and to the east the town was protected by the Garonne, some 600m wide. A successful siege would require a blockade on the river as well as operations by the army. At Lormont, 6km downstream from Bordeaux, the French built fortifications to harbour their shipping and to house troops and artillery. French shipping also patrolled the mouth of the Gironde.

The Bordelais constructed fortifications about 1km from the city to protect the English shipping. However, after the fall of Cadillac in late September the French could turn all of their resources to the submission of Bordeaux. The blockade became increasingly effective and famine was taking a grip on the population. That, and the collapse of morale after the defeat at Castillon, led to some Gascons negotiating with the French for the surrender of the city. They had hoped to negotiate safe-conduct and the retention of their possessions. Charles VII was not disposed to be generous after the events of the last year and said that they must surrender to his mercy. Roger de Camoys, the English commander, was determined to hold out and would not negotiate until it was clear that relief from England would not be forthcoming. To discourage desertion he had all the ships disabled and used as floating batteries to protect the port.

After the rejection of the approach by the Gascons seeking favourable terms hostilities were renewed vigorously, including attacks on the fortifications protecting the port. In early October famine was taking an increasing hold and an epidemic had broken out both within Bordeaux and among the besiegers. Camoys offered safe-conduct for a French representative to enter the city to arrange for negotiations. These started at Lormont on 5 October. It seems that two strands of negotiations were under way: one for the citizens who had to look to the future after the departure of the English when they were back under French jurisdiction and one for the English to secure their freedom. The terms were agreed on 9 October. Charles VII demanded that twenty of the most prominent citizens surrender to his mercy. Camoys pleaded for their lives in return for perpetual banishment. The king refused but in the end their lives were spared.

On 12 October twelve hostages, six Gascon and six English, were handed over to guarantee the terms of the surrender agreement. Two days later further hostages were handed over and the fortifications around the port surrendered. The gates were opened on 16 October and the surrender was formally completed three days later. The English were allowed to depart with full honours and to go either to England or to Calais. The only remaining Anglo-Gascon garrisons were Bénauges and Rions and these had surrendered by the end of October. After more than three centuries Aquitaine had ceased to be held by English kings as dukes of Aquitaine.

Chapter 10

Conclusions

The essentials of sieges are timeless. What changes over time are the means of defence and attack. The key change during the 116 years of the Hundred Years War was the development of artillery. At the start it was little more than some new-fangled curiosity. By the end it was a formidable arm in both siege warfare and set-piece battles. Charles VII had built upon earlier military reforms made by his grandfather, Charles V, and during his reign his master of artillery, Jean Bureau, brought great technical and organizational skills to bear. He capitalized on technical developments with the manufacture of guns and powder to bring the effectiveness of French artillery to new heights.

Of course, cannon could be used as a weapon of defence, but it was in the attack of fortifications that the effect of advances was most marked. The pace of technological change in artillery outpaced developments in the design of defences. Such expedients as the use of barbicans and the construction of banks of earth behind walls could help to counter the effectiveness of artillery to some extent, but the much-needed fundamental change to the design of fortifications had to wait a little longer.

The changes in artillery effectiveness when they finally came were dramatic. A look at the sieges considered in this book is illuminating. Of the eight sieges considered in the period of the English ascendancy between 1337 and 1360 only two were successfully brought to a conclusion by surrender and one by assault. The other five were abandoned. The mean duration of the sieges considered here was eighty-eight days.

During the French recovery from 1369 to 1383 ten of the seventeen sieges in this book were brought to a successful conclusion: three by assault and seven by composition. Seven sieges were abandoned. The average duration of these sieges was thirty-five days. Between the renewal of war in 1415 until the Truce of Tours in 1444 twenty-seven of the forty-four sieges considered here resulted in surrender, three places fell to assault and nine were abandoned. The average siege duration was higher than the previous periods at ninety-one days.

The samples here are, of course, small and skewed to some extent in all three of these periods by exceptionally long sieges: Calais in 1346–1347

(332 days), St-Sauveur-le-Vicomte in 1374–1375 (321 days), Tartas in 1441–1442 (330 days) and Dieppe 1442–1443 (292 days). Many factors came into play in determining the duration of sieges, but the pattern over these first three periods of the war does not seem to indicate a dramatic impact by artillery. Of the sixty-nine sieges 30 per cent were abandoned. Again, there could be many reasons for abandonment of a siege, but an inability to inflict significant damage on the fortifications was clearly important. The fact that only 10 per cent of sieges were concluded by a successful assault is also indicative that artillery was still not effective enough seriously to degrade well-built stone walls and towers.

In the final few years of the war, from the collapse of the Truce of Tours in 1449 until the expulsion of the English from Aquitaine four years later, the story was entirely different. Of the eighteen sieges covered in this book during these years all were of places held by the English. Without exception, all resulted in surrender. The average duration fell to twenty-five days. In Normandy the average duration of the sieges was barely three weeks. The speed of the collapse of English-held places in Normandy owed a good deal to the general erosion of English political power in the duchy and financial neglect. The growing military imbalance as the French army reforms took effect and the French began to put their differences aside to concentrate on defeating the common foe was also significant. Also, as the collapse accelerated, the obvious absence of any prospect of relief played a part in the decisions taken by commanders. Nevertheless, the effectiveness of artillery was the critical factor. Places that surrendered were not doing so because they were running out of supplies. They were doing so for several reasons: the array of heavy guns was sufficient to encourage their capitulation, damage to walls and towers was quickly and effectively achieved demonstrating that an assault would surely be forthcoming, or in some cases assaults were repulsed but it was obvious that as the degradation of defences continued the inevitable result would be a successful attack.

The days of medieval town walls and castles where high walls had pre-dominated in design were numbered. In the future lower profile walls would seek to reduce the effectiveness of artillery fire and geometric designs would enhance the use of artillery by the garrison.

Summary of Outcomes of Sieges Considered in this Book

	Years	Abandoned	Relieved	Taken by Assault	Surrendered
The English Ascendancy	1337–1360	5	0	1	2
The French Recovery	1369–1383	7	0	3	7
Renewal of War	1415–1443	10	5	3	33
Expulsion of the English	1449–1453	0	0	0	18

See Appendix II for detail of the outcome of the sieges discussed in this book.

Duration of Sieges

Note: In some cases the precise dates of sieges are not known, and approximations have been made.

Date	Town or Fortress	Duration of Siege (days)	Abandoned	Relieved	Taken by Assault	Composition or Surrender	Held By
The English Ascendancy, 1337–1360 (8 sieges)							
1339	Cambrai	20	✕				French
1340	Tournai	64	✕				French
1345–1346	La Réole	60				✕	French
1346	Aiguillon	142	✕				English
1346–1347	Calais	332				✕	French
1356	Breteuil	40	✕				Navarrese
1356	Romorantin	5			✕		French
1359–1360	Reims	39	✕				French
	Totals		5	–	1	2	
	Median Duration: 50 days						
	Average Duration: 88 days						
The French Recovery, 1369–1383 (17 Sieges)							
1369	Realville	15			✕		English
1369	Duraval	35	✕				French
1370	La-Roche-sur-Yonne	35					French
1370	Limoges	3				✕	English
1370	Limoges	4			✕		French
1370–1371	Montpon-Ménestérol	80				✕	French
1372	Soubise	5				✕	English
1373	Chizé	5			✕		English
1373	Brest	71	✕				English
1373	Derval	121	✕				English
1374	La Réole	6				✕	English
1374–1375	St-Sauveur-le-Vicomte	321				✕	English
1377	Bergerac	14				✕	English

Date	Town or Fortress	Duration of Siege (days)	Abandoned	Relieved	Taken by Assault	Composition or Surrender	Held By
1377	St-Macaire	4				×	English
1378	Cherbourg	18	×				English
1380-1381	Nantes	64	×				French
1383	Ypres	33	×				Flemish
	Totals		7	–	3	7	

Median Duration: 18 days
Average Duration: 35 days

The renewal of war in 1415 to the Truce of Tours, 1444 (51 sieges)

Date	Town or Fortress	Duration of Siege (days)	Abandoned	Relieved	Taken by Assault	Composition or Surrender	Held By
1415	Harfleur	37				×	French
1417	Caen	36				×	French
1417–1418	Falaise town	35				×	French
1417–1418	Falaise castle	80				×	French
1418	Louviers	16				×	Burgundians
1418	Pont-de-l'Arche	24				×	French
1418–1419	Rouen	155				×	French
1419	Ivry-la-Bataille	10				×	French
1419	La Roche-Guyon	28				×	French
1419–1420	Chateau-Gaillard	180				×	French
1420	Sens	5				×	French
1420	Montereau	17				×	French
1420	Melun	133				×	French
1421	Alencon	50	×				English
1421	Dreux	34				×	French
1421	Villeneuve-sur-Yonne	5				×	French
1421–1422	Meaux	217				×	French
1422	Cosne	42		×			Burgundians
1423	Meulan	57				×	French
1423–1424	Le Crotoy	252				×	French
1423	Cravant	30		×			Burgundians
1424	Compiègne	42				×	French
1424	Gaillon	60				×	French
1424	Ivry-la-Bataille	60				×	French
1424–1425	Guise	150				×	French
1424–1425	Mont-St-Michel	440	×				French
1427	Pontorson	71				×	Bretons/French
1427	Montargis	60		×			French
1427	La Gravelle	30	×				French

Date	Town or Fortress	Duration of Siege (days)	Abandoned	Relieved	Taken by Assault	Composition or Surrender	Held By
1428–1429	Orléans	211	✕				French
1429	Jargeau	3			✕		English
1429	Beaugency-sur-Loire	3				✕	English
1429	La Charité-sur-Loire	28	✕				Burgundians
1430	Compiègne	150	✕				French
1431	Louviers	150				✕	French
1432	St Céneri-le-Gérei	10	✕				French
1432	Lagny-sur-Marne	96	✕				French
1433	St Valery-sur-Somme	57				✕	French
1433	St Céneri-le-Gérei	90				✕	French
1433	Sillé-le-Guillaume	42			✕		French
1434	Creil	42				✕	French
1435	St-Denis	35				✕	French
1436	Calais	21	✕				English
1437	Le Crotoy	45	✕				English
1439	Meaux	58				✕	English
1439	Avranches	25		✕			English
1440	Harfleur	130				✕	French
1441	Creil	18				✕	English
1441	Pontoise	103			✕		English
1441–1442	Tartas	330				✕	English
1442–1443	Dieppe	292		✕			French
	Totals		10	5	3	33	

Median Duration: 45 days
Average Duration: 84 days

The Expulsion of the English, 1449–1453 (18 sieges)

1449	Verneuil-sur-Avre	36				✕	English
1449	Vernon	4				✕	English
1449	Harcourt	7				✕	English
1449	Rouen town	9				✕	English
1449	Rouen castle	27				✕	English
1449	Harfleur	25				✕	English
1450	Honfleur	35				✕	English
1450	Bayeux	16				✕	English
1450	Caen	27				✕	English
1450	Falaise	16				✕	English
1450	Cherbourg	38				✕	English

Date	Town or Fortress	Duration of Siege (days)	Abandoned	Relieved	Taken by Assault	Composition or Surrender	Held By
1449	Mauléon	7				✕	English
1451	Montguyon	7				✕	English
1451	Blaye	11				✕	English
1451	Bordeaux	18				✕	English
1451	Bayonne	15				✕	English
1453	Cadillac	60				✕	English
1453	Bordeaux	90				✕	English
	Totals		–	–	–	18	

Median Duration: 18 days
Average Duration: 25 days

Notes

There is a wide range of sources, both primary and secondary, which cover the Hundred Years War and the sieges. I have drawn extensively on printed narrative primary sources and secondary sources. Some of the work of the chroniclers needs to be treated with caution, particularly over numbers which are frequently conveniently round and often clearly exaggerated. Sometimes there are more accurate data available because of subsequent work on archival material, but in the absence of such figures the chroniclers' figures at least give an idea of relative strength. It also needs to be remembered that chroniclers were often writing for patrons and were not necessarily objective in their writing. Jean Froissart in particular, who during his time in the service of Edward III's queen, Philippa, from 1361 to 1369, was writing from an English perspective, while after his return to his native Flanders he was less sympathetic, notably in his telling of the siege of Limoges in 1370. His writing sometimes smacks of tabloid journalism, but is an invaluable source nonetheless. Some accounts, such as the contemporary report on the siege of Orléans by an anonymous inhabitant, are striking, however, for their even-handed approach.

Chapter 1: The Hundred Years War

There are currently four volumes of Jonathan Sumption's magisterial work on the Hundred Years War, with a final volume to come. There is no better secondary source, but the entire work runs to several thousand pages. There is a wide choice for those who prefer a more concise account, including *The Hundred Years' War: 1337–1453 (Essential Histories)* by Anne Curry, Robin Neillands' *The Hundred Years War*, and *The Hundred Years War: England and France at War, c.1300–c.1450* by Christopher Allmand.

Chapter 2: Siege Warfare

Clifford J. Rogers, *War Cruel and Sharp: English Strategy under Edward III, 1327–1360*, examines and analyses the strategy of Edward III and his use of *chevauchées* in the first phase of the war. For the quotation (author's translation) on the situation at Bourges see the *Chronique du religieux de Saint-Denis*, vol. 4, p. 681. See the *Collection Générale des Documents Français qui se Trouvent en Angleterre*, ed. Jules Delpit, vol. 1, Paris 1847, p. 223, item 346 for the letter from King Henry V to the City of London requiring transhipment of supplies to Harfleur. For the unfortunate Perrot Monein see Guy Gross, *Le Prince Noir en Berry*, and Louis Raynal, *Histoire du Berry, depuis les temps les plus anciens jusqu'en 1789*, vol. 2. Christine de Pisan's quote can be found in *The Book of Deeds of Arms and of Chivalry*. Descriptions for the division of spoils can be found in Andrew Ayton and Philip Preston's *The Battle of Crécy 1346*, and Michael Prestwich's *Armies and Warfare in the Middle Ages*. Susan Rose, in *Calais, An English Town in France, 1347–1558*, gives a detailed account of the history of English-held Calais. For the conduct of sieges, see Maurice Keen, *The Laws of War in the Late Middle Ages*. The Biblical reference to sieges, although no reference to this is known before Henry V's siege of Harfleur in 1415, can be found in *The Revised English Bible, with Apocrypha*, Oxford and Cambridge, 1989, Deuteronomy, 20:10–14. Primary sources used generally in this chapter include Enguerrand de Monstrelet's *Chronique*, vol. 2, and Siméon Luce's edition of *Chroniques de J Froissart*, vol. 7. My thanks to Guilhem Pépin for the letter from the Prince of Wales, dated 22 September 1370, written at Limoges after the sacking of the *cité*. See Maurice Keen, *The Laws of War in the Late Middle Ages*, for the charge of treason made against Sir William Chamberlain for the surrender of Meaux in 1439. Jonathan Sumption, *Cursed Kings*, cites the archives of Calvados for casualties at Caen in 1417.

Chapter 3: Fortifications – Attack and Defence

Descriptions of fortifications and their development can be found in *The Medieval Fortress, Castles, Forts and Walled Cities of the Middle Ages*, by J.E. Kaufmann, H.W. Kaufmann and Robert F. Jurga, and *Fortresses de la France Medievale* by J.-F. Finó. Nicolas Savy's *La ville fortifiée de la Guerre de cent ans* provides a valuable and interesting analysis of measures taken for the defence of towns in south-west France. For the division of costs between the crown and the inhabitants for the fortifications of *bastides* and their more general history see James Bentley's *Fort Towns of France*. There is a replica thirteenth-century castle under construction at Guédelon in France using traditional construction techniques and showing many typical features of castles of the Hundred Years War. Renaud Beffeyte has carried out extensive research with reconstructed siege machines and has written extensively on his research and experimentation in *L'Art de la Guerre au Moyen Âge*, and *War Machines in the Middle Ages*. See also *The Medieval Siege* by Jim Bradbury and *Medieval Siege Warfare* by Christopher Gravett for siege equipment. For artillery of the period see Robert D. Smith, 'Artillery and the Hundred Years War: Myth and Interpretation', in *Arms, Armies and Fortifications in the Hundred Years War*, and Dan Spencer's 'Artillery' in Anne Curry, Peter Hoskins, Thom Richardson and Dan Spencer, *The Agincourt Companion*, and Michael Prestwich, *Armies and Warfare in the Middle Ages*. See Richard Barber, *Edward III and the triumph of England*, for possible use of ribalds on the Crécy expedition of 1346 and Jim Bradbury, *The Medieval Siege*, and Susan Rose, *Calais, An English Town in France, 1347–1558*, for the use of cannon at Calais in the siege that followed. Anne Curry, in 'Guns and Goddams. Was there a military revolution in Lancastrian Normandy, 1415–50?', discusses the use of artillery by English armies during the war. In 'Gunners, Aides and Archers: The Personnel of the English Ordnance Companies in Normandy in the Fifteenth Century', Andy King gives an interesting insight into the organization of artillery in English armies in the later years of the war. Reconstructions of siege engines, many in working order, can be seen at the châteaux of Tiffauges and Castelnaud-la-Chapelle in France. Froissart in *Oeuvres de Froissart, Chroniques*, vol. 5, describes the impact of the Black Prince's expedition beyond the Garonne and the poor state of defences. Romain Guignard, in *Issoudun des Origines à 1850, Aperçu des Chroniques Locales*, recounts the drawn-out process over many years for the reconstruction of the fortifications of Issoudun. *La Guerre de Cent Ans vue à Travers les Registres du Parlement* records the case of the Lord of Lapenne and his efforts to persuade local inhabitants to contribute to the cost of maintenance of fortifications. Jacques Michaud and André Cabans in *Histoire de Narbonne* and Paul Carbonel in *Histoire de Narbonne, des origines à l'époque contemporaine* relate the dispute between the consuls and the bishop over the demolition of the town walls at Narbonne. Henri Ménard, *Carbonne, Huit*

Siècles d'Histoire, records the provisions for keeping buildings at set distances from walls to facilitate the movement of men engaged in defending the town. See Henri Ribadieu, *Les Campagnes du Comte de Derby en Guyenne*, for the creation of a breach in the walls of Meilhan-sur-Garonne.

Chapter 4: The English Ascendancy, 1337–1360

As always Jonathan Sumption, in *Trial by Battle*, gives an excellent and full account of the early years of the Hundred Years War. Clifford J. Rogers, *War Cruel and Sharp*, provides an invaluable analysis of Edward III's strategy, including the Crécy campaign and the siege of Calais, which he argues may well have been his objective from the outset of his 1346 campaign. Kenneth Fowler's *The King's Lieutenant, Henry of Grosmont, First Duke of Lancaster 1310–1361*, gives a good account of Lancaster's campaign in Aquitaine in 1345–1346, including Bergerac, La Réole and Aiguillon and the terms of his indenture. See Chaudru de Crazannes, 'Notice sur le Castrum d'Aiguillon' in the *Revue Archéologique*, for a description of the town and fortifications of Aiguillon. The *arrière-ban* was a royal summons to vassals, and in turn to lesser vassals, to muster in the service of the king. Richard Barber, *Edward III and the Triumph of England*, also gives useful material on the Crécy campaign and the siege of Calais. Susan Rose's history of the English occupation of Calais, *Calais, An English Town in France, 1347–1558*, provides an interesting and informative account of events during the siege. Craig Lambert's article on Calais, 'Edward III's siege of Calais: A reappraisal' describes the importance of maritime support for the siege and also analyses the numbers involved in the English forces. See Robert of Avesbury, *De Gestis Mirabilibus Regis Edwardi Tertii*, for Jean de Vienne's last appeal to King Philip for relief. See my *In the Steps of the Black Prince, The Road to Poitiers, 1355–1356* for events surrounding the siege of Romorantin. The *Eulogium Historiarum*, Froissart's *Oeuvres*, H.T. Riley's *Memorials of London Life* and Jean Le Bel all recount events before and during the siege. See also R. Crozet, 'Siège de Romorantin par le Prince de Galles (1356)', in *Revue Historique, Année 51*, and Alexandre Dupré, *Recherches Historiques sur Romorantin et la Sologne*. For negotiations leading to the Treaty of Brétigny and analysis of the terms of the First and Second Treaty of London, see Clifford J. Rogers, 'The Anglo-French Peace Negotiations of 1354–60 Reconsidered', in J.S. Bothwell, ed., *The Age of Edward III*. For accounts of events from the Battle of Poitiers until the renewal of war in 1359, see: Sumption, *Trial by Fire*, R. Delachenal, *Histoire de Charles V*, vols 1 and 2, Ian Mortimer, *The Perfect King*, and Richard Barber, *Edward Prince of Wales and Aquitaine*. See also Richard Barber, *Edward III and the Triumph of England*, and a short monograph by Henri Moranvillé, *Le siege de Reims 1359–60*, for the Reims campaign of 1359–1360.

Chapter 5: The French Recovery, 1369–1389

Among the primary sources for this stage of the war are Jean Froissart's *Chroniques*, the *Chronique de bon duc Loys de Bourbon*, Walsingham's *Chronica Maiora*, the *Chronique normande du xive siècle* and *Les Grandes Chroniques de France, Chroniques des Règnes de Jean II et Charles V*, vol. 2. For Ypres the richest primary source is the *Istore et Chroniques de Flandres*, edited by Kervyn de Lettenhove. Once again, the most comprehensive of secondary sources for this period of the war is by Jonathan Sumption: *Divided Houses*. In French a valuable secondary source is vol. 4 of Robert Delachenal's *Histoire de Charles V*. For events at Chizé see, *Histoire de Bertrand du Guesclin, Connestable de France et des Royaumes de Leon, de Castille, de Cordove et de Seville, Duc de Molines, Comte de Longueville Etc* by Paul Hay du Chastelet and, for the alternative story of the trap set with carts of wine, see L. Favre, *Duguesclin et Jeanne d'Arc, ou la France aux XIVe et XVe siècles*. For a reappraisal of casualties at Limoges see *The Black Prince*, by Michael Jones. Jean Froissart uses the term 'lance', which was occasionally used to describe a tactical unit in the medieval period. However, in the English armies of the fourteenth century it was used more as an administrative term for pay and recruiting purposes. There is an example of a lance in 1379 consisting of two men-at-arms, an archer and a page – see Prestwich, *Armies and Warfare in the Middle Ages*, and Ayton and Preston, *The Battle of Crécy, 1346*. Froissart probably used the term here as synonymous with a man-at-arms. *Routiers* were soldiers, often redundant during periods of truce or peace, who formed armed bands. Often they were little more than brigands pillaging and looting the countryside. Sometimes these bands were formidable fighting units with several hundred men and on occasion fought for England and France. They are often described as 'English' but in reality they comprised men from many nations, including the French. The Paris Bastille is of course well known, but 'bastille' is often used in the period of the Hundred Years War to describe temporary field forts. The word *bastide*, also used to describe fort towns, is likewise used to describe field forts.

Chapter 6: From Harfleur to the Death of Henry V, 1415–1422

General primary sources used for this period are *La Chronique d'Enguerrand de Monstrelet*, and the *Chronique du religieux de Saint-Denis*. The College of Arms MS M9, fos 31–66v gives a valuable account of events in France between 1415 and 1429 from the viewpoint of the English army, and the *Gesta Henrici Quinti* relates in detail events during the siege of Harfleur. See Anne Curry's paper, 'Representing War and Conquest, 1414–1429: The Evidence of College of Arms Manuscript M9' for analysis of MS M9. We also have the poem of John Page relating to the siege of Rouen. Once again Jonathan Sumption comes to the fore with *Cursed Kings* for a general account of the progress of the war. Juliet Barker in her *Conquest, The English Kingdom of France, 1417–50* relates the military and political history of English involvement in Normandy and northern France after Henry V's return in 1417. Anne Curry's *Agincourt, a New History* relates the story of Henry V's Agincourt expedition with detailed analysis of preparations for the campaign and events at the siege of Harfleur. Her article 'Guns and Goddams' brings useful information on a number of sieges in this book, notably Rouen in this chapter and Louviers and Montargis in the next. G. du Fresne de Beaucourt's *Histoire de Charles VII* is a very useful secondary source in French. Dan Spencer gives a detailed account of the deployment and use of artillery at Harfleur in '"The scourge of the stones": English gunpowder artillery at the siege of Harfleur'. See Craig Lambert's 'Henry V and the crossing to France: reconstructing naval operations for the Agincourt campaign, 1415' for a detailed analysis of shipping for the Agincourt campaign and the siege of Harfleur. In French, the *Siège et Prise de Caen par les Anglais en 1417, Épisode de la Guerre de Cent Ans* by Léon Puiseux is a useful reference for Henry's siege of Caen. For some points of detail, Jim Bradbury, *The Medieval Siege*, gives information on Henry V's logistic preparations for the 1415 expedition and the siege of Harfleur. The College of Arms MS details events at Montereau (including the transfer of John the Fearless' corpse to Dijon), Melun, Meaux, including the circumstances surrounding the execution of the Vaurus cousins, Cosne and Henry V's appointment of the Duke of Burgundy as his lieutenant.

Chapter 7: From the Death of Henry V to the Siege of Orléans, 1422–1429

The principal general primary sources used for this chapter were *La Chronique d'Enguer-rand de Monstrelet*, the *Chronique de Charles VII, Roi de France*, and the *Chronique du Mont-Saint-Michel, 1343–1468*. The College of Arms MS M9 gives a number of details not found in the principal chronicles: the threat to hang Remon at Compiègne, the lack of supplies for the garrison of Ivry and no sign of relief being forthcoming, the size of the English army, the distribution of that army and the French attack on the besiegers at Montargis. The same source gives detail on the deaths of the Earl of Salisbury and Sir Thomas Margrave at Orléans and the English preparations before the Battle of the Herrings. The account of the siege of Orléans is largely taken from the *Journal du Siège d'Orléans, 1428–1429, Augmenté des Plusieurs Documents, Notamment des Comptes de Ville 1429–1431*. The Duke of Bedford's letter to King Henry VI after the lifting of the siege of Orléans is in Rymer's Foedera. See Dan Spencer's article 'The Provision of Artillery for the 1428 Expedition to France' for the strength and artillery train of the expeditionary force sent to Orléans under the com-mand of Salisbury. The 'Song of Joan of Arc' is taken from *Christine de Pisan, Ditié de Jeanne d'Arc*. See Anne Curry's doctoral thesis 'Military Organisation in Lancastrian Normandy, 1422–1455', for numbers and organization of the besieging force and the maritime blockade of Mont-St-Michel and numbers for Pontorson. Once again, Juliet Barker's *Conquest, The English Kingdom of France, 1417–50* and G. Du Fresne de Beau-court's, *Histoire de Charles VII* are invaluable secondary sources.

Chapter 8: From Orléans to the Truce of Tours, 1429–1444

Primary sources for this chapter are the *Chronique de Charles VII, Roi de France, La Chron-ique d'Enguerrand de Monstrelet*, and *Les États de Normandie sous la Domination Anglaise*. Once again Juliet Barker's *Conquest, The English Kingdom of France, 1417–50* is a valuable secondary source, as is, in French, de Beaucourt's *Histoire de Charles VII*.

Chapter 9: The Expulsion of the English from France, 1449–1453

The main primary sources used for this chapter were the *Chronique du Mont-Saint-Michel, 1343–1468*, and the *Chronique de Charles VII, Roy de France par Jean Chartier*. Among secondary sources de Beaucourt's *Histoire de Charles VII* covers the whole period from the end of the Truce of Tours until the expulsion of the English in 1453. Juliet Barker's *Conquest, The English Kingdom of France*, covers the defeat of the English in Normandy, and David Nicolle's *The Fall of English France, 1449–53*, gives a comprehensive description of the final events in the north and in Aquitaine. A.J. Pollard gives a useful account of Sir John Talbot's exploits in *John Talbot & The War in France, 1427–53*.

Bibliography

Allmand, Christopher, *The Hundred Years War: England and France at War c.1300–c.1450* (Cambridge, 2008).

Ayton, Andrew and Philip Preston, *The Battle of Crécy 1346* (Woodbridge, 2005).

Barber, Richard, *Edward Prince of Wales and Aquitaine, a Biography of the Black Prince* (Woodbridge, 2003).

Barber, Richard, *Edward III and the Triumph of England* (London, 2013).

Barker, Juliet, *Conquest, The English Kingdom of France, 1417–50* (London, 2009).

Beaucourt, G. du Fresne de, *Histoire de Charles VII*, 7 Vols (Paris, 1881–1891).

Beaurepaire, Charles de, *Les États de Normandie sous la Domination Anglaise* (Évreux, 1859).

Beffeyte, Renaud, *War Machines in the Middle Ages* (Rennes, 2008).

Beffeyte, Renaud, *L'Art de la Guerre au Moyen Âge* (Rennes, 2105).

Bel, Jean Le, *Chronique*, ed. J. Viard and E. Déprez (Paris, 1904–1905).

Bentley, James, *Fort Towns of France* (London, 1993).

Bradbury, Jim, *The Medieval Siege* (Woodbridge, reprinted paperback 2007).

Carbonel, Paul, *Histoire de Narbonne, des origines à l'époque contemporaine* (Narbonne, 1956).

Charpentier, Paul and Cuissard, Charles, eds, *Journal du Siège d'Orléans, 1428–1429, Augmenté des Plusieurs Documents, Notamment des Comptes de Ville 1429–1431* (Orléans, 1896).

Chartier, Jean, *Chronique de Charles VII, Roi de France*, ed. Vallet de Viriville, 2 vols (Paris, 1858).

Chastelet, Paul Hay du, *Histoire de Bertrand du Guesclin, Connestable de France et des Royaumes de Leon, de Castille, de Cordove et de Seville, Duc de Molines, Comte de Longueville etc* (Paris, 1666).

Chaudru de Crazannes, 'Notice sur le Castrum d'Aiguillon', *Revue Archéologique*, Fifteenth Year, No. 1 (April to September 1858) (Paris, 1858).

Chronique du bon duc Loys de Bourbon, Chazaud, A-M. (Paris, 1876).

Chronique du religieux de Saint-Denis, ed. L. Balluguet, 6 vols (Paris, 1839–1852).

Chronique normande du xive siècle, ed. A. and E. Molinier (Paris, 1882).

Chroniques de J. Froissart, ed. Siméon Luce, 15 vols (Paris, 1869–1899).

Collection Générale des Documents Français qui se Trouvent en Angleterre, ed. Jules Delpit, vol. 1 (Paris, 1847).

Crozet, R., 'Siège de Romorantin par le Prince de Galles (1356)', in *Revue Historique*, Année 51, vol. 153 (Paris 1926).

College of Arms MS M9, fos 31–66v

Curry, Anne, 'Military Organisation in Lancastrian Normandy, 1422–1455', 2 vols (Teeside Polytechnic doctoral thesis, 1985).

Curry, Anne, *The Hundred Years' War: 1337–1453 (Essential Histories)* (Oxford, 2002).

Curry, Anne, *Agincourt, A New History* (Stroud, 2006).

Curry, Anne, 'Guns and Goddams. Was there a military revolution in Lancastrian Normandy, 1415–50?' *Journal of Medieval Military History*, VIII (2010): 171–88

Curry, Anne, 'Representing War and Conquest, 1414–1429: The Evidence of College of Arms Manuscript M9', in *Representing War and Violence, 1250–1600*, ed. Joanna Bellis and Laura Slater (Woodbridge, 2016).

Delachenal, R, *Histoire de Charles V*, Paris, 5 vols (1909–1931).

Delvey, Jean-Pierre, 'Carbonne sous l'Ancien Régime', in *Histoire et Traditions Carbonnaises*, vol. 4 (Toulouse, 1998).

Dupré, Alexandre, *Recherches Historiques sur Romorantin et la Sologne* (Paris, 1994).

Eulogium Historiarum, vol. 3, ed. F.S. Haydon (London, 1863).

Favre, L., *Duguesclin et Jeanne d'Arc, ou la France aux XIVe et XVe siècles* (Niort and Paris, 1853).

Finó, J.-F., *Fortresses de la France Medievale* (Paris, 1967).

Fowler, Kenneth, *The King's Lieutenant, Henry of Grosmont, First Duke of Lancaster 1310–1361* (London, 1969).

Froissart, Jean, *Oeuvres de Froissart, Chroniques*, ed. Kervyn de Lettenhove, 25 vols (Brussels, 1870–1887).

Galfridi Le Baker de Swynebroke, *Chronicon*, ed. E.M. Thompson (Oxford 1889).

Gesta Henrici Quinti, The Deeds of Henry the Fifth, ed. F. Taylor and J.S. Roskell (Oxford, 1975).

Gravett, Christopher, *Medieval Siege Warfare* (Oxford, 1990).

Gross, Guy, *Le Prince Noir en Berry* (Bourges, 2004).

Guignard, Romain, *Issoudun des Origines à 1850, Aperçu des Chroniques Locales* (Issoudun, 1943).

Hoskins, Peter, *In the Steps of the Black Prince, The Road to Poitiers, 1355–1356* (Woodbridge, 2012).

Istore et Chroniques de Flandres, ed. Kervyn de Lettenhove, vol. 2 (Brussels, 1880).

Jones, Michael, *The Black Prince* (London, 2017).

Kaufmann, J.E., Kaufmann, H.W. and Jurga, Robert F., *The Medieval Fortress, Castles, Forts and Walled Cities of the Middle Ages* (Cambridge (USA), paperback edition, 2004).

Keen, Maurice, *The Laws of War in the Late Middle Ages* (first published 1965, paperback edition Abingdon and New York, 2017).

Kennedy, Angus J. and Varty, Kenneth, eds, and Shopkow, L., tr., 'The Song of Joan of Arc', in *Christine de Pisan, Ditié de Jeanne d'Arc* (Oxford, 1977).

King, Andy, 'Gunners, Aides and Archers: The Personnel of the English Ordnance Companies in Normandy in the Fifteenth Century', *Journal of Medieval Military History*, IX (2011): 65–75

Lambert, Craig, 'Edward III's siege of Calais: A reappraisal', *Journal of Medieval History*, 37 (2011): 245–56

Lambert, Craig, 'Henry V and the crossing to France: reconstructing naval operations for the Agincourt campaign, 1415', *Journal of Medieval History*, 43(1) (2017): 59–73

Les Grandes Chroniques de France, Chronique des Règnes de Jean II and Charles V, ed. R. Delachenal, vol. 2 (Paris, 1916).

Luce, Simeon, *Chronique du Mont-Saint-Michel, 1343–1468*, 2 vols (Paris, 1879–1883).

Ménard, Henri, *Carbonne, Huit Siècles d'Histoire* (St-Girons, 1985).

Michaud, Jacques and Cabanis, André, eds, *Histoire de Narbonne* (Toulouse, 1981).

Monstrelet, Enguerrand de, *Chronique*, 6 vols, ed. L. Douet d'Arcq (Paris 1857–1862).

Moranvillé, Henri, *Le siege de Reims, 1359–60*, extract from Bibliothèque de l'Ecole de Chartres, vol. LVI (Nogent-le-Rotrou, 1895).

Mortimer, Ian, *The Perfect King, The Life of Edward III, Father of the English Nation* (London, 2006).

Neillands, Robin, *The Hundred Years War* (London, 1998).

Nicolle, David, *The Fall of English France, 1449–53* (Oxford, 2012).

Page, John, 'The Siege of Rouen: A poem', in *The Historical Collections of a Citizen of London in the Fifteenth Century*, ed. James Gairdner (London, 1876).

Pisan, Christine de, *The Book of Deeds of Arms and of Chivalry*, tr. Sumner Willard, ed. Charity Cannon Willard (Pennsylvania, 1999).

Pollard, A.J., *John Talbot & the War in France, 1427–1453* (Barnsley, 2005).

Prestwich, Michael, *Armies and Warfare in the Middle Ages, The English Experience* (New Haven and London, 1996).

Puiseux, Léon, *Siège et Prise de Caen par les Anglais en 1417, Épisode de la Guerre de Cent Ans* (Caen, 1868).

Raynal, Louis, *Histoire du Berry, depuis les temps les plus anciens jusqu'en 1789* (Paris, 1884).

Ribadieu, Henri, *Les Campagnes du Comte de Derby en Guyenne* (Paris, 1865).

Riley, H.T., ed., *Memorials of London and London Life in the XIIIth, XIVth, and XVth Centuries* (London, 1868).

Robert of Avesbury, *De Gestis Mirabilibus Regis Edwardi Tertii*, ed. E.M. Thompson (London, 1889).

Rogers, Clifford J., *War Cruel and Sharp: English Strategy under Edward III, 1327–1360* (Woodbridge, 1990).

Rogers, Clifford J., 'The Anglo-French Peace Negotiations of 1354–60 Reconsidered', in J.S. Bothwell, ed., *The Age of Edward III* (Woodbridge and Rochester, 2001).

Rose, Susan, *Calais, An English Town in France, 1347–1558* (Woodbridge, 2008).

Rymer, Thomas, ed., 'Rymer's Foedera with Syllabus: July–December 1428', in *Rymer's Foedera*, vol. 10 (London, 1727–1735).

Savy, Nicholas, *La ville fortifiée de la Guerre de cent ans (v. 1345–v. 1395), armement et tactique* (Pradines, 2017).

Smith, Robert D., 'Artillery and the Hundred Years War: Myth and Interpretation', in *Arms, Armies and Fortifications in the Hundred Years War*, ed. Anne Curry and Michael Hughes (Woodbridge, 1994).

Spencer, Dan, 'Artillery', in Anne Curry, Peter Hoskins, Thom Richardson and Dan Spencer, *The Agincourt Companion* (London, 2015).

Spencer, Dan, 'The Provision of Artillery for the 1428 Expedition to France', *Journal of Medieval Military History*, XIII (2015): 179–92

Spencer, Dan, '"The scourge of the stones": English gunpowder artillery at the siege of Harfleur', *Journal of Medieval History*, 43 (1) (2017): 59–73

Sumption, Jonathan, *Trial by Battle, The Hundred Years War, vol. I* (London, 1990).

Sumption, Jonathan, *Trial by Fire, The Hundred Years War, vol. II* (London, 1999).

Sumption, Jonathan, *Divided Houses, The Hundred Years War, vol. III* (London, 2009).

Sumption, Jonathan, *Cursed Kings, The Hundred Years War, vol. IV* (London, 2015).

The Revised English Bible, with Apocrypha (Oxford and Cambridge, 1989).

Timbal, P.-C., in collaboration with Gilles, M., Martin, H., Metman, J., Payen, J. and Poussin, B., *La Guerre de Cent Ans Vue à Travers les Registres du Parlement (1337–1369)* (Paris, 1961).

Walsingham, Thomas, *The St Alban's Chronicle, The Chronica Maiora of Thomas Walsingham, vol. 1, 1376–94*, ed. J. Taylor, W.R. Childs and L. Watkiss (Woodbridge, 2003).

Index

Abbeville, 137, 178, 179
Aberystwyth, 32
Agen, 49
Agenais, 66, 74
Agincourt, Battle of, 11, 12, 14, 21, 22, 103, 107, 122, 140, 147
Aiguillon, 6, 16, 49, 50–3, 64
Albany, Duke of, Governor of Scotland, 126
Albret, Bernadet d', 65
Albret, Bertucat d', 87–8
Albret, Charles d', 103, 164, 187
Albret, Guillaume d', 150–2
Albret, Lord d', 181, 187
Alençon, 110, 127, 169–70, 193
Alençon, Duchy of, 110
Alençon, Duke of, 139, 140, 160, 163, 168, 172, 173, 181–2
Ambrières-les-Vallées, 144
Amiens, 59, 182
Amiens, Treaty of, 142
Angers, 74, 91, 138, 143
Angoulême, 72, 79
Angoumois, 66
Anjou, 10, 66, 138, 141, 144, 176
Anjou, Charles d', 172, 185
Anjou, Duke of, 71–4, 79, 82–3, 86–8, 90
Anthenaise, Aimery d', 172
Antwerp, 3
Aquitaine, Duchy of, 2, 3, 7–10, 13–14, 20, 46, 51, 56, 62–3, 66, 71–3, 74, 78, 84, 93–4, 180, 203–5, 207–10
Aquitaine, Dukes of, 2
Aquitaine, Prince of, 8
Aragon, 83
Ardevon, 142
Argentan, 110, 193
Arques, 196
Arras, 59, 96

Arras, Treaty of, 10, 174–6
Artevelde, Jacob van, 4, 5, 44
Artevelde, Philip van, 92, 94
Artois, County of, 55, 57
Artois, Robert of, 2, 3, 41
Arundel, Earl of, 9, 102, 165, 168, 170–3
Arundel, John of, 89
Athens, Duke of, 49
Auberoche, Battle of, 6, 47, 50
Aubert, Étienne, Cardinal-Archbishop of Ostia, 62
Audebeuf, Pierre, 168
Audley, Sir James, 73
Aumale, 166
Aumale, Count of, 135, 138–40
Auray, 80, 84
Aurigan, Thomas, 197
Auvergne, 152
Auxerre, 138
Auxi, Lord of, 178–9
Avranches, 138, 141, 181–2

Balinghem, 177
Bar, Bourg de, 151
Bar, Count of, 140
Bar, Duke of, 140
Barbazan, Arnaud-Guilhem de, 124, 126
Baugé, Battle of, 13, 126–7
Bayeux, 12, 85, 112, 198–9
Bayonne, 207
Bearn, 204
Bearn, Bernard de, 207
Beauce, 77
Beaufort, Cardinal, 162, 176
Beaufort, Edmund, Earl later Duke of Somerset, 181–3, 188–9, 193–6, 200–1
Beaufort, Henry, Bishop of Winchester, 142
Beaufort, Roger de, 75

Beaugency-sur-Loire, 125, 160–2
Beaugener, Simon de, 150
Beaujeu, Edward de, 59
Beaulo, Enguerrand de, 55
Beaumont, Sir Thomas, 175–6
Beaumont-sur-Oise, 17, 173, 185
Beaumont-sur-Sarthe, 168
Beauvais, 118, 120, 167, 182
Beauvais, Bishop of, 49
Beauvaisis, 119
Bec-Hellouin, 112
Bécherel, 80, 85
Bedford, Duke of, 13, 14, 106, 133–44,
    156, 159, 162–4, 166, 168–70, 172–4,
    176
Bel, Jean le, 63
Bellême, 110, 196
Belon, Jean, 18, 73–4
Bénauges, 210
Bergerac, 6, 46–7, 53, 75, 87–8, 205
Berry, 133, 135
Berry, Duke of, 71, 75–7
Bétheney, 68
Béthune, 16, 59
Beuil, Lord of, 168
Beuzeville-la-Bastille, 84
Béziers, 37
Bigorre, 66, 204
Black Prince, 7, 8, 16, 19, 21, 25, 35–7,
    39, 63–4, 67–8, 70, 72, 75–7, 88
Blanche, Henry, 144
Blanchetaque, 11
Blanquefort, 208
Blaye, 46, 88, 205–6, 208
Blois, 150–1, 157
Blois, Charles de, 5, 59, 60
Blois, Count of, 25, 66
Bois-de-Vincennes, 175
Bolingbroke, Henry, *see* Henry IV, King
    of England
Bonport, 113
Bonsmoulins, 171
Bordeaux, 2, 6–8, 14, 46, 50, 52, 55,
    63–4, 66, 70, 76, 83, 87–8, 93, 99, 180,
    187, 203, 205–10
Bosche, Peter van Den, 94
Boulogne, 57, 60

Bourbon, Duke of, 48–9, 80, 83, 90
Bourbon, Jacques de, 59
Bourbon, Pierre de, 124
Bourbon, The Bastard of, 182
Bourbourg, 94, 97
Bourg, 88, 206, 208
Bourges, 16–18, 134, 149, 164
Bourguignon, Renaud Guillaume de, 197
Boussac, Marshal de, 166–7
Bouteiller, Sir Ralph, 136–7
Bouteillier, Guy Le, 115, 118–20, 122
Bouvines, 45
Brabant, 4
Brabant, Duke of, 41, 43–5
Braquemont, Robert de, 113
Brest, 5, 80–2, 84, 89
Breteuil, 63–4
Brétigny, 69
Brétigny, Treaty of, 1–3, 7, 8, 10, 14, 21,
    39, 69, 70, 101
Brézé, Pierre de, 190
Briquebec, 111, 199
Brittany, Duchess of, 80
Brittany, Duchy of, 5–7, 10, 59, 60, 63,
    66, 72, 80–4, 86, 90–1, 112, 142
Brittany, Duke of, *see* John III, John IV,
    John V, John de Montfort
Bruges, 85–6, 92, 178
Buch, Captal de, 65, 79
Buchan, Earl of, 126–7, 133, 135,
    138–40, 150
Buckingham, Duke of, 91–2
Budes, Sylvester, 78
Burdet, Sir Nicholas, 142, 186
Bureau, Gaspard, 198
Bureau, Jean, 184, 186, 198, 201–2
Burgh, Thomas, 141
Burghersh, Bartholomew de, 65
Burghersh, Bishop Henry, 43
Burgundy, Dukes of, *see* Philip the Bold,
    John the Fearless and Philip the Good

Cadillac, 208–9
Caen, 12, 22, 24, 107–11, 116, 137, 173,
    196–201
Caernarvon, 18

Cahors, 35, 37, 73
Cajarc, 38
Calais, 1, 7, 8, 11, 12, 14, 16–18, 22–5,
　31–2, 39, 53–63, 66–7, 69, 72, 74,
　76–7 81–2 86, 89, 91, 94, 97–8, 106–7,
　125, 127, 140, 166, 170, 176–80, 187,
　190, 210
Calveley, Sir Hugh, 83
Cambrai, 4, 40, 42
Cambridge, Earl of, 11, 73, 76, 78, 84–6
Camoys, Roger de, 210
Campbell, Robin, 201
Carbonne, 35
Carcassonne, 36
Carentan, 89, 111, 193
Cassel, 59
Castelmoron, 49
Castile, 70, 83
Castillon, 206, 208–9
Castillon, Battle of, 14, 15, 22, 209
Catherine de Valois, Queen of England,
　10, 11, 13, 122
Catterton, Thomas, 85–6
Caudebec, 116, 120, 175, 196
Caumont, Alexander de, 50, 51
Caumont, Bertrand de, 126
Caumont, Lord of, 64
Ceccano, Annibale, Cardinal-Archbishop
　of Naples, 62
Cercanceaux, Abbot of, 148
Chaliers, 37
Chamberlain, Sir William, 18, 181
Champagne, 129
Chandler, William, 88
Chandos, Sir John, 72–3
Channel Islands, 82, 143
Charles II, King of Navarre, 63, 90
Charles IV, King of France, 2
Charles V, King of France, 1, 2, 8, 14, 21,
　69–71, 74, 77, 80, 82, 84, 90–1, 123
Charles VI, King of France, 8–10, 12, 13,
　91, 96, 100, 105, 109, 120–2, 124, 134
Charles VII, King of France, 1, 13–15,
　134, 162–5 167, 169–70, 174, 176,
　180–4, 186–7, 191, 193–5, 197–9, 201,
　203, 206–10

Charles, Dauphin of France, 12, 13, 67,
　117, 119, 122–3, 125, 127–8, 130,
　132–6, 138, 150, 152, 157, 159, 160–2
Chartres, 64, 69, 127, 136
Chastel, Tanneguy du, 133, 135
Chastellux, Lord of, 113
Château-Gaillard, 121–2, 166, 196
Châteauroux, 65
Châtellerault, 75
Châtillon, Gaucher de, 67
Châtillon-sur-Indre, 48–9
Chatterton, Dickon, 202
Chaumont, Guillaume de, 122–3
Chécy, 157
Cherbourg, 22, 88–90, 112, 114, 196,
　198, 199, 201–2
Chin, 41
Chinon, 152
Chissay, Guichard de, 129, 132
Chizé, 79–80
Clairac, 51
Clarence, Duke of, 9, 13, 101–2, 104–5,
　108, 109, 112–13, 115, 126–7
Clarence, The Bastard of, 164–5
Clement VI, Pope, 5
Clement VII, Pope, 93
Clermont, Count of, 151–2, 209
Clifford, Thomas, Lord, 131
Clinton, Lord, 186
Clisson, Olivier de, 81–2, 91–2
Coblenz, 3
Coëtivy, Prégent de, Admiral of France,
　185, 187, 202
Cognac, 76, 84, 86, 203
Cognac, Lord of, 187
Comminges, Count of, 204
Compiègne, 17, 56–7, 138–9, 164–5
Conches-en-Ouche, 166, 184
Condé-sur-Noireau, 111
Corbeil, 124, 175
Cornwall, John, 130–1
Cornwall, Sir John, 113, 115, 130
Cosne, 16, 132–3
Courtenay, Richard, Bishop of Norwich,
　104
Coutances, 112, 193
Craon, Armury de, 74

Craon, Jean de, Archbishop of Reims, 67
Cravant, 138
Crécy, Battle of, 6–8, 12, 14, 16, 20–1, 31, 39, 51, 53–4, 57, 70, 89
Creil, 173, 184
Cresswell, Edmund, 88
Croy, Lord, 179
Culant, Louis de, Admiral of France, 148, 152

Dagworth, Sir John, 6
Damazan, 50–1
Dangu, 192
Dauphin, *see* Louis, 5ᵗʰ Dauphin (1401–15), John (1415–17) and Charles (1417–22 – King Charles VII), and Louis, 8ᵗʰ Dauphin (1423–61)
Dauphiné, 152
David, King of Scotland, 57
Delisle, Lancelot, 150
Derby, Earl of, 6, 46, 47, 87
Derval, 80–2
Despenser, Henry, Bishop of Norwich, 19, 93–7
Devereux, Sir John, 79–80
Dieppe, 61, 120, 176, 179–80, 187–9
Domfront, 110, 112–14, 116, 201
Dordogne, 75, 77
Dorset, Earl of, 105–6
Douglas, Earl, 127, 139, 140
Dreux, 17, 128, 138
Duke of Burgundy, *see* Philip the Bold, John the Fearless and Philip the Good
Dunkirk, 94, 97
Dunois, Count of, 190–1, 193–4, 198–9, 201, 205–8
Duravel, 73

Edinburgh, 32
Edward III, King of England, 1–8, 12, 14–17, 19–21, 24, 31, 39–46, 48, 51–6, 58–9, 61–3, 66–70, 74, 77, 84, 89, 102, 107–8, 112–13, 116
Eleanor of Aquitaine, 2
Elmham, Sir William, 88
Entwhistle, Bertrand, 142
Erpingham, Sir Thomas, 105

Esplechin, Truce of, 5
Essay, 193
Estouteville, Louis, Sire d', 102
Estouteville, Jean d', 183
Estrac, Count of, 204
Eu, 120
Eu, Count of, 183, 187, 192
Évreux, 163
Exeter, Duke of, 114–15, 122, 129, 133
Exmes, 110, 193
Eymet, 87

Falaise, 110–11, 201
Fastolf, Sir John, 139, 144, 149, 151, 160, 162
Fauconberg, Lord, 178–81, 183
Fécamp, 120, 175–6, 193
Felton, Sir Thomas, 87, 92
Fitzhugh, Lord, 105
Flanders, 4, 5, 10, 52, 56, 58–9, 93–8, 176
Flanders, Count of, 92, 95
Flanders, Joan of, 5
Flavy, Guillaume de, 165
Flote de Revel, Pierre, Admiral of France, 58
Foix, 204
Foix, Count of, 42, 181, 187, 203–5, 207–9
Folleville, 182
Formigny, Battle of, 22, 198
Fosseux, Jean du, 55
Fougères, 196
Fresnay, 110
Frogenhalle, Richard, 193
Froissart, Jean, 24, 76
Fronsac, 206, 208–9

Gaillardet, 209
Gaillon, 139
Gallardon, 127
Gascony, 6, 7, 22, 59, 86, 90, 91
Gast, Louis, 132
Gaucourt, Raoul de, 102, 106, 169, 188
Gaure, 66
Gençay, 80, 84, 86
Ghent, 4, 5, 41, 92, 94–5, 97, 178
Gien, Robert de, 66

Gisors, 121, 193, 196
Glasdale, Sir William, 157, 159
Glendower, Owen, 9, 18, 78–9
Gloucester, Duke of, 111–12, 114, 142, 177–8, 202
Gough, Matthew, 161–2, 168–9, 198
Gournay, 192
Gower, Richard, 202
Gower, Thomas, 202
Gravelines, 55, 94, 97, 178
Graville, 101
Graville, Jean Malet de, 113
Gressart, Perrinet, 164
Grey, Sir Thomas, 11
Grosmont, Henry of, Earl of Derby, later Earl and then Duke of Lancaster, 46
Guesclin, Bertrand du, Constable of France, 8, 70–1, 75, 77–82, 85–7, 89–91
Guesclin, Olivier du, 90
Guiche, 203
Guienne, 2
Guînes, 66, 177
Guise, 140–2

Hacqueville, Sire de, 105
Hainault, 4
Hainault, Count of, 43–5
Harcourt, 112, 191, 193
Harcourt, Godefroy d', 6
Harcourt, Jacques d', 136–7
Harfleur, 11, 17, 18, 22, 23, 32, 34, 35, 53, 54, 99–107, 113–17, 175–6, 180, 182–4, 196–7
Harlech, 18
Hastings, Sir Hugh, 6, 16, 52–3
Haye, Jehan de la, 142
Hennebout, 5
Henry II, King of England, 2, 66, 107
Henry IV, King of England, 2, 8, 9, 17, 99
Henry V, King of England, 1, 2, 8–15, 17, 18, 21–4, 32, 54, 99–112, 114–34, 183, 195–6, 200
Henry VI, King of England and France, 13, 122, 133–4, 145, 155–6, 159, 165–7, 174–6, 208

Hereford, Earl of, 74
Heron, Robin, 155
Herrings, Battle of the, 151
Hesdin, 59–61, 179
Hewitt, Sir Walter, 79
Holden, Laurence, 142
Honfleur, 112, 114, 120, 195–8, 201
Hungerford, Sir Walter, 131
Huntingdon, Earl of, 104, 115, 124, 126, 165–6, 170, 181, 187

Île-de-France, 103, 121
Illiers, Florant d', 191
Isabella, de Valois, Queen of England, 8
Isle-Adam, Sire de l', 174, 176
Issoudun, 36
Ivry-la-Bataille, 121, 139

James I, King of Scotland, 122, 124, 126–7
James II, King of Scotland, 32
Jargeau, 147, 153, 160, 164
Jean I, Count of Armagnac, 7–8, 47, 70
Joan of Arc, 13, 152, 155, 157–60, 162–6
John II, King of France, 2, 3, 5, 7–8, 10–12, 33, 47, 53, 63–6, 70, 120
John III, Duke of Brittany, 5
John IV, Duke of Brittany, John de Montford, 81, 86, 90–2
John of Gaunt, 8, 74, 76–8, 80–3, 89, 93–4, 98, 102
John the Fearless, Duke of Burgundy, 9–12, 18, 21, 117–23, 126, 132, 136–7, 141
John V, Duke of Brittany, 10, 13, 125, 127, 142–3, 174
John, Duke of Normandy, *see* John II, King of France
John, King of England, 114
Joigny-sur-Yonne, 123
Jonzac, 205
Jouy, 173

Kermoysan, Tugdual de, 202
Knolles, Sir Robert, 72–4, 77, 80–2
Kyriell, Sir Thomas, 179, 196, 198, 203

La Bossinière, 138
La Capelle, 4
La Charité-sur-Loire, 133, 164
La Fayette, Gilbert de, 111, 151
La Gravelle, 144
La Hire, 143, 149–52, 155, 158, 160, 166–7, 172–3, 177, 183–5
La Réole, 6, 48–50, 52, 63, 75, 83, 87
La Roche-Derrien, Battle of, 59–60
La Roche-Guyon, 121, 193
La Rochelle, 72, 79
La Roche-sur-Yon, 18, 73–4
Lagny-sur-Marne, 169–70
Lalinde, 75
Lancaster, Earl of, later Duke of and earlier Earl of Derby, 33, 48, 50–2, 56–7, 59, 62–4, 67–8, 83
Langon, 46, 88, 208
Languedoc, 152, 181
Laon, 172
Lapenne, *see* Thibaud de Lévis-Montbrun
Larchant, *see* St-Mathurin-de-Larchant
Laval, Lord of, 181
Le Crotoy, 54, 89, 133, 136–7, 140–1, 178–9
Le Fossat d'Aiguillon, 50
Le Mans, 77
Léer, Olivier de, 126
Lesparre, Lord of, 206
Leulinghem, Truce of, 8, 97, 99
Libourne, 78, 88, 206, 208
Lille, 178
Lillebonne, 106, 175, 196
Limoges, 16, 24, 75–7
Limoges, Bishop of, 75
Limousin, 66, 75, 77–8
Lisieux, 192
Loches, 36
Lohéac, Lord, 181
Lomagne, Viscount of, 181
London, First Treaty of, 66
London, Second Treaty of, 66
Longny, 192
Loré, Ambroise de, 144, 168–9, 171, 173
Lormont, 209–10
Lorraine, Duke of, 140
Louis of Bavaria, Holy Roman Emperor, 3

Louis, 5th Dauphin of France, 2, 10, 12–13, 23, 103, 105
Louis, 8th Dauphin of France, 186, 188
Louviers, 112, 166, 168, 184, 192
Lunac-d'Aiguillon, 50
Luppé, Peron de, 129, 132
Lusignan, 79
Luxembourg, John of, 125, 140, 165–6
Luxembourg, Louis of, 174
Lyonnais, 152

Maine, 10, 14, 66, 144, 170, 176, 189
Maine, Count of, 187
Mâle, Louis de, 92–3, 98
Malestroit, Jean de, 78
Malestroit, Truce of, 5
Manny, Sir Walter, 24
Mantes-la-Jolie, 17, 121, 128, 192
March, Earl of, 129
Marche, de la, Count of, 187
Marck, 177
Marennes, 79
Margrave, Sir Thomas, 147
Martel, 31
Martel, Guillaume VIII, Sire de Bacqueville, 103
Mauléon, 203–5
Mauny, Olivier de, 111, 122
Mauny, Walter, 50
Meaux, 13, 18, 128–32, 180–2
Mehun-sur-Yèvre, 125
Meilhan-sur-Garonne, 33
Melun, 123–6
Menil, Hugh, 50
Menin, 95
Meudrac, Henry, 141
Meuillon, Guillaume de, 111
Meulan, 17, 121, 134–6, 175
Meung-sur-Loire, 147, 160–2
Mignon, Berthault, 154
Moissac, 49, 72, 75
Moncontour, 77
Monein, Perrot, 19
Monségur, 48
Montargis, 125, 143–4, 170, 180
Montauban, 72–3
Montcuq, 46, 88

Montdidier, 138
Montenay, Guillaume de, 108, 110
Montereau, 123, 180
Montfort, John IV, Duke of Brittany, 5,
  80, 82, 84–5, 90, 92
Montgiscard, 27
Montguyon, 205
Montivilliers, 101, 104, 120, 175, 183,
  196–7
Montmor, Morelet de, 79
Montpon, Guillaume de, 78
Montpon-Ménestérol, 78
Montreuil-Bellay, 80, 137
Mont-St-Michel, 136–7, 141–2
Morlaix, 5
Mortagne, 110
Morton, Robert, 79
Mowbray, Sir Thomas, 115
Mussidan, 46

Nájera, Battle of, 8, 70
Nantes, 73, 90–2
Narbonne, 37, 63
Narbonne, Archbishop of, 37
Navarre, King of, 74, 205
Nemours, 180
Nesle, Guy de, 130
Neufchâtel-en-Bray, 196
Neville, Sir John, 80–1
Neville's Cross, Battle of, 57
Nieulay, 61–2
Niort, 79–80
Normandy, Duchy of, 2, 6, 10–13, 17, 22,
  54, 56, 63, 66, 74, 85, 89, 103, 107,
  110–13, 116–17, 120–2, 127, 129, 132,
  134, 136, 138–9, 142, 162, 166–8, 170,
  173–6, 180–2, 184–5, 187, 190, 193,
  198–203, 205
Normandy, Duke of, 16, 48–53, 56–7
Northampton, Earl of, 5, 6, 62
Norwich, Bishop of, *see* Despenser,
  Henry
Noyons, 40

Orléans, 13, 17, 18, 34, 57, 64, 144–60,
  162, 164–5
Orléans, Bishop of, 152

Orléans, Duke of, 9, 126, 147, 153, 156
Orléans, Philip of, Count of Vertus, 125
Orléans, The Bastard of, 143, 147,
  149–55, 157–8, 169, 183, 187–8, 190,
  192, 196–8
Ormond, John of, 192
Ouistreham, 200
Owen of Wales, 78–9
Oye, 177

Page, John, 114
Pallière, Géraud de la, 139
Paris, 5, 8, 13, 17–19, 32, 36, 67, 69, 70,
  77, 83, 85, 90, 92, 96, 103, 110, 117–19,
  121–3, 126, 128–9, 132–4, 136, 138–40,
  143–4, 151, 156, 160, 162–3, 166–7,
  169–70, 172–6, 180, 184–6
Patay, Battle of, 13, 162
Pavilly, Eustache de, 118
Pedro the Cruel, 8, 70
Pellegrue, 48
Pembroke, Earl of, 73–4, 76
Perche, County of, 110
Percy, Sir Thomas, 77
Périgord, 66, 86
Périgord, Cardinal of, 66
Périgueux, 38, 46, 78
Peyto, Sir William, 184, 188
Philip Augustus, King of France, 114
Philip III, King of France, 3
Philip IV, King of France, 2, 37
Philip of Navarre, 63
Philip the Bold, Duke of Burgundy, 9, 71,
  86, 95, 98, 177–8
Philip the Good, Duke of Burgundy,
  12–14, 121–4, 127–8, 133, 142, 152,
  156, 162–5, 167, 170–2, 175–9, 184
Philip VI, King of France, 2–7, 16, 20,
  23, 39–41, 45, 52–5, 57–63
Philippa, Queen of England, 24
Picardy, 103, 119, 125, 128, 179, 182
Picauville, 84
Pisan, Christine de, 20, 159
Pointoise, 118, 175
Poissy, 185
Poitiers, 6, 57, 73, 78, 84, 86, 134, 152

Poitiers, Battle of, 2, 7–8, 12, 14, 21, 36, 39, 63, 66, 70, 73
Poitiers, Louis of, 47
Poitou, 66, 73, 79–80
Pole, Sir John de la, 136–8, 141, 143, 160
Pomport, 88
Pont-Audemer, 192
Pont-de-l'Arche, 112–14, 117, 193, 194
Pont-Douve, 202
Pont-Gilbert, 181
Ponthieu, County of, 66, 72, 178
Pont-l'Abbé, 84
Pont-l'Évêque, 192
Pontoise, 17, 19, 118, 176, 181, 184–6
Pontorson, 143
Pont-Ste-Maxence, 173
Pontvallain, Battle of, 77
Port-Ste-Marie, 49, 51
Provins, 19

Quercy, 37, 66, 72, 74–5, 78
Quillebeuf, 116

Réalville, 72
Reims, 7, 13, 16, 17, 66–9, 91, 116, 138, 140, 152, 160, 162, 167
Remon, Guillaume, 139
Rempston, Sir Thomas, 140, 142, 187
Rennes, 80, 142
Ricarville, Guillaume de, 167–8
Richard I, the Lionheart, King of England, 48, 113
Richard II, King of England, 8, 9, 11, 88, 93–4, 98–9, 107
Richemont, Arthur de, Constable of France, 143, 161, 172, 180–1, 184, 187, 199–201
Rieu, Marshal of, 174–5
Rions, 206, 208, 210
Rivière, Perrette de la, 121
Robert II, King of Scotland, 126
Roche, Hugh de la, 75
Rohan, Viscount of, 80
Romorantin, 16, 21, 25, 64–6
Roosebeke, Battle of, 94
Rouen, 12, 17, 22, 64, 92, 103–4, 112–22, 165–7, 173–5, 180–2, 185, 191–6, 201–2

Rouergue, 66, 72, 74
Rouvres, Jean de, 132
Rue, 137, 173
Rutel, 130

St-Germain-en-Laye, 175
St-James-de-Beuvron, 142
St-Jean-d'Angely, 79
St-Leonard, 181
St-Lô, 85, 111, 138, 193
St-Macaire, 49, 78, 88, 208
St-Maigrin, 203
St-Malo, 73, 80, 89
St-Mathurin-de-Larchant, 143
St-Nicholas-de-la-Grave, 72
St-Omer, 41, 59
St-Per, Augerot de, 187
St-Pierre-le-Moûtier, 164
St-Pol, Count of, 170, 188, 192
St-Pol, The Bastard of, 174
St-Pol-de-Léon, 6
St-Rémy-du-Val, 110
St-Sauveur, 111
St-Sauveur-de-Pierrepont, 84
St-Sauveur-le-Vicomte, 84–6, 201
St-Sevère, Marshal, 150–2, 154, 158
St-Vaast-la-Hougue, 6, 89
St-Valery-sur-Somme, 137, 170–3, 179
Saintes, 79
Saintonge, 66, 80
Salisbury, Earl of, 80–2, 102, 115, 127, 136, 144–6, 153
San Vitale, Cardinal of, 66
Sancerre, 133
Sangatte, 61, 177
Saumur, 137
Saumur, Treaty of, 142
Scales, Lord, 139, 153, 160, 174, 176, 180–1, 185
Scott, Martin, 79
Scrope, Henry, Lord, 11
Sées, 110
Sens, 122
Sigismund, Holy Roman Emperor, 12
Sillé-le-Guillaume, 172
Sluys, 177
Sluys, Battle of, 4, 41

Soissons, 19
Somerset, Earl of and later Duke of,
   see Beaufort, Edmund
Somerton, Castle, 66
Soubise, 79
Southampton, 82, 99
Spain, Charles of, 59
Stafford, Lord Ralph, 46, 50
St-Céneri-le-Gérei, 167–9, 171–2
St-Denis, 58, 167, 173–6
St-Denis-Chef-de-Caux, 100
St-Émilion, 88, 206
Stewart, John, 138, 150–2
Stewart, William, 150–2
Suffolk, Earl of, 65, 104, 136, 139, 142–3,
   153–4, 160

Talbot, Sir John, 147, 153, 160, 162, 171,
   173–4, 176, 178–81, 183, 185–6, 191,
   193, 194–6, 201, 208–9
Tancarville, 175, 196
Tartas, 186–7
Thérouanne, 57
Thibaud de Lévis-Montbrun, 36
Thorigny-sur-Marne, 129
Thouars, 73
Thun-l'Évêque, 41
Tombelaine, 141–2, 199
Tonneau, Jehan, 154
Tonneins, 50–1
Torcy, 166
Torigny, 111
Toulouse, 49, 52, 72, 134
Touques, 107, 193
Touraine, 10, 66, 77, 117
Tournai, 5, 40–6, 116
Tours, 64, 117, 119, 139
Tours, Truce of, 14, 188–9, 211
Trastámara, Henry of, 8, 70, 79
Trivet, Sir Thomas, 85–6
Troyes, 122
Troyes, Treaty of, 12, 122, 132, 134, 136,
   143

Umfraville, Sir Gilbert, 126
Urban VI, Pope, 93

Vaas, 77
Vallebreton, Hennequin, 85
Valognes, 89, 111, 193, 198
Valois, Catherine de, Queen of England,
   10
Vannes, 80
Vaurus, Dennis, 132
Vaurus, The Bastard of, 129, 132
Vendée, 73
Vendôme, 128
Vendôme, Count of, 165
Vendômois, 77
Verneuil, 110, 139
Verneuil, Battle of, 139–40
Verneuil-sur-Avre, 190–2
Vernon, 23, 105, 121, 192
Verzy, 68
Vienne, Jean de, 55, 60, 63, 84
Vignolles, Amado de, 172–3
Vignolles, Etienne de, *see* La Hire
Villefranche-sur-Cher, 64–5
Villemur, John de, 75
Villeneuve-sur-Yonne, 123, 128–9
Vire, 111, 198
Vitanval, 100
Vivoin, 168–9

Warwick, Earl of, 74, 112, 116, 121–2,
   124, 129, 131, 133, 143–4, 178
Waurin, Robert of, 59
William I, King of England, 2, 64
Willoughby, Lord, 168–71, 173
Wissant, 54
Woodville, Richard, 205
Worcester, Earl of, 131

Xaintrailles, Poton de, 140, 150–2, 156,
   184, 201

York, Duke of, 175–6, 178, 185–6, 188
Ypres, 19, 34, 92–7

Zype, Peter van der, 94